WORDS THAT CHANGED THE WORLD

25 SPEECHES THAT SHAPED THE WORLD WE LIVE IN

WORDS THAT CHANGED THE WORLD

25 SPEECHES THAT SHAPED THE WORLD WE LIVE IN

C. EDWIN VILADE

METRO BOOKS

NEW YORK

We would like to thank the following organisations for the permission
to reproduce copyright material:

Frank D. Roosevelt Presidential Library and Museum

Reproduced with permission of Curtis Brown Ltd, London on behalf
of The Estate of Winston Churchill Copyright © Winston S. Churchill

John F. Kennedy Presidential Library and Museum

Printed with the permission of the General Douglas MacArthur
Foundation, MacArthur Square, Norfolk, Virginia 23510

Reprinted by arrangement with The Heirs to the Estate of Martin
Luther King Jr., c/o Writers House as agent for the proprietor New York,
NY. © 1963 Dr. Martin Luther King Jr; copyright renewed 1991
Coretta Scott King

Courtesy of the Ronald Reagan Presidential Foundation

Lyndon Baines Johnson Library

© The Nobel Foundation 1979

Nelson Mandela Foundation

The Richard Nixon Foundation

Text by C. Edwin Vilade
Designed by Rawshock

Metro Books
122 Fifth Avenue
New York, NY 10011

978-1-4351-2407-3

Printed and bound in China

1 3 5 7 9 10 8 6 4 2

Contents

Words That Changed The World

THE GREEK MATHEMATICIAN ARCHIMEDES was fond of saying, "Give me a lever long enough and a place to stand, and I will move the Earth." He never found either, but speakers throughout the ages have used another tool, rhetoric, to figuratively achieve that end. The right person using the right words in the right way in the right place can alter the course of history.

The ancient art of public speaking, or rhetoric, has fallen somewhat into disrepute. The term "rhetoric" is as often used as a pejorative now as in any other sense. However, it has an ancient and honorable history. A man named Corax, who lived in the Greek colony of Syracuse on Sicily about 2,500 years ago, wrote down the first recorded rules of rhetoric. At that time, the local ruler confiscated all private lands in the area and forced citizens to go to court to get them back. The eloquence of their arguments was, in many instances, the deciding factor as to whether their case failed or not. Many of the less articulate Syracusans began to consult with Corax to help them frame their arguments. He soon developed a thriving business and eventually set down his principles in writing. Some scholars say he went further, actually writing out the arguments for clients, which would make him history's first speechwriter.

Nothing remains of Corax's treatise, but reference is made to it in the bible of rhetoricians, Aristotle's *Rhetoric*. The great philosopher devoted considerable time to laying out the rules of public speaking, and his framework stands today as a matchless guide for anyone preparing a speech. Aristotle defined rhetoric as the "ability to see, in each case, the available means of persuasion." Rhetoric has also been called "situated speech", matching the arguments to the external circumstances and the needs and expectations of the audience to achieve the speaker's communications aims. In other words, effective speech.

Aristotle's basics have come down to us as the five canons (principles) of rhetoric: invention, arrangement, style, memory, and delivery. Essentially they mean that the speaker should find the strongest arguments, lay them out for maximum impact, use the most apt language, practice the speech (no texts or teleprompters in Ancient Greece), and bring the words to life through the proper vocal emphasis and inflection.

Aristotle also divided rhetorical arguments into three parts: *ethos*, *logos*, and *pathos*. *Ethos* is the credibility and stature of the speaker. In some societies – notably in structured Asian societies – their place in society confers *ethos* upon a speaker. Elsewhere in the world, *ethos* is normally earned through accomplishment or conspicuous virtue. In this volume, one could point to Mother Teresa and Nelson Mandela as speakers whose *ethos* is strong, and certain politicians as the opposite. The second form of argument, *logos*, is the appeal to logic – facts and figures. Lawyers' courtroom statements might be good examples. *Logos* is always good to have in a speech to bolster the more emotional arguments of the third form of argument: *pathos*.

Charismatic leaders such as Winston Churchill have effectively used *pathos* to mobilize their countrymen to achieve great ends though, regrettably, sociopaths such as Hitler and Mussolini have been equally effective using the same technique. Perhaps the most famous use of *pathos* to sway a crowd was Mark Antony's oration over the body of Julius Caesar. The "Friends, Romans, Countrymen" opening comes from Shakespeare's superb dramatization, but the speech was based on historical fact and Antony was, by all accounts, a wonderful orator. His words that day indisputably altered the course of Roman history. Many centuries later, a young Henry V stood before his sick and weary troops at Agincourt as, vastly outnumbered, they prepared to do battle with the French. Again, we remember Shakespeare's peerless version of his words, but whatever the king said it rallied his "band of brothers" to victory. More than 500 years afterward, Churchill steeled the British people against the Nazi peril by the sheer force of his oratory. Over all the centuries, leaders around the world have inspired and cajoled their people to feats of individual and collective courage through their words, and written new chapters in the annals of humankind.

A speech will almost always combine elements of all three types of argument to varying degrees, and a great speech will have them in near-perfect proportions. Nevertheless, a speech consisting almost solely of one or another element can achieve the speaker's objective, and can take its place in history even if deficient, or entirely lacking, in one or both of the others. This volume contains several of that type.

In the ancient world, no person who was not adept at oratory could aspire to a public career, and a public figure was always presumed to write his own speeches. That was not always the case – professional speechwriters have always lurked in the shadows, but were usually unacknowledged. However, the presumption of self-authorship persisted to modern times and was often the fact. Through to the 20th Century, great statesmen were generally great speechwriters and orators and their words fuelled the revolutions not only of the United States but also France, Italy, South America, and all the other areas that radically changed the map of the world. Eloquence has historically been as much a hallmark of leadership as prowess with the sword.

That changed somewhat during the 20th Century: a change that has been one of many to the public speaking process. To confine analysis to Presidents of the United States, we find that the Presidents of the early part of the century – from the stirring and eloquent Teddy Roosevelt and Woodrow Wilson, to the wretchedly incoherent Warren G. Harding, the surprisingly effective Calvin Coolidge, and the leaden Herbert Hoover – more than likely wrote most of their own speeches.

The modern trend began with Franklin Delano Roosevelt, who employed two Pulitzer Prize winners and a New York State Supreme Court Justice among his many speechwriters. Their efforts, together with his own contributions, combined in a remarkable 13-year period of oratory that sustained the American people through the Great Depression and a World War. Truman, no natural orator, nevertheless benefited from Roosevelt's example and his own plainspoken style served him well. From all accounts, Eisenhower needed a lot of help with his speeches, and Kennedy's speechwriters included the masterful Ted Sorenson, craftsman of the "ask not..." call to action.

By the time Richard Nixon took office, the trend toward seeking professional word-smithing help was well established and each White House since has employed a cadre of speechwriters, some more successful than others. The use of professionals to help craft speeches has spread around the world and it is probable that nearly all the speeches delivered by government and private-sector officials of all stripes in the last several decades have been tweaked, massaged, or entirely drafted by speechwriters.

This has played a role in an increase in the number of speeches delivered. The number of public statements given by President Barack Obama, for instance, is many times the number required of even so voluble a President as FDR. Interestingly, this proliferation has taken place at the same time as two other trends. First, analysts claim that traditional rhetoric, marked by conscious eloquence and the use of formal techniques, is in decline. Plain, ordinary speech communicates more clearly and effectively, some scholars of rhetoric claim. The validity of that assertion is doubtful. The eloquence of such as John F. Kennedy, Ronald Reagan, and Barack Obama clearly contributed both to their attainment of high office and to any success they had in achieving their policy goals.

They also benefited from the second trend: the size of the audience. Where a 19th or early 20th Century speech might directly reach an audience of a few thousand, the advent of radio, television, and the Internet has put the speaker before millions. Certainly, neither Roosevelt nor Churchill would have been as effective if the bulk of the people had only been able to read their words in the *Washington Post* or *The Times*. That impact has only been heightened over the decades by the advances in the electronic media.

Nothing matches the immediacy of a speech – whether viewed and heard, either in person or electronically – to convey information or to exercise persuasion by a leader. The speeches considered in this volume, and many more, are proof that the lever of words and the fulcrum of the proper speaker in the proper venue can move the world.

January 30, 1882	Franklin Delano Roosevelt is born in Hyde Park, New York.
June 24, 1903	Receives his A.B. from Harvard College.
March 17, 1905	Marries Anna Eleanor Roosevelt.
December 8, 1910	Elected to the New York State Senate.
March 17, 1913	Appointed Assistant Secretary of the Navy under President Woodrow Wilson.
1920	Runs as the Democrat candidate for Vice-President on the ticket with James N. Cox, who is defeated by Warren G. Harding.
August 1921	Roosevelt is stricken with poliomyelitis at Campobello, New Brunswick, Canada. He never walks unaided again.
November 6, 1928	Elected Governor of New York over Republican challenger Albert Ottinger.
July 1932	The Democratic Party nominates Roosevelt for President. In his acceptance speech he pledges "a new deal for the American people."
November 8, 1932	Roosevelt is elected United States President, defeating Herbert Hoover.
March 12, 1933	Roosevelt delivers his first radio "fireside chat" in which he discusses the banking crisis.
November 3, 1936	Roosevelt is re-elected President with John N. Garner as Vice-President.
November 5, 1940	Elected to an unprecedented third term. Henry Wallace is elected as Vice-President.
January 6, 1941	In his State of the Union message, Roosevelt recommends lend lease aid to Great Britain.
December 7, 1941	Japan attacks Pearl Harbor. Roosevelt asks Congress to declare war the following day.
December 11, 1941	Germany and Italy declare war on the United States.
October 1944	On the 21st and 27th, respectively, FDR campaigns in an open car in cold rain in New York City and Philadelphia to dispel rumors he is in poor health.
November 7, 1944	Roosevelt is re-elected to a fourth term with Harry Truman as Vice-President.
February 4–11, 1945	Roosevelt, Churchill, and Stalin meet at Yalta and discuss postwar settlements.
March 1, 1945	Roosevelt addresses Congress on the results of the Yalta Conference.
March 29, 1945	Travels to Warm Springs for rest and recuperation.
April 12, 1945	Roosevelt dies at Warm Springs, Georgia.
April 15, 1945	Roosevelt is buried in the Rose Garden of his home at Hyde Park, New York.

President Franklin Delano Roosevelt

"The only thing we have to fear is fear itself."

WHEN FRANKLIN DELANO ROOSEVELT TOOK office, the United States had sunk to the lowest depths of the Great Depression that had begun more than three years earlier with the stock market crash of October 1929. By March 1933, most of America's banks were closed and industrial production had dropped by more than half. One-quarter of the U.S. workforce – about 13 million people – was out of work. Small farms were being foreclosed by the thousands and 10 percent of single-family homes were bank-owned.

The sense of hopelessness had only deepened in the five months since Roosevelt had defeated Herbert Hoover for re-election. During the campaign, Roosevelt had traveled the country, radiating optimism and outlining in general terms the programs for economy recovery and reform that later came to be known as the New Deal. After the election, however, he stayed virtually silent. For whatever reason – conscious strategy or honest ideological disagreement – Roosevelt refused either to endorse Hoover's proposed economic remedies, or to provide more details about his own programs prior to his inauguration. Meanwhile, the U.S. economic condition continued to deteriorate.

The agonizing five-month interregnum (the March date was the last before the Inauguration moved to its present January date) only served to build support for Roosevelt's programs, whatever they might be. And on Inauguration day the national sense of anticipation was palpable. The people waited for relief, for inspiration, for leadership. In his maiden address as U.S. President, Roosevelt did not disappoint.

Franklin Delano Roosevelt delivers his Inaugural Address on March 4, 1933.

FIRST TERM INAUGURAL ADDRESS

MARCH 4, 1933

UNITED STATES CAPITOL, WASHINGTON, D.C.

President Hoover, Mr. Chief Justice, my friends:

This is a day of national consecration. And I am certain that on this day my fellow Americans expect that on my induction into the Presidency, I will address them with a candor and a decision which the present situation of our people impels.

This is preeminently the time to speak the truth, the whole truth, frankly and boldly. Nor need we shrink from honestly facing conditions in our country today. This great Nation will endure, as it has endured, will revive and will prosper.

So, first of all, let me assert my firm belief that the only thing we have to fear is fear itself – nameless, unreasoning, unjustified terror which paralyzes needed efforts to convert retreat into advance. In every dark hour of our national life, a leadership of frankness and of vigor has met with that understanding and support of the people themselves which is essential to victory. And I am convinced that you will again give that support to leadership in these critical days.

In such a spirit on my part and on yours we face our common difficulties. They concern, thank God, only material things. Values have shrunk to fantastic levels; taxes have risen; our ability to pay has fallen; government of all kinds is faced by serious curtailment of income; the means of exchange are frozen in the currents of trade; the withered leaves of industrial enterprise lie on every side; farmers find no markets for their produce; and the savings of many years in thousands of families are gone.

Franklin D. Roosevelt takes the oath of office as 32nd President of the United States of America.

More important, a host of unemployed citizens face the grim problem of existence, and an equally great number toil with little return. Only a foolish optimist can deny the dark realities of the moment.

And yet our distress comes from no failure of substance. We are stricken by no plague of locusts. Compared with the perils which our forefathers conquered, because they believed and were not afraid, we have still much to be thankful for. Nature still offers her bounty and human efforts have multiplied it. Plenty is at our doorstep, but a generous use of it languishes in the very sight of the supply.

Primarily, this is because the rulers of the exchange of mankind's goods have failed, through their own stubbornness and their own incompetence, have admitted their failure, and have abdicated. Practices of the unscrupulous money changers stand indicted in the court of public opinion, rejected by the hearts and minds of men.

True, they have tried. But their efforts have been cast in the pattern of an outworn tradition. Faced by failure of credit, they have proposed only the lending of more money. Stripped of the lure of profit by which to induce our people to follow their false leadership, they have resorted to exhortations, pleading tearfully for restored confidence. They only know the rules of a generation of self-seekers. They have no vision, and when there is no vision the people perish.

Yes, the money changers have fled from their high seats in the temple of our civilization. We may now restore that temple to the ancient truths. The measure of that restoration lies in the extent to which we apply social values more noble than mere monetary profit.

Happiness lies not in the mere possession of money; it lies in the joy of achievement, in the thrill of creative effort. The joy, the moral stimulation of work no longer must be forgotten in the mad chase of evanescent profits. These dark days, my friends, will be worth all they cost us if they teach us that our true destiny is not to be ministered unto but to minister to ourselves, to our fellow men.

Recognition of that falsity of material wealth as the standard of success goes hand in hand with the abandonment of the false belief that public office and high political position are to be valued only by the standards of pride of place and personal profit; and there must be an end to a conduct in banking and in business which too often has given to a sacred trust the likeness of callous and selfish wrongdoing. Small wonder that confidence languishes, for it thrives only on honesty, on honor, on the sacredness of obligations, on faithful protection, and on unselfish performance; without them it cannot live.

Restoration calls, however, not for changes in ethics alone. This Nation is asking for action, and action now.

Roosevelt was elected to the Oval Office with America still reeling from the Great Depression. Here, unemployed squatters wait for eviction by the police from the Hard Luck Camp in New York City.

Our greatest primary task is to put people to work. This is no unsolvable problem if we face it wisely and courageously. It can be accomplished in part by direct recruiting by the Government itself, treating the task as we would treat the emergency of a war, but at the same time, through this employment, accomplishing great – greatly needed projects to stimulate and reorganize the use of our great natural resources.

Hand in hand with that we must frankly recognize the overbalance of population in our industrial centers and, by engaging on a national scale in a redistribution, endeavor to provide a better use of the land for those best fitted for the land.

Yes, the task can be helped by definite efforts to raise the values of agricultural products, and with this the power to purchase the output of our cities. It can be helped by preventing realistically the tragedy of the growing loss through foreclosure of our small homes and our farms. It can be helped by insistence that the Federal, the State, and the local governments act forthwith on the demand that their cost be drastically reduced. It can be helped by the unifying of relief activities which today are often scattered, uneconomical, unequal. It can be helped by national planning for and supervision of all forms of transportation and of communications and other utilities that have a definitely public character. There are many ways in which it can be helped, but it can never be helped by merely talking about it.

We must act. We must act quickly.

And finally, in our progress towards a resumption of work, we require two safeguards against a return of the evils of the old order. There must be a strict supervision of all banking and credits and investments. There must be an end to speculation with other people's money. And there must be provision for an adequate but sound currency.

These, my friends, are the lines of attack. I shall presently urge upon a new Congress in special session detailed measures for their fulfillment, and I shall seek the immediate assistance of the 48 States.

Through this program of action we address ourselves to putting our own national house in order and making income balance outgo. Our international trade relations, though vastly important, are in point of time, and necessity, secondary to the establishment of a sound national economy. I favor, as a practical policy, the putting of first things first. I shall spare no effort to restore world trade by international economic readjustment; but the emergency at home cannot wait on that accomplishment.

The basic thought that guides these specific means of national recovery is not nationally – narrowly nationalistic. It is the insistence, as a first consideration, upon the interdependence of the various elements in and parts of the United States of America – a recognition of the old and permanently important manifestation of the American spirit of the pioneer. It is the way to recovery. It is the immediate way. It is the strongest assurance that recovery will endure.

In the field of world policy, I would dedicate this Nation to the policy of the good neighbor: the neighbor who resolutely respects himself and, because he does so, respects the rights of others; the neighbor who respects his obligations and respects the sanctity of his agreements in and with a world of neighbors.

If I read the temper of our people correctly, we now realize, as we have never realized before, our interdependence on each other; that we can not merely take, but we must give as well; that if we are to go forward, we must move as a trained and loyal army willing to sacrifice for the good of a common discipline, because without such discipline no progress can be made, no leadership becomes effective.

We are, I know, ready and willing to submit our lives and our property to such discipline, because it makes possible a leadership which aims at the larger good. This, I propose to offer, pledging that the larger purposes will bind upon us, bind upon us all as a sacred obligation with a unity of duty hitherto evoked only in times of armed strife.

With this pledge taken, I assume unhesitatingly the leadership of this great army of our people dedicated to a disciplined attack upon our common problems.

Action in this image, action to this end is feasible under the form of government which we have inherited from our ancestors. Our Constitution is so simple, so practical that it is possible always to meet extraordinary needs by changes in emphasis and arrangement without loss of essential form. That is why our constitutional system has proved itself the most superbly enduring political mechanism the modern world has ever seen.

It has met every stress of vast expansion of territory, of foreign wars, of bitter internal strife, of world relations. And it is to be hoped that the normal balance of executive and legislative authority may be wholly equal, wholly adequate to meet the unprecedented task before us. But it may be that an unprecedented demand and need for undelayed action may call for temporary departure from that normal balance of public procedure.

I am prepared under my constitutional duty to recommend the measures that a stricken nation in the midst of a stricken world may require. These measures, or such other measures as the Congress may build out of its experience and wisdom, I shall seek, within my constitutional authority, to bring to speedy adoption.

But, in the event that the Congress shall fail to take one of these two courses, in the event that the national emergency is still critical, I shall not evade the clear course of duty that will then confront me. I shall ask the Congress for the one remaining instrument to meet the crisis – broad Executive power to wage a war against the emergency, as great as the power that would be given to me if we were in fact invaded by a foreign foe.

A poster portraying President Roosevelt as "Dr. New Deal", trying several remedies to cure an ailing Uncle Sam; Congress is portrayed as a nurse following the doctor's orders.

For the trust reposed in me, I will return the courage and the devotion that befit the time. I can do no less.

We face the arduous days that lie before us in the warm courage of national unity; with the clear consciousness of seeking old and precious moral values; with the clean satisfaction that comes from the stern performance of duty by old and young alike. We aim at the assurance of a rounded, a permanent national life.

We do not distrust the – the future of essential democracy. The people of the United States have not failed. In their need they have registered a mandate that they want direct, vigorous action. They have asked for discipline and direction under leadership. They have made me the present instrument of their wishes. In the spirit of the gift I take it.

In this dedication – In this dedication of a Nation, we humbly ask the blessing of God.

May He protect each and every one of us.

May He guide me in the days to come.

Analysis

FDR's first inaugural speech is a powerful example of the optimal situation for rhetorical effectiveness – when the man and the moment come together. After 12 years of Presidential statements delivered by the barely coherent Warren G. Harding, the literate but distant Calvin Coolidge, and the leaden Hoover, Roosevelt represented a return to eloquence in the bully pulpit of the U.S. Presidency. Eloquence proved to be just what a dire situation required.

Roosevelt was a superb orator who valued the power of words, particularly as amplified by the relatively new medium of radio. He took great care that his first speech as President carried maximum impact. His audience, the American people, were more than receptive – they were desperate for hope and for leadership, both of which Roosevelt was well prepared to deliver.

The patrician Roosevelt was not a man who merely relied on his own considerable verbal resources, however. He was not reluctant to call on the best rhetorical talents available to shape his addresses. His principal assistance on the Inaugural Address most likely came from Sam Rosenman, a longtime friend and associate who had assisted on many speeches during Roosevelt's term as Governor of New York, and during the Presidential campaign. Rosenman served as a sort of unofficial chief of speechwriting during Roosevelt's Presidency, despite his pressing duties as a judge on the New York State Supreme Court. He coordinated the efforts of at least a dozen prominent contributors to FDR's speeches, including poet Archibald MacLeish and playwright Robert Sherwood, each of whom won the Pulizer Prize in his field. Roosevelt's

enormous success completely transformed the nature of the White House communications process. Every President since has employed speechwriters, either talented colleagues or paid professionals, though not always with the same degree of success that Roosevelt enjoyed.

Roosevelt himself was clearly in command of the product, however, and was probably the most significant contributor, according to contemporary accounts. The Inaugural speech is, today, most known for the inspirational quote, "The only thing we have to fear is (dramatic pause) fear itself," which has come to be the speech's unofficial title. That famous affirmation appears in the third paragraph, and is quite obviously designed for immortality. It sets the ringing oratorical tone for what follows, though the whole speech is dense with memorable turns of phrase and blunt avowals that times were going to change. Roosevelt followed the "fear itself" construction immediately with the reassurance that America's darkest hours had produced leadership of "frankness and vigor." It went without saying that he was the vigorous leader for this crisis.

What came after was a terrific, almost throwaway, line that put the privations of the Great Depression into a kind of perspective. He said that the nation's troubles concerned, "thank God, only material things." In other words, that there were more important things – spiritual matters and qualities of character – which would bring the American people through difficult times. This test was nothing compared to those their forefathers faced and conquered. They were suffering want in the midst of plenty not because of the failures of the people, but the failures of "the money changers." The bankers and industrial giants had overreached and stumbled, abetted by their leaders in government. Hoover, sitting nearby, must have squirmed at the force of the indictment of his Administration.

The speech pulled no punches and remains a strong and unalloyed indictment of Wall Street and the captains of industry. It is of interest that the sophisticated Roosevelt, not known to be overly religious, littered the speech with biblical references, most notably repeatedly decrying the depredations of the "money changers." No wonder then that the moneyed establishment of which he was a member disowned him as a traitor.

Roosevelt offered no real specifics of the programs to come in the surprisingly brief speech – less than 2,000 words. However, he clearly laid out his priorities. One was putting people to work by "direct recruiting by the Government itself…" foreshadowing the great corps of workers later employed by the U.S. on public works projects such as the Civilian Conservation Corps and the Works Progress Administration. Surprisingly, he also advocated moving people out of cities and into rural areas in a "national scale of redistribution" – a social engineering scheme that quickly fell by the wayside. He strongly signalled his intent that government would play a much larger role in communications and transportation, as well as reining in the power of

Roosevelt delivers one of his "fireside chats" to the nation. The President pioneered the use of the relatively new media in politics.

the investment sector through regulation. Roosevelt also found room to speak of the need to restore trade and for the U.S. to become a "good neighbor" in international relations. Overall, throughout the speech, the prospect of a greatly expanded, activist Federal government was clear. He would seek the cooperation of the Congress, he said, but if the Congress was not up to the task, he would proceed without it.

The reaction was immediate and affirmative. The speech cemented Roosevelt's national mandate and he seized the moment in the historic first 100 days of his Administration. He launched a broad array of measures designed to bring about quick recovery and also to reform the financial system that he blamed for the national economic collapse. During his first two terms, Roosevelt fundamentally altered the nature of the U.S. government, massively increasing its size and creating a social safety net and system of economic regulation that has persisted, and grown further, to the present day.

November 30, 1874	Winston Leonard Spencer-Churchill is born at Blenheim Palace in Oxfordshire, England.
February 20, 1895	Commissioned as a Second Lieutenant in the 4th Hussar Regiment.
1899	Resigns from the Army after seeing action in India and the Sudan and becomes a Conservative Party candidate in a by-election, which he loses.
1900	Returns to England and stands again for Parliament as a Conservative. This time he is elected.
1904	Leaves the Conservative Party to become a member of the Liberal Party.
September 12, 1908	Marries Clementine Hozier.
1911	Churchill is made First Lord of the Admiralty.
1915	After the disaster of Gallipoli, for which he takes much of the blame, Churchill resigns from the Cabinet and rejoins the army.
1916	Churchill commands the 6th Battalion Royal Scots Fusiliers for several months then resumes his political career.
1922	Loses his seat as a Member of Parliament for Dundee in the General Election.
1924	Churchill leaves the Liberals to rejoin the Conservative Party. Re-elected to Parliament, he is appointed the Chancellor of the Exchequer.
September 3, 1939	Britain declares war on Germany.
May 10, 1940	Churchill succeeds Neville Chamberlain as British Prime Minister.
1940–1945	Churchill leads the British government during World War II.
July 26, 1945	Churchill's government is defeated in the General Election.
October 25, 1951	Becomes British Prime Minister again.
1953	Churchill is knighted by Queen Elizabeth II and wins the Nobel Prize for Literature.
1955	Because of poor health, Churchill resigns as Prime Minister.
October 15, 1964	Churchill decides not to seek re-election and retires from politics.
January 24, 1965	Dies in London.

Prime Minister Winston Churchill

"I have nothing to offer but blood, toil, tears and sweat."

THE PERIOD 1929 TO 1939 marked a long low point in Winston Churchill's brilliant political career. During the first chapter of his life in politics – which spanned World War I and its aftermath – he had alienated, in one way or another, top officials from every major party in Britain. When the Conservative party (of which he was then a member) reassumed power, government posts were repeatedly denied him and he was relegated to Parliament's backbenches, a political wilderness reserved for cranks and the powerless. During this exile, Churchill's became a lonely voice in Parliament, warning of the growing military strength of Hitler's Germany and entreating the government to take action to curb the Nazis before it was too late. Only when Prime Minister Neville Chamberlain's policy of appeasement was proven a failure by Germany's invasion of Poland, did Churchill's star begin to rise again.

On September 3, 1939, the day Britain declared war on Germany after that invasion, Chamberlain appointed Churchill as First Lord of the Admiralty, a position he had held throughout World War I. Churchill's efforts in that post failed to energize the Anglo-French alliance during the following few months (a period of inaction on both sides that became known as "the phony war"). Then, in April 1940, the German army invaded Norway and two Anglo-French counteroffensives failed. When the Nazis overran Belgium, the Netherlands, and Luxembourg the following month, Chamberlain resigned.

All the British political parties realized that only Churchill could unite and lead the country against the Nazi peril, and he was named Prime Minister at the head of a coalition government. He also assumed the portfolio of the Ministry of Defence. The five members of the War Cabinet, as it was called, represented all mainstream political

Winston Churchill addresses the officers and men of H.M.S. *Hardy* at Horse Guards Parade, London, after their destroyer was sunk in action of the coast of Norway in April 1940.

parties, but Churchill was clearly the one man on whom Britain's hope of survival depended. Three days after the hasty formation of the coalition the new Prime Minister went before the Parliament.

FIRST SPEECH AS PRIME MINISTER

MAY 13, 1940

HOUSE OF COMMONS, LONDON

I beg to move, that this House welcomes the formation of a Government representing the united and inflexible resolve of the nation to prosecute the war with Germany to a victorious conclusion.

On Friday evening last I received His Majesty's Commission to form a new Administration. It was the evident wish and will of Parliament and the nation that this should be conceived on the broadest possible basis and that it should include all parties, both those who supported the late Government and also the parties of the Opposition. I have completed the most important part of this task. A War Cabinet has been formed of five Members, representing, with the Opposition Liberals, the unity of the nation. The three party Leaders have agreed to serve, either in the War Cabinet or in high executive office. The three Fighting Services have been filled. It was necessary that this should be done in one single day, on account of the extreme urgency and rigour of events. A number of other positions, key positions, were filled yesterday, and I am submitting a further list to His Majesty tonight. I hope to complete the appointment of the principal Ministers during tomorrow. The appointment of the other Ministers usually takes a little longer, but I trust that, when Parliament meets again, this part of my task will be completed, and that the Administration will be complete in all respects.

I considered it in the public interest to suggest that the House should be summoned to meet today. Mr. Speaker agreed, and took the necessary steps, in accordance with the powers conferred upon him by the Resolution of the House. At the end of the proceedings today, the Adjournment of the House will be proposed until Tuesday, 21st May, with, of course, provision for earlier meeting, if need be. The business to be considered during that week will be notified to Members at the earliest opportunity. I now invite the House, by the resolution which stands in my name, to record its approval of the steps taken and to declare its confidence in the new Government.

To form an Administration of this scale and complexity is a serious undertaking in itself, but it must be remembered that we are in the preliminary stage of one of the greatest battles in history, that we are in action at many other points in Norway and in Holland, that we have to be prepared in the Mediterranean, that the air battle is continuous and that many preparations have to be made here at home. In this crisis I hope I may be pardoned if I do not address the House at any length today. I hope that any of my friends and colleagues, or former colleagues, who are affected by the political reconstruction, will make all allowances for any lack of ceremony with which it has been necessary to act. I would say to the House, as I said to those who have joined this Government: "I have nothing to offer but blood, toil, tears and sweat."

We have before us an ordeal of the most grievous kind. We have before us many, many long months of struggle and of suffering. You ask, what is our policy? I will say: It is to wage war, by sea, land and air, with all our might and with all the strength that God can give us; to wage war against a monstrous tyranny never surpassed in the dark and lamentable catalogue of human crime. That is our policy. You ask, what is our aim? I can answer in one word: Victory. Victory at all costs, victory in spite of all terror, victory, however long and hard the road may be; for without victory, there is no survival. Let that be realised; no survival for the British Empire, no survival for all that the British Empire has stood for, no survival for the urge and impulse of the ages, that mankind will move forward towards its goal. But I take up my task with buoyancy and hope. I feel sure that our cause will not be suffered to fail among men. At this time I feel entitled to claim the aid of all, and I say, come then, let us go forward together with our united strength.

Winston Churchill inspects damage caused by an air raid in Battersea, London.

An inspirational British wartime poster featuring Churchill's line "Let us go forward together" from this speech.

Analysis

Winston Churchill was one of the greatest orators of the 20th, or any other, century; a fact that was recognized even while he was a lone voice in the wilderness, crying out against the coming evil. Now, he had been summoned to employ his great gift of words in the service of his country, and he did not disappoint. Churchill would go on, during the course of the war, to inspire the British people and electrify the world in addresses to Parliament and on radio. His oratory arguably played as much of a role in Britain's war effort as his indomitable will, prodigious energy, and strategic capabilities.

Churchill's maiden speech as Prime Minister would, in lesser hands, have been a perfunctory procedural address. His task was to ask formally for the approval of the House of Commons of the new government with Churchill at its head. Indeed, much of the short address was taken up with the business of moving for the necessary vote of confidence, and in apologizing both for the short notice and the brevity of the speech, both of which were attributed to the demanding circumstances.

As delivered by a master, however, the address becomes immortal. The last half sums up the task ahead with remarkable clarity and force. No one in the audience would have accused Churchill of hyperbole as he characterized the situation as "the preliminary stage of one of the greatest battles in history." A little later came the sentence by which the speech has become known, "I have nothing to offer but blood, toil, tears and sweat." Another vigorous and emphatic orator, Theodore Roosevelt, originally uttered those words when he was appointed U.S. Assistant Secretary of the Navy three years before he became President. Churchill, with his naval background, undoubtedly read Roosevelt's speech and was impressed enough to remember the phrase. Although he used it without attribution, it did not matter. From that day forward, the words belonged not to Teddy Roosevelt, but to Churchill.

The final paragraph of the speech is an extraordinary example of Churchill's rhetorical technique. He asks and answers two rhetorical questions: what is our policy and what is our aim? The answers both employ one of Churchill's favorite rhetorical devices – repetition – which he used with unparalleled effectiveness.

"You ask, what is our policy? I will say it is to wage war…." "You ask, what is our aim? I can answer in one word: victory…." Churchill followed that with another repetition, repeating the phrase "no survival" several times. Each of the three repetitions built the dramatic effect further, to a crescendo of defiance of the "monstrous tyranny never surpassed in the dark and lamentable catalogue of human crime." Using the word "crime" in regard to the Nazis was a masterful stroke. Branding the Nazis as criminals reduced them in stature, and was also a calculated insult to "Herr Hitler", as Churchill always called the Nazi leader. Indeed, Churchill calculated the effect of his every word. For instance, he always carefully mispronounced "Nazi" as "Nozzi", in another subtle provocation. Churchill's oratory abounded with such sly touches, used throughout his political career to discomfit his opponents. In his speeches as Prime Minister, however, Churchill hoped that his aggravating remarks might goad the megalomaniac Hitler into rash errors. According to historical accounts, the ploy worked.

Churchill closed the speech on a note of "buoyancy and hope," expressing in his gruff voice, tinged with the accent of the aristocracy, the "surety that our cause will not be suffered to fail among men." The archaic, faintly biblical, language was intended to be memorable, and quotable. Like most of his rhetorical constructions, it succeeded.

That Churchill changed history with his words, as well as his deeds, is undeniable. He painted the Nazi threat – and the consequences of defeat – in the direst possible terms, but never once entertained the notion that actual defeat was possible. When he gave this speech, the combined British and French armies were being pushed inexorably back toward the beaches of Dunkirk. There was a very real danger that they would be annihilated and that Hitler would then invade Britain. Hearing Churchill, every Briton knew that they would resist to the end the fate that had befallen the rest of Europe; that they had found a leader worth following with, as Churchill said, "all our might and with all the strength that God can give us."

Winston Churchill leaves a Cabinet meeting at 10 Downing Street on 10 May, 1940: the day of his appointment as Prime Minister. With him are Air Minister, Sir Kingsley Wood (left), and Foreign Secretary Anthony Eden (right).

Allied troops wade out to the waiting flotilla of ships during the evacuation of Dunkirk.

Prime Minister Winston Churchill

"We shall fight on the beaches."

WINSTON CHURCHILL ONCE FAMOUSLY SAID "history will be kind to me, for I intend to write it." After World War II, during the years he was out of power, he did write a superb six-volume account of it, as only one who was intimately involved could have done. In 1940, however, he was busy making the history that he would later recount.

His aim, as he said in his initial speech, was, in one word, victory. In his first days as Prime Minister, Churchill mobilized all of Britain to that goal. Although he was politically a conservative and his positions were actively anti-socialist, he rammed through Parliament the most comprehensive emergency powers in modern British history, placing all "persons, their services and their property at the disposal of the Crown."

From the first days in his new post, Churchill was seemingly ubiquitous. He appeared at RAF headquarters, inspected bomb damage and comforted victims of the "blitz" in London, and reviewed coastal defenses. His ever-present cigar and "V for Victory" sign were familiar to the whole country, as were his Parliamentary and radio addresses, which mixed frank assessments of the peril with grim but welcome humor. Single-handedly, he lifted the beleaguered nation by the sheer force of his personality.

And the nation needed lifting, because the news was not good. The British and French armies had been battered and routed in France, Belgium had fallen, and its army had surrendered. Nevertheless, British pride had been somewhat eased by the "miracle of Dunkirk" – the successful evacuation of more than 335,000 soldiers from the Allied armies against overwhelming odds by a motley flotilla of naval vessels and private craft. The evacuation took more than a week: a week of anxiety and prayer throughout

FOR WINSTON CHURCHILL TIMELINE, PLEASE SEE PAGE 16

WORDS THAT CHANGED THE WORLD

Britain. In its aftermath, Churchill appeared before Parliament. It was an appearance he had scheduled a week earlier to provide a full account of what he had thought would be a devastating military disaster. Although his news was somewhat better than he had expected, he took pains to dampen the euphoria of the Dunkirk rescue with a heavy dose of reality.

SPEECH TO PARLIAMENT

JUNE 4, 1940

HOUSE OF COMMONS, LONDON

From the moment that the French defences at Sedan and on the Meuse were broken at the end of the second week of May, only a rapid retreat to Amiens and the south could have saved the British and French Armies who had entered Belgium at the appeal of the Belgian King, but this strategic fact was not immediately realised. The French High Command hoped they would be able to close the gap, and the Armies of the north were under their orders. Moreover, a retirement of this kind would have involved almost certainly the destruction of the fine Belgian Army of over 20 divisions and the abandonment of the whole of Belgium. Therefore, when the force and scope of the German penetration were realised and when a new French Generalissimo, General Weygand, assumed command in place of General Gamelin, an effort was made by the French and British Armies in Belgium to keep on holding the right hand of the Belgians and to give their own right hand to a newly created French Army which was to have advanced across the Somme in great strength to grasp it.

However, the German eruption swept like a sharp scythe around the right and rear of the Armies of the north. Eight or nine armoured divisions, each of about 400 armoured vehicles of different kinds, but carefully assorted to be complementary and divisible into small self-contained units, cut off all communications between us and the main French Armies. It severed our own communications for food and ammunition, which ran first to Amiens and afterwards through Abbeville, and it shore its way up the coast to Boulogne and Calais, and almost to Dunkirk. Behind this armoured and mechanised onslaught came a number of German divisions in lorries, and behind them again there plodded comparatively slowly the dull brute mass of the ordinary German Army and German people, always so ready to be led to the trampling down in other lands of liberties and comforts which they have never known in their own.

I have said this armoured scythe-stroke almost reached Dunkirk – almost but not quite. Boulogne and Calais were the scenes of desperate fighting. The Guards defended Boulogne for a while and were then withdrawn by orders from this country. The Rifle Brigade, the 60th Rifles, and the Queen Victoria's Rifles, with a battalion of British tanks and 1,000 Frenchmen, in all about 4,000 strong, defended Calais to the last. The British Brigadier was given an hour to surrender. He spurned

the offer, and four days of intense street fighting passed before silence reigned over Calais, which marked the end of a memorable resistance. Only 30 unwounded survivors were brought off by the Navy and we do not know the fate of their comrades. Their sacrifice, however, was not in vain. At least two armoured divisions, which otherwise would have been turned against the British Expeditionary Force, had to be sent for to overcome them. They have added another page to the glories of the Light Division, and the time gained enabled the Graveline waterlines to be flooded and to be held by the French troops.

Thus it was that the port of Dunkirk was kept open. When it was found impossible for the Armies of the north to reopen their communications to Amiens with the main French Armies, only one choice remained. It seemed, indeed, forlorn. The Belgian, British and French Armies were almost surrounded. Their sole line of retreat was to a single port and to its neighbouring beaches. They were pressed on every side by heavy attacks and far outnumbered in the air.

When a week ago today I asked the House to fix this afternoon as the occasion for a statement, I feared it would be my hard lot to announce the greatest military disaster in our long history. I thought – and some good judges agreed with me – that perhaps 20,000 or 30,000 men might be re-embarked. But it certainly seemed that the whole of the French First Army and the whole of the British Expeditionary Force north of the Amiens-Abbeville gap, would be broken up in the open field or else would have to capitulate for lack of food and ammunition. These were the hard and heavy tidings for which I called upon the House and the nation to prepare themselves a week ago. The whole root and core and brain of the British Army, on which and around which we were to build, and are to build, the great British Armies in the later years of the war, seemed about to perish upon the field or to be led into an ignominious and starving captivity.

That was the prospect a week ago. But another blow which might well have proved final was yet to fall upon us. The King of the Belgians had called upon us to come to his aid. Had not this Ruler and his Government severed themselves from the Allies, who rescued their country from extinction in the late war, and had they not sought refuge in what has proved to be a fatal neutrality, the French and British Armies might well at the outset have saved not only Belgium but perhaps even Poland. Yet at the last moment, when Belgium was already invaded, King Leopold called upon us to come to his aid, and even at the last moment we came. He and his brave, efficient Army, nearly half a million strong, guarded our eastern flank and thus kept open our only line of retreat to the sea. Suddenly, without prior consultation, with the least possible notice, without the advice of his Ministers and upon his own personal act, he sent a plenipotentiary to the German Command, surrendered his Army and exposed our whole flank and means of retreat.

I asked the House a week ago to suspend its judgment because

British and French troops wait on the dunes at Dunkirk to be picked up by Naval and merchant vessels.

the facts were not clear, but I do not feel that any reason now exists why we should not form our own opinions upon this pitiful episode. The surrender of the Belgian Army compelled the British at the shortest notice to cover a flank to the sea more than 30 miles in length. Otherwise all would have been cut off, and all would have shared the fate to which King Leopold had condemned the finest Army his country had ever formed. So in doing this and in exposing this flank, as anyone who followed the operations on the map will see, contact was lost between the British and two out of the three corps forming the First French Army, who were still further from the coast than we were, and it seemed impossible that any large number of Allied troops could reach the coast.

The enemy attacked on all sides with great strength and fierceness, and their main power, the power of their far more numerous air force, was thrown into the battle or else concentrated upon Dunkirk and the beaches. Pressing in upon the narrow exit, both from the east and from the west, the enemy began to fire with cannon upon the beaches by which alone the shipping could approach or depart. They sowed

magnetic mines in the channels and seas; they sent repeated waves of hostile aircraft, sometimes more than 100 strong in one formation, to cast their bombs upon the single pier that remained, and upon the sand dunes upon which the troops had their eyes for shelter. Their U-boats, one of which was sunk, and their motor launches took their toll of the vast traffic which now began. For four or five days an intense struggle reigned. All their armoured divisions – or what was left of them – together with great masses of German infantry and artillery, hurled themselves in vain upon the ever-narrowing, ever-contracting appendix within which the British and French Armies fought.

Meanwhile, the Royal Navy, with the willing help of countless merchant seamen, strained every nerve to embark the British and Allied troops. Two hundred and twenty light warships and 650 other vessels were engaged. They had to operate upon the difficult coast, often in adverse weather, under an almost ceaseless hail of bombs and an increasing concentration of artillery fire. Nor were the seas, as I have said, themselves free from mines and torpedoes. It was in conditions such as these that our men carried on, with little or no rest, for days and nights on end, making trip after trip across the dangerous waters, bringing with them always men whom they had rescued. The numbers they have brought back are the measure of their devotion and their courage. The hospital ships, which brought off many thousands of British and French wounded, being so plainly marked were a special target for Nazi bombs; but the men and women on board them never faltered in their duty.

Meanwhile, the Royal Air Force, which had already been intervening in the battle, so far as its range would allow, from home bases, now used part of its main metropolitan fighter strength, and struck at the German bombers, and at the fighters which in large numbers protected them. This struggle was protracted and fierce. Suddenly the scene has cleared, the crash and thunder has for the moment – but only for the moment – died away. A miracle of deliverance, achieved by valour, by perseverance, by perfect discipline, by faultless service, by resource, by skill, by unconquerable fidelity, is manifest to us all. The enemy was hurled back by the retreating British and French troops. He was so roughly handled that he did not harry their departure seriously. The Royal Air Force engaged the main strength of the German Air Force, and inflicted upon them losses of at least four to one; and the Navy, using nearly 1,000 ships of all kinds, carried over 335,000 men, French and British, out of the jaws of death and shame, to their native land and to the tasks which lie immediately ahead. We must be very careful not to assign to this deliverance the attributes of a victory. Wars are not won by evacuations. But there was a victory inside this deliverance, which should be noted. It was gained by the Air Force. Many of our soldiers coming back have not seen the Air Force at work; they saw only the bombers which escaped its protective attack. They underrate its achievements. I have heard much talk of this; that is why I go out of my way to say this. I will tell you about it.

This was a great trial of strength between the British and German Air Forces. Can you conceive a greater objective for the Germans in the air than to make evacuation from these beaches impossible, and to sink all these ships which were displayed, almost to the extent of thousands? Could there have been an objective of greater military importance and significance for the whole purpose of the war than this? They tried hard, and they were beaten back; they were frustrated in their task. We got the Army away; and they have paid fourfold for any losses which they have inflicted. Very large formations of German aeroplanes – and we know that they are a very brave race – have turned on several occasions from the attack of one-quarter of their number of the Royal Air Force, and have dispersed in different directions. Twelve aeroplanes have been hunted by two. One aeroplane was driven into the water and cast away, by the mere charge of a British aeroplane, which had no more ammunition. All of our types – the Hurricane, the Spitfire and the new Defiant – and all our pilots have been vindicated as superior to what they have at present to face.

When we consider how much greater would be our advantage in defending the air above this island against an overseas attack, I must say that I find in these facts a sure basis upon which practical and reassuring thoughts may rest. I will pay my tribute to these young airmen. The great French Army was very largely, for the time being, cast back and disturbed by the onrush of a few thousands of armoured vehicles. May it not also be that the cause of civilisation itself will be defended by the skill and devotion of a few thousand airmen? There never had been, I suppose, in all the world, in all the history of war, such an opportunity for youth. The Knights of the Round Table, the Crusaders, all fall back into a prosaic past: not only distant but prosaic; but these young men, going forth every morn to guard their native land and all that we stand for, holding in their hands these instruments of colossal and shattering power, of whom it may be said that "When every morning brought a noble chance, And every chance brought out a noble knight," deserve our gratitude, as do all of the brave men who, in so many ways and on so many occasions, are ready, and continue ready, to give life and all for their native land.

I return to the Army. In the long series of very fierce battles, now on this front, now on that, fighting on three fronts at once, battles fought by two or three divisions against an equal or somewhat larger number of the enemy, and fought fiercely on some of the old grounds that so many of us knew so well, in these battles our losses in men have exceeded 30,000 killed, wounded and missing. I take occasion to express the sympathy of the House to all who have suffered bereavement or who are still anxious. The President of the Board of Trade is not here today. His son has been killed, and many in the House have felt the pangs of affliction in the sharpest form. But I will say this about the missing. We have had a large number of wounded come home safely to this country – the greater part – but I would say about the missing that there may be very many reported missing who will come back home, some day, in one way or another. In the confusion of this fight it is inevitable that many have been left in positions where honour required no further resistance from them.

Against this loss of over 30,000 men, we can set a far heavier loss certainly inflicted upon the enemy. But our losses in material are enormous. We have perhaps lost one-third of the men we lost in the opening days of the battle of 21st March, 1918, but we have lost nearly as many guns – nearly 1,000 guns – and all our transport, all the armoured vehicles that were with the Army in the North. This loss will impose a further delay on the expansion of our military strength. That expansion had not been proceeding as fast as we had hoped. The best of all we had to give had gone to the British Expeditionary Force, and although they had not the numbers of tanks and some articles of equipment which were desirable, they were a very well and finely equipped Army. They had the first-fruits of all that our industry had to give, and that is gone. And now here is this further delay. How long it will be, how long it will last, depends upon the exertions which we make in this island. An effort the like of which has never been seen

Winston Churchill broadcasts to the nation from Downing Street, London.

in our records is now being made. Work is proceeding everywhere, night and day, Sundays and week-days. Capital and labour have cast aside their interests, rights and customs and put them into the common stock. Already the flow of munitions has leapt forward. There is no reason why we should not in a few months overtake the sudden and serious loss that has come upon us, without retarding the development of our general programme.

Nevertheless, our thankfulness at the escape of our Army and so many men, whose loved ones have passed through an agonising week, must not blind us to the fact that what has happened in France and Belgium is a colossal military disaster. The French Army has been weakened, the Belgian Army has been lost, a large part of those fortified lines upon which so much faith had been reposed is gone, many valuable mining districts and factories have passed into the enemy's possession, the whole of the Channel ports are in his hands, with all the tragic consequences that follow from that, and we must expect another blow to be struck almost immediately at us or at France. We are told that Herr Hitler has a plan for invading the British Isles. This has often been thought of before. When

Napoleon lay at Boulogne for a year with his flat-bottomed boats and his Grand Army, he was told by someone, "There are bitter weeds in England." There are certainly a great many more of them since the British Expeditionary Force returned.

The whole question of home defence against invasion is, of course, powerfully affected by the fact that we have for the time being in this island incomparably more powerful military forces than we have ever had at any moment in this war or the last. But this will not continue. We shall not be content with a defensive war. We have our duty to our Ally. We have to reconstitute and build up the British Expeditionary Force once again, under its gallant Commander-in-Chief, Lord Gort. All this is in train; but in the interval we must put our defences in this island into such a high state of organisation that the fewest possible numbers will be required to give effective security and that the largest possible potential of offensive effort may be realised. On this we are now engaged. It will be very convenient, if it be the desire of the House, to enter upon this subject in a secret Session. Not that the Government would necessarily be able to reveal in very great detail military secrets, but we like to have our discussions free, without the restraint imposed by the fact that they will be read the next day by the enemy, and the Government would benefit by views freely expressed in all parts of the House by Members with their knowledge of so many different parts of the country. I understand that some request is to be made upon this subject, which will be readily acceded to by His Majesty's Government.

We have found it necessary to take measures of increasing stringency, not only against enemy aliens and suspicious characters of other nationalities, but also against British subjects who may become a danger or a nuisance should the war be transported to the United Kingdom. I know there are a great many people affected by the orders which we have made who are the passionate enemies of Nazi Germany. I am very sorry for them, but we cannot, at the present time and under the present stress, draw all the distinctions which we should like to do. If parachute landings were attempted and fierce fighting attendant upon them followed, these unfortunate people would be far better out of the way, for their own sakes as well as for ours. There is, however, another class, for which I feel not the slightest sympathy. Parliament has given us the powers to put down Fifth Column activities with a strong hand, and we shall use those powers, subject to the supervision and correction of the House, without the slightest hesitation until we are satisfied, and more than satisfied, that this malignancy in our midst has been effectively stamped out.

Turning once again, and this time more generally, to the question of invasion, I would observe that there has never been a period in all these long centuries of which we boast when an absolute guarantee against invasion, still less against serious raids, could have been given to our people. In the days of Napoleon, of which I was speaking just now, the same wind which would have carried his transports across the Channel might have driven away the blockading fleet. There was always the chance, and it is that chance which has excited and befooled the imaginations of many Continental tyrants. Many are the tales that are told. We are assured that novel methods will be adopted, and when we see the originality of malice, the ingenuity of aggression, which our enemy displays, we may certainly prepare ourselves for every kind of novel stratagem and every kind of brutal and treacherous manœuvre. I think that no idea is so outlandish that it should not be considered and viewed with a searching, but at the same time, I hope, with a steady eye.

Men of the British Expeditionary Force arrive at a London railway station on their return home from the evacuation of Dunkirk, to be greeted by young women handing out fruit and cigarettes.

Winston Churchill (center), seen during a visit to inspect coastal defenses in the North East of England during July 1940.

We must never forget the solid assurances of sea power and those which belong to air power if it can be locally exercised.

I have, myself, full confidence that if all do their duty, if nothing is neglected, and if the best arrangements are made, as they are being made, we shall prove ourselves once again able to defend our island home, to ride out the storm of war, and to outlive the menace of tyranny, if necessary for years, if necessary alone. At any rate, that is what we are going to try to do. That is the resolve of His Majesty's Government – every man of them. That is the will of Parliament and the nation. The British Empire and the French Republic, linked together in their cause and in their need, will defend to the death their native soil, aiding each other like good comrades to the utmost of their strength. Even though large tracts of Europe and many old and famous States

29

have fallen or may fall into the grip of the Gestapo and all the odious apparatus of Nazi rule, we shall not flag or fail. We shall go on to the end. We shall fight in France, we shall fight on the seas and oceans, we shall fight with growing confidence and growing strength in the air, we shall defend our island, whatever the cost may be. We shall fight on the beaches, we shall fight on the landing grounds, we shall fight in the fields and in the streets, we shall fight in the hills; we shall never surrender, and even if, which I do not for a moment believe, this island or a large part of it were subjugated and starving, then our Empire beyond the seas, armed and guarded by the British Fleet, would carry on the struggle, until, in God's good time, the new world, with all its power and might, steps forth to the rescue and the liberation of the old.

Analysis

This was the second of three legendary speeches Churchill delivered shortly after assuming the office of Prime Minister. Each has become known by an inspirational quote it contained. The first has gone down in history as his "Blood, toil, tears and sweat" speech; this one "We shall fight on the beaches"; and the third, "This was their finest hour".

The bulk of the speech is an account of the events leading up to Dunkirk and an assessment of the current situation. It could have been a dry recitation, but not in Churchill's hands. He delivered a galloping, enthralling description that kept both his fellow House of Commons members and the vast listening audience in Britain spellbound with suspense, even though they knew the outcome.

Churchill liberally sprinkled the address, as he did all his speeches, with extraordinary turns of phrase. For instance, he related that the German "eruption swept like a sharp scythe …" and behind the armored onslaught "plodded comparatively slowly the dull brute mass of the ordinary German army...." After his moving and memorable tale of the gallant British defense of Calais, which kept open the port of Dunkirk and preserved a slim chance of rescue, he characterized the peril still ahead: "The whole root and core and brain of the British Army … seemed about to perish upon the field or to be led into an ignominious and starving captivity."

He was also characteristically blunt, calling King Leopold's surrender of the Belgian army a "pitiful episode." The Belgian king had begged the Allied armies to come to his aid, then left them almost without means of retreat when he abruptly capitulated to the Germans, in the process delivering his "brave, efficient army" into Nazi hands.

Churchill offered a description of the courage and sacrifice of all parties in the evacuation, singling out the RAF for particular praise. Ground troops had undervalued its contribution in the past, he said, but never again. British airmen had taken out four German aircraft for every one they lost. Their deeds drove the Knights of the Round Table and the Crusaders "back into a prosaic past." The rhetoric in this speech does not come up to the standard of another, made later in the year, which has come to be known for the line "Never in the field of human endeavour was so much owed by so many to so few," but it presages a continuing theme of accolades for the role of the RAF in the Battle of Britain.

After lamenting at length the loss of men and machines, Churchill cautioned the people against being too buoyed by the Dunkirk evacuation, reminding them that "what has happened in France and Belgium is a colossal military disaster" which it would take some time, and heroic effort, to overcome. The fact that the virtually intact army was now on British soil mitigated the immediate threat of invasion, he said, but Britain would not be content to fight a defensive war. When the army again took the fight to continental Europe, Britain must have arranged its defenses against the prospect of invasion. The temptation to invade Britain had "excited and befooled the imagination of many Continental tyrants," in the past and was now being contemplated again.

That passage set up the customary Churchillian peroration – the end piece intended to inflame and inspire his countrymen – which, in so many instances, has provided immortal quotes. He used, again as per custom, the technique of repetition, combined with the technique of joining together related phrases without conjunctions. The "we shall fight" series of repetitions was followed by a simple statement, "We shall never surrender." Churchill was telling the world that no matter what the rest of Europe had done, Britain would stand.

At the very end of the speech is a warning to Germany that can also be interpreted as an entreaty to America. Even if the Nazis succeeded in invading and subjugating "this island" the "Empire beyond the seas" would carry on the struggle. Churchill implicitly included the former colony in stating his conviction that "the new world, with all its power and might" would step forth to the rescue.

History, which Churchill both made and wrote, records the impacts of his words on this and other occasions. His island survived and prevailed, and his words reached across the Atlantic where they moved America to play its own part in World War II.

Churchill gives his famous "V for victory" sign outside 10 Downing Street, London.

President Franklin Delano Roosevelt

"A date which will live in infamy."

B Y 1939, FOREIGN POLICY WAS overshadowing domestic policy as Roosevelt's second term neared its end, even though economic recovery from the Great Depression was far from realized. U.S. attention was now focused on Europe, where the gathering storm clouds of the mid-decade had finally coalesced into war with Nazi Germany. Roosevelt had strongly backed arms sales to countries combating German aggression and, after the fall of France in 1940, he joined with Congress in escalating defense preparations and "all aid short of war" to Great Britain.

With war in Europe looming, Roosevelt declared his candidacy for an unprecedented third term. Isolationist sentiment remained strong throughout the country and both Roosevelt and his opponent, Wendell Willkie, pledged to keep the country out of war. Isolationists favored Willkie, while those supporting U.S. entry into the fray tended to back Roosevelt. Roosevelt won handily.

Throughout 1941, the eyes of America remained focused on Germany, as the country moved closer to actual hostilities. War across the Atlantic was inevitable. It was a question of when, and how. The answer came, unexpectedly, from the direction of the Pacific. FDR had taken note of Japan's increasing belligerency and its formal alliance with Germany and Italy. The U.S. cut off exports essential to Japan's capacity to wage war and, throughout 1941, unsatisfactory negotiations were conducted while Japan continued the build-up of men and arms in the Pacific region. Nevertheless, Roosevelt was convinced the Japanese were bluffing.

December 7, 1941, proved him wrong. On that day, the Japanese bombed Pearl Harbor, the main American navy base in the Pacific. Roosevelt was surprised and the

FOR FRANKLIN DELANO ROOSEVELT TIMELINE, PLEASE SEE PAGE 8

A view of Pearl Harbor after the Japanese attack, with smoke pouring from USS *Shaw* while the minelayer USS *Oglana* lies capsized in the foreground.

President Franklin D. Roosevelt addresses Congress the day after Japanese forces attacked Pearl Harbor.

American people were stunned. The day after the attack, he went before the Congress to ask for a declaration of war with Japan, which would almost automatically send the U.S. to war against Germany and Italy, too.

ADDRESS TO THE U.S. CONGRESS

DECEMBER 8, 1941
UNITED STATES CAPITOL, WASHINGTON, D.C.

Mr. Vice President, and Mr. Speaker, and Members of the Senate and House of Representatives:

Yesterday, December 7, 1941 – a date which will live in infamy – the United States of America was suddenly and deliberately attacked by naval and air forces of the Empire of Japan.

The United States was at peace with that Nation and, at the solicitation of Japan, was still in conversation with its Government

and its Emperor looking toward the maintenance of peace in the Pacific. Indeed, one hour after Japanese air squadrons had commenced bombing in the American Island of Oahu, the Japanese Ambassador to the United States and his colleague delivered to our Secretary of State a formal reply to a recent American message. And while this reply stated that it seemed useless to continue the existing diplomatic negotiations, it contained no threat or hint of war or of armed attack.

It will be recorded that the distance of Hawaii from Japan makes it obvious that the attack was deliberately planned many days or even weeks ago. During the intervening time the Japanese Government has deliberately sought to deceive the United States by false statements and expressions of hope for continued peace.

The attack yesterday on the Hawaiian Islands has caused severe damage to American naval and military forces. I regret to tell you that very many American lives have been lost. In addition American ships have been reported torpedoed on the high seas between San Francisco and Honolulu.

Yesterday the Japanese Government also launched an attack against Malaya.

Last night Japanese forces attacked Hong Kong.

Last night Japanese forces attacked Guam.

Last night Japanese forces attacked the Philippine Islands.

Last night the Japanese attacked Wake Island. And this morning the Japanese attacked Midway Island.

Japan has, therefore, undertaken a surprise offensive extending throughout the Pacific area. The facts of yesterday and today speak for themselves. The people of the United States have already formed their opinions and well understand the implications to the very life and safety of our Nation.

As Commander in Chief of the Army and Navy I have directed that all measures be taken for our defense.

But always will our whole Nation remember the character of the onslaught against us.

No matter how long it may take us to overcome this premeditated invasion, the American people in their righteous might will win through to absolute victory. I believe that I interpret the will of the Congress and of the people when I assert that we will not only defend ourselves to the uttermost but will make it very certain that this form of treachery shall never again endanger us.

Hostilities exist. There is no blinking at the fact that our people, our territory, and our interests are in grave danger.

With confidence in our armed forces – with the unbounding determination of our people – we will gain the inevitable triumph – so help us God.

I ask that the Congress declare that since the unprovoked and dastardly attack by Japan on Sunday, December 7, 1941, a state of war has existed between the United States and the Japanese Empire.

Analysis

One hallmark of a great orator is knowing the right note to strike – what to say and, just as important, what not to say. The American people had grown used to FDR's oratorical prowess – his dense and sometimes overblown rhetoric. For nine years, he had cajoled and inspired them through the depths of the Depression and then into the run-up to armed conflict.

On December 8, 1941, the largest radio audience in history – 81 percent of the American people – heard a different Roosevelt. The master communicator knew that the events of the previous day spoke for themselves and that eloquence and bombast would be superfluous. He largely achieved success for the speech in the first line, intoning magisterially the immortal phrase, "a date which will live in infamy." Interestingly, the original manuscript of the "Infamy" speech in the U.S. National Archives shows that as originally drafted it began with the much milder "a date which will live in world history." Roosevelt's superb instincts as a wordsmith are clearly on display here. Replacing the two words with only one, he produced a phrase that not only had the desired immediate effect, but which has taken its place in history. His speech that day affects public officials' rhetorical choices to this day, shaping the responses to such events as the September 11, 2001, terrorist attacks.

The original manuscript, prepared only in the afternoon and evening of December 7, also shows Roosevelt at work tightening and strengthening the speech in other places to heighten its impact. He made no attempt to soft-peddle the damage the attacks had done. Quite the opposite. He wanted to underscore the grievous harm Americans had suffered and the grave threat to the nation as a whole. Roosevelt also rejected Secretary of State Cordell Hull's urging to offer a full and detailed account of Japanese duplicity leading up to the attack, though he did note that the Japanese Ambassador had delivered a message to the White House even after his nation's planes had struck Pearl Harbor, containing no threat or even acknowledgment of the aggression. Instead of a detailed and angry account, Roosevelt solemnly recited in simple and stark terms the litany of the Japanese attacks, using the rhetorical technique of repetition to heighten the impact, hammering home each separate incident by repeating the words "last night …"

The speech itself is strikingly brief at 520 words – perhaps the greatest impact per word this side of the Gettysburg Address – and is almost devoid of Roosevelt's usual metaphoric flights. Simplicity was, on this occasion, much more effective. Roosevelt's words and demeanor radiated aggrieved determination. The nation has suffered grave harm, he said, but would do everything necessary to win ultimate victory. He made no attempt to make a case for going to war, or to include any concessions to the still-considerable isolationist sentiment in the country. He made no appeal for support from the people. The clear implication was that total support for, and total commitment to, facing and defeating U.S. enemies was a given. The American people responded exactly as Roosevelt had hoped: with anger, and with expressions of support for exacting vengeance.

Within an hour after the speech, Congress acted almost unanimously to declare war on Japan. Only one representative voted against the declaration, pacifist Republican Jeannette Rankin of Montana. Three days later, Germany and Italy declared war on the United States and the U.S. was fully engaged in the global war that would occupy it for the next four years.

Political scientists and rhetoricians alike have declared Roosevelt's brief, uncomplicated speech one of the greatest of the 20th Century. It is certainly one of the most famous, and its effects among the most far-reaching.

President Roosevelt signs the declaration of war against Japan while wearing a black armband.

January 26, 1880	Douglas MacArthur is born in Little Rock, Arkansas.
June 11, 1903	Graduates first in his class from the U.S. Military Academy and is commissioned a Second Lieutenant in the U.S. Army Corps of Engineers.
1908–1912	Becomes troop commander, adjutant, and Army Service Schools instructor at Fort Leavenworth, Kansas. While there, he is promoted to Captain.
December 1915	Promoted to Major.
August 1917	Promoted to Colonel, MacArthur becomes Chief of Staff of the 42nd Division in France.
June 1918	Promoted to Brigadier General in the National Army, MacArthur takes part in Marne operations and commands the 84th Infantry Brigade in the St. Mihiel and Meuse-Argonne offensives.
November 1918	Takes command of the 42nd Division in the Sedan offensive.
1919–1922	After World War I, MacArthur serves as Superintendent of the U.S. Military Academy.
January 1920	Promoted to Brigadier General in the Regular Army.
January 1925	MacArthur is promoted to Major General.
November 1930	Becomes Army Chief of Staff with the rank of General.
1935	Resumes his rank of Major General and becomes military advisor to the government of the Philippines.
December 1937	Retires from active service, but continues as advisor to the Philippine government.
July 1941	MacArthur is recalled to active service as Lieutenant General and given command of Unites States Army Forces in the Far East.
1941–1945	Leads American forces in Pacific campaigns as Supreme Allied Commander.
April 1, 1942	Receives Medal of Honor for the preparation of Philippines defenses.
December 1944	Promoted to temporary General of the Army.
September 2, 1945	Accepts formal Japanese surrender aboard the battleship *Missouri*, ending World War II.
September 1945	Appointed Supreme Allied Commander in Japan.
April 1946	The rank of General of the Army is made permanent.
July 1950	Upon the North Korean invasion of South Korea, MacArthur is designated Commander of the United Nations Command in the Far East.
April 1951	Relieved of command by President Truman.
May 12, 1962	Delivers farewell speech to U.S. Military Academy corps of cadets.
April 5, 1964	Dies in Washington, D.C.

General Douglas MacArthur

"A great victory has been won."

B Y THE SUMMER OF 1945, General Douglas MacArthur had spent a decade in the Far East, first as Chief Military Advisor to the government of the Philippines and then, after being recalled to active duty in mid-1941, as commander of U.S. forces in the Pacific. He conducted a valiant delaying action in the Philippines when the Japanese invaded following Pearl Harbor, famously declaring "I shall return" when ordered to evacuate to Australia in March 1942. He was in charge of Allied forces that fought their way back across the South Pacific over the next two years, finally making good on his promise with a successful invasion of the Philippines in autumn 1944.

The war in Europe ended in May 1945, but the long, savage slog toward the Japanese homeland continued throughout that summer with some of the bloodiest island-to-island fighting of the war. MacArthur was preparing a two-phase invasion of Japan that was to commence in November 1945 with a thrust onto the southern island of Kyushu. Military strategists projected more than a million casualties, including a quarter of a million dead, before Japan was subjugated.

That invasion became unnecessary when American planes dropped atomic bombs on Hiroshima on August 6 and Nagasaki three days later. The Japanese government swiftly capitulated. The war ended with stunning, disorienting suddenness.

MacArthur, by now promoted to General of the Army, was in charge of the surrender ceremony aboard the battleship U.S.S. *Missouri* in Tokyo Bay. As Supreme Commander of the Allied armed forces that would occupy Japan, he knew that he would become a virtual dictator of the defeated country. He thus knew that the remarks accompanying the surrender of swords and signing of documents would have to be more than *pro forma*. As of that day, he would have to be more statesman than soldier, and his words should reflect that. He made brief remarks at the ceremony itself, and then expanded on them later that day in a radio address.

General Douglas MacArthur broadcasts while Japanese Foreign Minister Mamoru Shigemitsu signs the unconditional surrender document on board the USS *Missouri*.

ADDRESS ON THE SURRENDER OF JAPAN

SEPTEMBER 2, 1945

ONBOARD THE U.S.S. *MISSOURI*

We are gathered here, representatives of the major warring powers, to conclude a solemn agreement whereby peace may be restored. The issues, involving divergent ideals and ideologies, have been determined on the battlefields of the world and hence are not for our discussion or debate. Nor is it for us here to meet, representing as we do a majority of the people of the earth, in a spirit of distrust, malice or hatred. But rather it is for us, both victors and vanquished, to rise to that higher dignity which alone befits the sacred purposes we are about to serve, committing all our people unreservedly to faithful compliance with the understanding they are here formally to assume.

It is my earnest hope, and indeed the hope of all mankind, that from this solemn occasion a better world shall emerge out of the blood and carnage of the past – a world dedicated to the dignity of man and the fulfillment of his most cherished wish for freedom, tolerance and justice.

The terms and conditions upon which the surrender of the Japanese Imperial Forces is here to be given and accepted are contained in the instrument of surrender now before you.

As supreme Commander for the Allied Powers, I announce it my firm purpose, in the tradition of the countries I represent, to proceed in the discharge of my responsibilities with justice and tolerance, while taking all necessary dispositions to ensure that the terms of surrender are fully, promptly, and faithfully complied with.

Let us pray that peace be now restored to the world and that God will preserve it always.

General Douglas MacArthur tours the Bataan Peninsula after his return to the Philippines.

RADIO ADDRESS TO A WORLD AUDIENCE AFTER THE SURRENDER CEREMONY

Today the guns are silent. A great tragedy has ended. A great victory has been won ….

As I look back upon the long, tortuous trail from those grim days of Bataan and Corregidor, when an entire world lived in fear, when democracy was on the defensive everywhere, when modern civilization trembled in the balance, I thank a merciful God that he has given us the faith, the courage and the power from which to mold victory. We have known the bitterness of defeat and the exultation of triumph, and from both we have learned there can be no turning back. We must go forward to preserve in peace what we won in war.

A new era is upon us. Even the lesson of victory itself brings with it profound concern, both for our future security and the survival of civilization. The destructiveness of the war potential, through progressive advances in scientific discovery, has in fact now reached a point which revises the traditional concepts of war.

Men since the beginning of time have sought peace …. Military alliances, balances of power, leagues of nations, all in turn failed, leaving the only path to be by way of the crucible of war. We have had our last chance. If we do not now devise some greater and more equitable system, Armageddon will be at our door. The problem basically is theological and involves a spiritual recrudescence and improvement of human character that will synchronize with our almost matchless advances in science, art, literature and all material and cultural development of the past two thousand years. It must be of the spirit if we are to save the flesh.

Analysis

MacArthur was a highly skilled speaker with a sense of occasion that he demonstrated throughout his career. In his remarks, both at the ceremony and on the radio, he adopted a formal oratorical style that, in itself, signalled the momentousness of the event. His words and cadences were Lincolnesque, obviously intended for posterity. The opening paragraph of the speech carries strong echoes of the Gettysburg Address, as in, "But rather it is for us, both victors and vanquished, to rise to that higher dignity which alone befits the sacred purposes we are about to serve, committing all our people unreservedly to faithful compliance with the understanding they are here formally to assume."

On the *Missouri*, he alluded to his intention to discharge his responsibilities "with justice and tolerance," but that was his last reference to his coming official duties. In his radio address, he struck global themes, perhaps intended to demonstrate his qualifications for the high office that eventually went to his counterpart in the European Theater of Operations, Dwight D. Eisenhower. In the radio address, MacArthur's focus was on the future, on the survival of civilization, and not reparation or vindictiveness for the events of the past. The war had taught the lesson that "there can be no turning back." The potential of weaponry, as demonstrated by the bombs that ended the war, was so great that it "revises the traditional concepts of war."

His final call for spiritual revival to match mankind's scientific and cultural achievements was rather marred by his poor choice of the word "recrudescence", which means, roughly, regeneration, but with which most of his audience would have been unfamiliar. Rhetorically speaking, it may be satisfying to a speaker to display the extent of his or her vocabulary, but it is a barrier to audience understanding. Simpler is better, as a rule.

He warned, "We have had our last chance. If we do not now devise some greater and more equitable system, Armageddon will be at our door." Certainly the stunning advent of the nuclear age would put a man in a spiritual mood, as he seemed to be when he closed his remarks by saying, "It must be of the spirit if we are to save the flesh."

Overall, MacArthur's remarks were graceful and statesmanlike. They marked the onset of what is generally considered to be one of the greatest chapters in his long and storied career: administration of post-war recovery in Japan. He was autocratic in his methods, coming to be known as the "Gaijin Shogun" (*gaijin* being a somewhat pejorative term for a non-Japanese, *shogun* the feudal warlord of Japan). Certainly, the fact that he was half a world away from Washington led him to assume more authority than the U.S. government would have liked. Nevertheless, he was energetic and effective. He demobilized Japanese military forces and purged the government of the militarists who had seized control and led the country to war. He is credited with initiating economic recovery policies that turned Japan into one of the world's leading industrial powers. He launched democratic governmental reforms that reduced the Emperor to a figurehead. He drafted a liberal, pacifist constitution that is still in use in Japan and inaugurated reforms in land redistribution, education, labor, public health, and women's rights.

MacArthur ceded control to the reconstituted Japanese government in 1949, though he stayed in Japan as Supreme Commander until 1951, when President Truman disagreed with his actions during the Korean War and relieved him of command.

In his farewell address to a joint session of the U.S. Congress following his dismissal, MacArthur said of Japan: "The Japanese people since the war have undergone the greatest reformation recorded in modern history. With a commendable will, eagerness to learn, and marked capacity to understand, they have from the ashes left in war's wake erected in Japan an edifice dedicated to the supremacy of individual liberty and personal dignity, and in the ensuing process there has been created a truly representative government committed to the advance of political morality, freedom of economic enterprise, and social justice."

Ending that address, he delivered the line for which he has become most famous, "... old soldiers never die; they just fade away."

General Douglas MacArthur speaks during ceremonies to mark the founding of the Korean Republic.

November 14, 1889	Jawaharlal Nehru is born to a wealthy family in Allahabad, Uttar Pradesh, India.
1905–1912	Nehru is educated in England, first at Harrow and then at Cambridge University. Qualifies as a barrister and is admitted to the English Bar.
1912	Returns to India to practice law and joins the Allahabad High Court.
February 8, 1916	Marries Kamala Kaul.
November 19, 1917	The couple's only child, Indira, is born. As Indira Gandhi, she will eventually serve as Prime Minister of India.
1919	Nehru meets Mahatma Gandhi and joins the Indian National Congress.
1924–1926	Serves as President of the Allahabad Municipal Corporation.
1926	While traveling to Europe for medical treatment of his wife, Nehru meets with many political leaders.
1926–1928	Serves as the General Secretary of the United Provinces Congress Committee.
February 28, 1936	Kamala Kaul Nehru dies of tuberculosis in Switzerland. Nehru never remarries.
1929	Nehru is elected President of the Congress Party. Re-elected six times, he is often imprisoned for civil disobedience. During this time, Nehru becomes Gandhi's heir apparent as leader of the independence movement.
1942	Joins with Gandhi and the Congress Party in the "Quit India" movement. Their refusal to support the British in World War II leads to Nehru's imprisonment until 1945.
1945–1947	Takes part in talks with the British that result in independence and the partition of India and Pakistan.
August 15, 1947	Becomes the first Prime Minister when India becomes independent. He holds the post until his death.
1962	India fights a border war with China, in which China scores military victories but incurs world disapproval. Nehru is blamed for India's military being unprepared for the conflict and responds with sweeping reforms of the nation's armed forces.
May 27, 1964	Nehru dies of a heart attack.

Prime Minister Jawaharlal Nehru

"At the stroke of the midnight hour, when the world sleeps, India will awake to life and freedom."

GREAT BRITAIN OCCUPIED PARTS OF India from the 17th Century onward and, for the final 90 years of this period, the country was officially part of the British Empire under the colonial rule known as the British Raj. India – an ancient, proud, and sophisticated society – naturally chafed under foreign rule and continually rebelled against it. In the early part of the 20th Century, the spirit of rebellion coalesced into a nationalist movement under Mohandas K. (Mahatma) Gandhi. He took over leadership of the Indian National Congress Party and transformed it into a formidable force for Indian independence. Gandhi launched widespread programs of non-violent civil disobedience. He and his followers were repeatedly jailed by the British but gradually gained a series of concessions that moved them closer to self-rule.

Jawaharlal Nehru came from a wealthy *Brahmin* (high-caste) family and was educated in England. He joined the Congress Party in 1916 and gradually emerged as leader of the country's intellectuals and youth. This led Gandhi to elevate him to the presidency of the Congress Party in 1929, over the heads of several more senior officials. For the next 18 years, Nehru and Gandhi wore away at the British; at the negotiating tables and in the streets. During World War II, Gandhi and Nehru took the position that they could not support Britain unless India was an independent nation. They, and other top Congress Party officials, were imprisoned for the duration of the war.

After the war, the Labour Party came to power in Britain and moved steadily toward granting independence to India. A growing enmity between Hindus and Muslims led to the partition of the former Raj into the nations of India and Pakistan. As leader of the

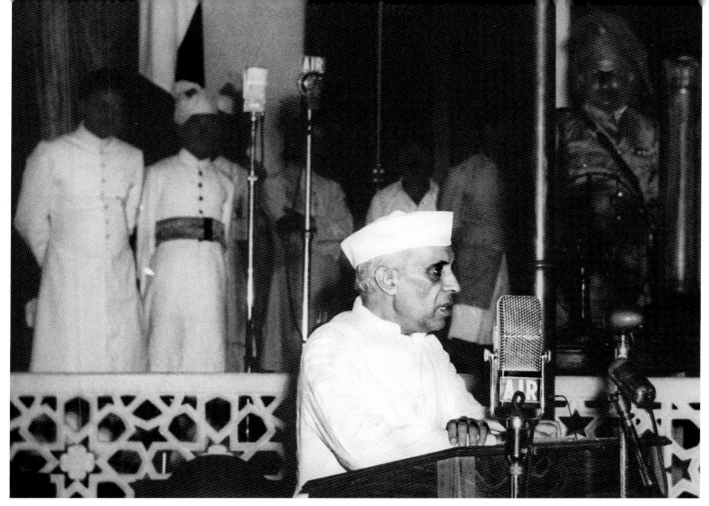

Jawaharlal Nehru, India's first Prime Minister, delivers his "tryst with destiny" speech at Parliament House in New Delhi.

Congress Party, Nehru became the first Prime Minister of a free India. On the eve of the date set for independence, he addressed the Indian Parliament.

SPEECH ON THE GRANTING OF INDIAN INDEPENDENCE

AUGUST 4, 1947

CONSTITUENT ASSEMBLY OF INDIA, NEW DELHI

Long years ago we made a tryst with destiny, and now the time comes when we shall redeem our pledge, not wholly or in full measure, but very substantially. At the stroke of the midnight hour, when the world sleeps, India will awake to life and freedom. A moment comes, which comes but rarely in history, when we step out from the old to the new, when an age ends, and when the soul of a nation, long suppressed, finds utterance. It is fitting that at this solemn moment we take the pledge of dedication to the service of India and her people and to the still larger cause of humanity.

At the dawn of history India started on her unending quest, and trackless centuries are filled with her striving and the grandeur of her success and her failures. Through good and ill fortune alike she has never lost sight of that quest or forgotten the ideals which gave her strength. We end today a period of ill fortune and India discovers herself again. The achievement we celebrate today is but a step, an opening of opportunity, to the greater triumphs and achievements that await us. Are we brave enough and wise enough to grasp this opportunity and accept the challenge of the future?

Freedom and power bring responsibility. The responsibility rests upon this Assembly, a sovereign body representing the sovereign people of India. Before the birth of freedom we have endured all the pains of labour and our hearts are heavy with the memory of this sorrow. Some of those pains continue even now. Nevertheless, the past is over and it is the future that beckons to us now.

That future is not one of ease or resting but of incessant striving so that we may fulfil the pledges we have so often taken and the one we shall take today. The service of India means the service of the millions who suffer. It means the ending of poverty and ignorance and disease and inequality of opportunity. The ambition of the greatest man of our generation has been to wipe every tear from every eye. That may be beyond us, but as long as there are tears and suffering, so long our work will not be over.

And so we have to labour and to work, and work hard, to give reality to our dreams. Those dreams are for India, but they are also for the world, for all the nations and peoples are too closely knit together today for any one of them to imagine that it can live apart. Peace has been said to be indivisible; so is freedom, so is prosperity now, and so also is disaster in this One World that can no longer be split into isolated fragments.

To the people of India, whose representatives we are, we make an appeal to join us with faith and confidence in this great adventure. This is no time for petty and destructive criticism, no time for ill-will or blaming others. We have to build the noble mansion of free India where all her children may dwell.

II.

The appointed day has come – the day appointed by destiny – and India stands forth again, after long slumber and struggle, awake, vital, free and independent. The past clings on to us still in some measure and we have to do much before we redeem the pledges we have so often taken. Yet the turning-point is past, and history begins anew for us, the history which we shall live and act and others will write about.

It is a fateful moment for us in India, for all Asia and for the world. A new star rises, the star of freedom in the East, a new hope comes into being, a vision long cherished materializes. May the star never set and that hope never be betrayed!

We rejoice in that freedom, even though clouds surround us, and many of our people are sorrow stricken and difficult problems encompass us. But freedom brings responsibilities and burdens and we have to face them in the spirit of a free and disciplined people.

On this day our first thoughts go to the architect of this freedom, the Father of our Nation [Gandhi], who, embodying the old spirit of India, held aloft the torch of freedom and lighted up the darkness that surrounded us. We have often been unworthy followers of his and have strayed from his message, but not only we but succeeding generations will remember this message and bear the imprint in their hearts of this great son of India, magnificent in his faith and strength and courage and humility. We shall never allow that torch of freedom to be blown out, however high the wind or stormy the tempest.

Jawaharlal Nehru (left) and Mohandas K. Gandhi confer in August 1942.

Our next thoughts must be of the unknown volunteers and soldiers of freedom who, without praise or reward, have served India even unto death.

We think also of our brothers and sisters who have been cut off from us by political boundaries and who unhappily cannot share at present in the freedom that has come. They are of us and will remain of us whatever may happen, and we shall be sharers in their good or ill fortune alike.

The future beckons to us. Whither do we go and what shall be our endeavour? To bring freedom and opportunity to the common man, to the peasants and workers of India; to fight and end poverty and ignorance and disease; to build up a prosperous, democratic and progressive nation, and to create social, economic and political institutions which will ensure justice and fullness of life to every man and woman.

We have hard work ahead. There is no resting for any one of us till we redeem our pledge in full, till we make all the people of India what destiny intended them to be. We are citizens of a great country on the verge of bold advance, and we have to live up to that high standard. All of us, to whatever religion we may belong, are equally the children of India with equal rights, privileges and obligations. We cannot encourage communalism or narrow-mindedness, for no nation can be great whose people are narrow in thought or in action.

To the nations and peoples of the world we send greetings and pledge ourselves to cooperate with them in furthering peace, freedom and democracy.

And to India, our much-loved motherland, the ancient, the eternal and the ever-new, we pay our reverent homage and we bind ourselves afresh to her service.

Analysis

Nehru was a superb speaker and this relatively short speech demonstrates his mastery of words and imagery. The opening passages are lyrical, with the exception of the rather strange choice of the word "tryst", with its connotation of illicit activity, to describe the country's dedication to the cause of independence. The speech was delivered in English, a language in which Nehru was fluent, so we cannot blame an awkward translation. Nevertheless, the expressiveness of the language in phrases such as "at the stroke of the midnight hour, when the world sleeps, India will awake to life and freedom," and "trackless centuries are filled with her striving and the grandeur of her successes and her failures," could not fail to move an audience.

While Gandhi's perspective on independence was religious and traditionalist, stressing a return to India's former glories, Nehru's

thinking was more secular and internationalist, and the speech reflects that. He struck two major themes: India's place in the world, and the elevation of his people from poverty and toward equality.

Signalling his interest in foreign affairs, he said that the dreams of the Indian people were for their country, but "they are also for the world, for all the nations and peoples are too closely knit together today for any one of them to imagine that it can live apart." In his closing he went on, "To the nations and peoples of the world we send greetings and pledge ourselves to cooperate with them in furthering peace, freedom and democracy."

In regard to the second theme, Nehru was a leftist who had toured Russia in the 1920s and was taken with the philosophy of Communism, though not the methods of the Soviet Union. He modified his views somewhat during his long tenure as Congress Party leader, but in this speech he set out goals in language of the sort frequently used by socialists, asking rhetorically, then answering, "Whither do we go and what shall be our endeavour? To bring freedom and opportunity to the common man, to the peasants and workers of India; to fight and end poverty and ignorance and disease; to build up a prosperous, democratic and progressive nation, and to create social, economic and political institutions which will ensure justice and fullness of life to every man and woman."

Nehru at a December 1946 reception held at India House, London, for Indian leaders and representatives to discuss the future of their country.

Nehru moves the resolution for an independent republic in a historic moment at the Constituent Assembly in New Delhi.

In setting out his aspirations to end poverty and suffering, he invoked Gandhi's spirit without mentioning him by name, noting that the "ambition of the greatest man of our generation has been to wipe every tear from every eye. That may be beyond us, but as long as there are tears and suffering, so long our work will not be over."

Nehru later paid specific and lengthy tribute to Gandhi as "the architect of this freedom, the Father of our Nation." He also acknowledged the sacrifices his people had made, speaking of the "unknown volunteers and soldiers of freedom who, without praise or reward, have served India even unto death," and he referred to the split with Pakistan by speaking of "our brothers and sisters who have been cut off from us by political boundaries."

The speech is considered in India to be a landmark address, capturing the essence of a triumphant moment in the country's history and its aspirations for the future. It launched Nehru's career as Prime Minister on a graceful and inspirational note. He was already a hero in India when he took office and went on to serve in that office for 17 years, until his death. One of his great legacies, signalled in the speech, was establishing for India a place in the international community. It was said of him that if Gandhi made Indians aware of India, Nehru made them aware of the world. He became, to the world, the face of India during his lifetime.

Nehru also stayed true to his pledge to fight poverty and promote equality, though the great mass of poor in India was such that he came nowhere near to solving the nation's economic or social problems. Nevertheless, he made some progress, particularly in the areas of education and equal rights, and remains immensely popular in India as a man who not only helped to secure independence, but set the country on the path to modernization.

Prime Minister Nehru pays tribute to Mahatma Gandhi following his death in 1948.

October 11, 1884	Anna Eleanor Roosevelt is born in New York City.
1890s	Eleanor Roosevelt's mother dies in 1892 and her father in 1894. She is raised by her maternal grandmother.
1899–1902	Attends a private school outside London, then makes her society debut in New York City.
1903	Becomes engaged to Franklin D. Roosevelt, her fifth cousin, once removed.
1903	Joins the Consumers' League to investigate working conditions in the garment districts.
March 17, 1905	Marries Franklin Delano Roosevelt in New York City. Her uncle, Theodore Roosevelt, gives her away.
1911	Endorses the Women's Suffrage Movement.
1912	Moves to Washington when her husband is appointed Assistant Secretary of the Navy.
1918–1919	Volunteers at St. Elizabeth Hospital, working with the Red Cross and the Navy League to help World War I servicemen. Volunteers at the International Congress of Working Women as a translator.
1920	Campaigns in her husband's unsuccessful bid for Vice-President and joins the League of Women Voters.
1921	Eleanor Roosevelt intensifies her political activities after her husband contracts a paralytic illness. She starts writing and lecturing, became editor of *Women's Democratic News*.
1932	Franklin Roosevelt is elected President. As First Lady, Eleanor becomes the "eyes and ears" for her husband, carrying on a schedule of speeches and public appearances. She is the first First Lady to hold regular press conferences.
1936	Begins writing the syndicated weekly newspaper column "My Day".
1943	Takes an extended, successful, trip to the South Pacific, visiting hospitalized troops to boost morale.
1944	Travels throughout Latin America on a mission to improve diplomatic relations in the region.
April 12, 1945	Franklin Roosevelt dies.
1945	Eleanor Roosevelt is named by President Truman as a delegate to the United Nations.
1948	As Chair of the United Nations Commission on Human Rights, she plays a major role in the drafting and adoption of the Universal Declaration of Human Rights.
1953	Resigns from her U.N. post when Dwight D. Eisenhower becomes President.
1961	Re-appointed by President John F. Kennedy as delegate to the United Nations General Assembly.
November 7, 1962	Eleanor Roosevelt dies in New York City of complications stemming from bone-marrow tuberculosis.

Eleanor Roosevelt

"We stand today at the threshold of a great event both in the life of the United Nations and in the life of mankind."

ELEANOR ROOSEVELT ESSENTIALLY INVENTED THE role of the modern First Lady. Before her husband, Franklin Delano Roosevelt, took office in 1932 the First Lady was simply the wife of the President, sometimes seen at her husband's side or presiding at ladies' teas and ribbon-cuttings, but rarely speaking up. Eleanor, however, was intelligent, articulate, and passionate about human rights. She carved out her own niche on the American political landscape – one that transcended her role at the White House and which continued after her husband's death. Succeeding First Ladies either sought or shunned the spotlight as they chose, but after Eleanor Roosevelt, the role of the activist Presidential partner was available to them.

She was born to wealth and social position and further enhanced both by marrying her distant cousin Franklin. Shy and awkward as a girl, Eleanor retreated into domestic life during their early marriage, bearing five children. However, when Franklin contracted a paralytic illness in 1921, she became his surrogate at political events, keeping his name and ambitions alive in political circles while he was recuperating.

As First Lady she kept up a heavy travel schedule, visiting places that would have been awkward for her wheelchair-bound husband. During World War II she traveled hundreds of thousands of miles domestically and overseas, making extensive visits to the South Pacific and to Latin America. By all accounts, both her activities in buoying the morale of servicemen and improving diplomatic relations with the countries she visited were very successful.

Eleanor Roosevelt was an active advocate for humanitarian causes from the beginning of FDR's Administration. After leaving the White House, she continued those interests, and was soon named by President Harry S. Truman as a delegate to the United Nations. She was instrumental in drafting the United Nations Universal Declaration of Human Rights, and spoke on behalf of its adoption.

Eleanor Roosevelt stands during a meeting of the United Nations drafting committee.

SPEECH TO THE UNITED NATIONS ON THE ADOPTION OF THE UNIVERSAL DECLARATION OF HUMAN RIGHTS

DECEMBER 9, 1948

PALAIS DE CHAILLOT, PARIS

Mr. President, fellow delegates:

The long and meticulous study and debate of which this Universal Declaration of Human Rights is the product means that it reflects the composite views of the many men and governments who have contributed to its formulation. Not every man nor every government can have what he wants in a document of this kind. There are of course particular provisions in the Declaration before us with which we are not fully satisfied. I have no doubt this is true of other delegations, and it would still be true if we continued our labors over many years. Taken as a whole the Delegation of the United States believes that this is a good document – even a great document – and we propose to give it our full support. The position of the United States on the various parts of the Declaration is a matter of record in the Third Committee. I shall not burden the Assembly, and particularly my colleagues of the Third Committee, with a restatement of that position here.

Eleanor Roosevelt is flanked by Queen Elizabeth and King George VI at the unveiling of a memorial to her husband in Grosvenor Square, London.

I should like to comment briefly on the amendments proposed by the Soviet delegation. The language of these amendments has been dressed up somewhat, but the substance is the same as the amendments which were offered by the Soviet delegation in committee and rejected after exhaustive discussion. Substantially the same amendments have been previously considered and rejected in the Human Rights Commission. We in the United States admire those who fight for their convictions, and the Soviet delegation has fought for their convictions. But in the older democracies we have learned that sometimes we bow to the will of the majority. In doing that, we do not give up our convictions. We continue sometimes to persuade, and eventually we may be successful. But we know that we have to work together and we have to progress. So, we believe that when we have made a good fight, and the majority is against us, it is perhaps better tactics to try to cooperate.

I feel bound to say that I think perhaps it is somewhat of an imposition on this Assembly to have these amendments offered again here, and I am confident that they will be rejected without debate.

The first two paragraphs of the amendment to article 3 deal with the question of minorities, which committee 3 decided required further study, and has recommended, in a separate resolution, their reference to the Economic and Social Council and the Human Rights Commission. As set out in the Soviet amendment, this provision clearly states "group," and not "individual," rights.

The Soviet amendment to article 20 is obviously a very restrictive statement of the right to freedom of opinion and expression. It sets up standards which would enable any state practically to deny all freedom of opinion and expression without violating the article. It introduces the terms "democratic view," "democratic systems," "democratic state," and "fascism," which we know all too well from debates in this Assembly over the past two years on warmongering and related subjects are liable to the most flagrant abuse and diverse interpretations.

The statement of the Soviet delegate here tonight is a very good case in point on this. The Soviet amendment of article 22 introduces new elements into the article without improving the committed text and again introduces specific reference to "discrimination." As was repeatedly pointed out in committee 3, the question of discrimination is comprehensively covered in article 2 of the Declaration, so that its restatement elsewhere is completely unnecessary and also has the effect of weakening the comprehensive principles stated in article 2. The new article proposed by the Soviet delegation is but a restatement of State obligation, which the Soviet delegation attempted to introduce into practically every article in the Declaration. It would convert the Declaration into a document stating obligations on states, thereby changing completely its character as a statement of principles to serve as a common standard of achievement for the members of the United Nations.

The Soviet proposal for deferring consideration of the Declaration to the 4th session of the Assembly requires no comment. An identical text was rejected in committee 3 by a vote of 6 in favor and 26 against. We are all agreed, I am sure, that the Declaration, which has been worked on with such great effort and devotion, and over such a long period of time, must be approved by this Assembly at this session.

Certain provisions of the Declaration are stated in such broad terms as to be acceptable only because of the provisions in article 30 providing for limitation on the exercise of the rights for the purpose of meeting the requirements of morality, public order, and the general welfare. An example of this is the provision that everyone has the right to equal access to the public service in his country. The basic principle of equality and of nondiscrimination as to public employment is sound, but it cannot be accepted without limitation. My government, for example, would consider that this is unquestionably subject to limitation in the interest of public order and the general welfare. It would not consider that the exclusion from public employment of persons holding subversive political beliefs and not loyal to the basic principles and practices of the constitution and laws of the country would in any way infringe upon this right.

Likewise, my government has made it clear in the course of the development of the Declaration that it does not consider that the economic and social and cultural rights stated in the Declaration imply an obligation on governments to assure the enjoyment of these rights by direct governmental action. This was made quite clear in the Human Rights Commission text of article 23 which served as a so-called "umbrella" article to the articles on economic and social rights. We consider that the principle has not been affected by the fact that this article no longer contains a reference to the articles which follow it. This in no way affects our whole-hearted support for the basic principles of economic, social, and cultural rights set forth in these articles.

In giving our approval to the Declaration today it is of primary importance that we keep clearly in mind the basic character of the document. It is not a treaty; it is not an international agreement. It is not and does not purport to be a statement of law or of legal obligation. It is a Declaration of basic principles of human rights and freedoms, to be stamped with the approval of the General Assembly by formal vote of its members, and to serve as a common standard of achievement for all peoples of all nations.

We stand today at the threshold of a great event both in the life of the United Nations and in the life of mankind. This Universal Declaration of Human Rights may well become the international Magna Carta of all men everywhere. We hope its proclamation by the General Assembly will be an event comparable to the proclamation of the Declaration of the Rights of Man by the French people in 1789, the adoption of the Bill of Rights by the people of the United States, and the adoption of comparable declarations at different times in other countries.

At a time when there are so many issues on which we find it difficult to reach a common basis of agreement, it is a significant fact that 58 states have found such a large measure of agreement in the complex field of human rights. This must be taken as testimony of our common aspiration first voiced in the Charter of the United Nations to lift men everywhere to a higher standard of life and to a greater enjoyment of freedom. Man's desire for peace lies behind this Declaration. The realization that the flagrant violation of human rights by Nazi and Fascist countries sowed the seeds of the last world war has supplied the impetus for the work which brings us to the moment of achievement here today.

In a recent speech in Canada, Gladstone Murray said:

"The central fact is that man is fundamentally a moral being, that the light we have is imperfect does not matter so long as we are always trying to improve it … we are equal in sharing the moral freedom that distinguishes us as men. Man's status makes each individual an end in himself. No man is by nature simply the servant of the state or of another man … the ideal and fact of freedom – and not technology – are the true distinguishing marks of our civilization."

This Declaration is based upon the spiritual fact that man must have freedom in which to develop his full stature and through common effort to raise the level of human dignity. We have much to do to fully achieve and to assure the rights set forth in this Declaration. But having them put before us with the moral backing of 58 nations will be a great step forward.

As we here bring to fruition our labors on this Declaration of Human Rights, we must at the same time rededicate ourselves to the unfinished task which lies before us. We can now move on with new courage and inspiration to the completion of an international covenant on human rights and of measures for the implementation of human rights.

In conclusion, I feel that I cannot do better than to repeat the call to action by Secretary Marshall in his opening statement to this Assembly:

"Let this third regular session of the General Assembly approve by an overwhelming majority the Declaration of Human Rights as a standard of conduct for all; and let us, as Members of the United Nations, conscious of our own short-comings and imperfections, join our effort in good faith to live up to this high standard."

President Harry Truman appointed Eleanor Roosevelt to the U.N. committee and called her the "First Lady of the World" in tribute to her human rights achievements.

Analysis

Eleanor Roosevelt was, from the time of her husband's illness, an active public speaker who represented FDR at substantive, as well as ceremonial, events. Over time, and gaining in confidence, she also became active in her own causes, notably workers' rights and child labor laws. Her network of women's political leaders was invaluable to her husband when he recovered sufficiently to resume his career, first as Governor of New York, then as President of the United States. During his Presidency, she maintained a separate schedule, frequently and forcefully expressing opinions that her husband could not, particularly in the areas of equal rights for African-Americans and equal opportunity for women. Her frequent and eloquent advocacy of liberal causes made her very nearly as controversial a figure as her husband.

She also cultivated the media, holding weekly press conferences and, beginning in 1936, writing her own syndicated weekly column, entitled "My Day". By the time of FDR's death she was a world-famous public figure in her own right, and one whose opinions carried considerable weight. Her appointment as Chair of the United Nations Human Rights Commission was much more than symbolic. She brought considerable stature, but also a well-honed rhetorical capability, to the podium from which she addressed the General Assembly on behalf of the United States delegation in support of the Universal Declaration of Human Rights.

She devoted the first part of her speech to the rebuttal of a series of amendments offered by the Soviet Union, partially on parliamentary grounds, and partially in disagreement with specifics of the amendments. Her arguments were, of course, diplomatically necessary but in reality *pro forma*, since by 1948 the attitudes were already hardening that would escalate into the Cold War between the United States and the Soviets.

After dispensing with the diplomatic necessities with regard to the Soviet Union, she turned to her advocacy of the document, reminding the delegates that it is not a treaty or a statement of law, but an affirmation of the basic principles of human rights – a standard to which all nations should aspire. Calling its passage "a great event," she expressed the hope that, "This Universal Declaration of Human Rights may well become the international Magna Carta of all men everywhere." She then likened the proclamation to the Declaration of the Rights of Man by the French in 1789, the Bill of Rights in the United States, and comparable events in other countries.

The fact that 58 nations could find agreement in the "complex field of human rights" she took as "testimony of our common aspiration first voiced in the charter of the United Nations to lift men everywhere to a higher standard of life and to a greater enjoyment of freedom." She ended by urging its adoption by an overwhelming majority, quoting Secretary of State George Marshall's opening statement to the Assembly.

In an era when few women had careers, the former First Lady had an active business and speaking agenda.

In fact, 48 nations wound up voting for the Declaration, with none voting against it. The Soviet bloc and several Muslim states abstained. At a time when the United Nations was still in its formative stages, the Declaration became the basis for many of the subsequent U.N. organizations and initiatives. Its 30 articles affirm rights for all without regard to race, gender, religion, or any other conditions. The rights begin with "life, liberty and security of person" and go on to freedom from slavery and torture, arbitrary detention, and many more. In the years since its adoption, the Declaration has become part of the constitutional documents of many nations and an accepted standard of international law. As such, it has had a profound impact on the world in the more than 60 years since its adoption.

Eleanor Roosevelt went on to serve as a U.S. delegate to the United Nations until 1953, chairing the U.N. Commission on Human Rights for much of that time. She had stayed active in Democratic politics during her time at the U.N., backing Adlai Stevenson against Eisenhower in the 1952 election and resigning when Eisenhower became President. After her departure, she maintained her interest, taking part in many U.N.-related projects and keeping up a heavy speaking schedule around the world. She averaged about 150 lectures per year during the 1950s. To the end of her life, she remained a passionate and effective advocate for human rights.

January 9, 1913	Richard Milhous Nixon is born in Yorba Linda, California, to Quaker parents.
1937	Graduates third in his class from Duke University Law School in North Carolina.
June 21, 1940	Marries Thelma Catherine ("Pat") Ryan in Riverside, California.
January 9, 1942	Nixon joins the Office of Price Administration, the Federal agency charged with regulating wartime prices and overseeing rationing.
September 2, 1942–March 10, 1946	Though eligible for an exemption from military service, Nixon serves as a commissioned officer in the U.S. Navy.
November 5, 1946	Elected as a Representative to the U.S. Congress where he serves two terms.
November 7, 1950	Elected to the U.S. Senate.
July 11, 1952	Selected by Republican candidate Dwight D. Eisenhower as his running mate in the 1952 Presidential election.
September 23, 1952	After disclosures that California businessmen have paid some of his expenses, Nixon defends his actions in a nationally televised speech. Eisenhower keeps him on the ticket.
November 4, 1952	Eisenhower is elected U.S. President with Nixon as Vice-President. Both men are re-elected on November 6, 1956.
November 8, 1960	Loses the Presidential election to John F. Kennedy.
November 6, 1962	Loses the California gubernatorial race to Democratic incumbent Edmund G. "Pat" Brown.
November 5, 1968	Nixon is elected President of the United States over Hubert H. Humphrey and independent candidate George Wallace. Spiro T. Agnew is his Vice-President.
June 17, 1972	Five burglars working for Nixon's re-election committee are arrested inside the Watergate office of the Democratic National Committee.
November 7, 1972	Nixon is re-elected President in a landslide election.
October 10, 1973	Vice-President Agnew resigns after being charged with bribery, tax evasion, and money laundering. Nixon chooses Gerald Ford to replace Agnew.
May 1, 1973	A special prosecutor is appointed by the Senate to investigate the Watergate break-in.
August 8, 1974	In the face of almost certain impeachment, Nixon announces his resignation, to be effective the next day.
September 8, 1974	President Gerald Ford grants Nixon a "full, free, and absolute pardon."
1974–1994	In retirement, Nixon practices law and writes books. In 1977, he admits some Watergate culpability in a series of televised interviews.
April 22, 1994	Nixon dies of a massive stroke in New York City.

Senator Richard M. Nixon

"Let me say this: I don't believe that I ought to quit because I'm not a quitter."

RICHARD NIXON WAS A 39-YEAR-OLD Senator from California in 1952 when he was chosen as the Vice-Presidential candidate on the Republican ticket headed by General Dwight Eisenhower. Nixon had been an ardent anti-Communist during his two terms in the House of Representatives and made headlines by spearheading the investigation of Alger Hiss, a State Department official accused of being a Soviet spy and later convicted of perjury. In his Senate race in 1950, he accused his opponent, Democratic Representative and former actress Helen Gahagan Douglas, of being "pink right down to her underwear." Douglas countered by dubbing him "Tricky Dicky", but Nixon won.

Two months into the 1952 campaign, the press became aware of a Nixon political fund, allegedly through a leak by a disgruntled supporter of California Governor Earl Warren, who blamed Nixon for secretly supporting Eisenhower over California favorite-son candidate Warren for the Presidential nomination. Nixon's supporters had been contributing since shortly after his election to the Senate and the funds were used to defray travel and other political expenses. The $18,000 fund was not illegal at the time, but it exposed Nixon – a vocal opponent of government corruption – to allegations that he might be giving special favors to his contributors. Within a matter of days, the controversy, which became known as "The Fund Crisis", grew until it threatened Nixon's place on the ticket. The Democrats began calling for his resignation from the campaign and Eisenhower went so far as to start looking for a replacement for Nixon as his running mate.

At the suggestion of Republican National Committee officials, Nixon decided to go on national television and radio to try to reverse public opinion. The RNC bought a half hour of time on Tuesday night on NBC, following Milton Berle's immensely popular *Texaco Star Theatre,* and Nixon went on the air to give an unprecedented address.

Richard M. Nixon makes his famous "Checkers" speech on television during the fund controversy in September 1952.

TELEVISED ADDRESS (KNOWN AS THE "CHECKERS" SPEECH)

SEPTEMBER 23, 1952

EL CAPITAN THEATRE, HOLLYWOOD, CALIFORNIA

My Fellow Americans:

I come before you tonight as a candidate for the Vice Presidency and as a man whose honesty and integrity have been questioned.

The usual political thing to do when charges are made against you is to either ignore them or to deny them without giving details.

I believe we've had enough of that in the United States, particularly with the present Administration in Washington, D.C. To me the office of the Vice Presidency of the United States is a great office and I feel that the people have got to have confidence in the integrity of the men who run for that office and who might obtain it.

I have a theory, too, that the best and only answer to a smear or to an

honest misunderstanding of the facts is to tell the truth. And that's why I'm here tonight. I want to tell you my side of the case.

I am sure that you have read the charge and you've heard that I, Senator Nixon, took $18,000 from a group of my supporters.

Now, was that wrong? And let me say that it was wrong – I'm saying, incidentally, that it was wrong and not just illegal. Because it isn't a question of whether it was legal or illegal, that isn't enough. The question is, was it morally wrong?

I say that it was morally wrong if any of that $18,000 went to Senator Nixon for my personal use. I say that it was morally wrong if it was secretly given and secretly handled. And I say that it was morally wrong if any of the contributors got special favors for the contributions that they made.

And now to answer those questions let me say this:

Not one cent of the $18,000 or any other money of that type ever

Nixon and his wife Pat are welcomed by a large crowd at Los Angeles airport.

went to me for my personal use. Every penny of it was used to pay for political expenses that I did not think should be charged to the taxpayers of the United States.

It was not a secret fund. As a matter of fact, when I was on "Meet the Press", some of you may have seen it last Sunday – Peter Edson came up to me after the program and he said, "Dick, what about this fund we hear about?" And I said, "Well, there's no secret about it. Go out and see Dana Smith, who was the administrator of the fund."

And I gave him his address, and I said that you will find that the purpose of the fund simply was to defray political expenses that I did not feel should be charged to the Government.

And third, let me point out, and I want to make this particularly clear, that no contributor to this fund, no contributor to any of my

campaign, has ever received any consideration that he would not have received as an ordinary constituent.

I just don't believe in that and I can say that never, while I have been in the Senate of the United States, as far as the people that contributed to this fund are concerned, have I made a telephone call for them to an agency, or have I gone down to an agency in their behalf. And the records will show that, the records which are in the hands of the Administration.

But then some of you will say and rightly, "Well, what did you use the fund for, Senator? Why did you have to have it?"

Let me tell you in just a word how a Senate office operates. First of all, a Senator gets $15,000 a year in salary. He gets enough money to pay for one trip a year, a round trip that is, for himself and his family between his home and Washington, D.C.

And then he gets an allowance to handle the people that work in his office, to handle his mail. And the allowance for my State of California is enough to hire thirteen people.

And let me say, incidentally, that that allowance is not paid to the Senator – it's paid directly to the individuals that the Senator puts on his payroll, but all of these people and all of these allowances are for strictly official business. Business, for example, when a constituent writes in and wants you to go down to the Veterans Administration and get some information about his GI policy. Items of that type for example.

But there are other expenses which are not covered by the Government. And I think I can best discuss those expenses by asking you some questions.

Do you think that when I or any other Senator makes a political speech, has it printed, should charge the printing of that speech and the mailing of that speech to the taxpayers? Do you think, for example, when I or any other Senator makes a trip to his home state to make a purely political speech that the cost of that trip should be charged to the taxpayers? Do you think when a Senator makes political broadcasts or political television broadcasts, radio or television, that the expense of those broadcasts should be charged to the taxpayers?

Well, I know what your answer is. It is the same answer that audiences give me whenever I discuss this particular problem. The answer is, "no." The taxpayers shouldn't be required to finance items which are not official business but which are primarily political business.

But then the question arises, you say, "Well, how do you pay for these and how can you do it legally?" And there are several ways that it can be done, incidentally, and that it is done legally in the United States Senate and in the Congress.

The first way is to be a rich man. I don't happen to be a rich man so I couldn't use that one.

Another way that is used is to put your wife on the payroll. Let me say, incidentally, my opponent, my opposite number for the Vice Presidency on the Democratic ticket, does have his wife on the payroll. And has had her on his payroll for the ten years – the past ten years.

Now just let me say this. That's his business and I'm not critical of him for doing that. You will have to pass judgment on that particular point. But I have never done that for this reason. I have found that there are so many deserving stenographers and secretaries in Washington that needed the work that I just didn't feel it was right to put my wife on the payroll.

My wife's sitting over here. She's a wonderful stenographer. She used to teach stenography and she used to teach shorthand in high school.

That was when I met her. And I can tell you folks that she's worked many hours at night and many hours on Saturdays and Sundays in my office and she's done a fine job. And I'm proud to say tonight that in the six years I've been in the House and the Senate of the United States, Pat Nixon has never been on the Government payroll.

There are other ways that these finances can be taken care of. Some who are lawyers, and I happen to be a lawyer, continue to practice law.

Richard Nixon reading paperwork on his hotel bed.

But I haven't been able to do that. I'm so far away from California that I've been so busy with my Senatorial work that I have not engaged in any legal practice.

And also as far as law practice is concerned, it seemed to me that the relationship between an attorney and the client was so personal that you couldn't possibly represent a man as an attorney and then have an unbiased view when he presented his case to you in the event that he had one before the Government.

And so I felt that the best way to handle these necessary political expenses of getting my message to the American people and the speeches I made, the speeches that I had printed, for the most part, concerned this one message – of exposing this Administration, the communism in it, the corruption in it – the only way that I could do that was to accept the aid which people in my home state of California who contributed to my campaign and who continued to make these contributions after I was elected were glad to make.

And let me say I am proud of the fact that not one of them has ever asked me for a special favor. I'm proud of the fact that not one of them has ever asked me to vote on a bill other than as my own conscience would dictate. And I am proud of the fact that the taxpayers by subterfuge or otherwise have never paid one dime for expenses which I thought were political and shouldn't be charged to the taxpayers.

Let me say, incidentally, that some of you may say, "Well, that's all right, Senator; that's your explanation, but have you got any proof?"

And I'd like to tell you this evening that just about an hour ago we received an independent audit of this entire fund. I suggested to Governor Sherman Adams, who is the chief of staff of the Dwight Eisenhower campaign, that an independent audit and legal report be obtained. And I have that audit here in my hand.

It's an audit made by the Price, Waterhouse & Co. firm, and the legal opinion by Gibson, Dunn & Crutcher, lawyers in Los Angeles, the biggest law firm and incidentally one of the best ones in Los Angeles.

I'm proud to be able to report to you tonight that this audit and this legal opinion is being forwarded to General Eisenhower. And I'd like to read to you the opinion that was prepared by Gibson, Dunn & Crutcher and based on all the pertinent laws and statutes, together with the audit report prepared by the certified public accountants.

"It is our conclusion that Senator Nixon did not obtain any financial gain from the collection and disbursement of the fund by Dana Smith; that Senator Nixon did not violate any Federal or state law by reason of the operation of the fund, and that neither the portion of the fund paid by Dana Smith directly to third persons nor the portion paid to Senator Nixon to reimburse him for designated office expenses constituted income to the Senator which was either reportable or taxable as income under applicable tax laws. (signed) Gibson, Dunn & Crutcher by Alma H. Conway."

Now that, my friends, is not Nixon speaking, but that's an independent audit which was requested because I want the American people to know all the facts and I'm not afraid of having independent people go in and check the facts, and that is exactly what they did.

But then I realize that there are still some who may say, and rightly so, and let me say that I recognize that some will continue to smear regardless of what the truth may be, but that there has been understandably some honest misunderstanding on this matter, and there's some that will say: "Well, maybe you were able, Senator, to fake this thing. How can we believe what you say? After all, is there a

The Nixons smiling for photographers on the set of his "Checkers" speech.

possibility that maybe you got some sums in cash? Is there a possibility that you may have feathered your own nest?" And so now what I am going to do – and incidentally this is unprecedented in the history of American politics – I am going at this time to give this television and radio audience a complete financial history; everything I've earned; everything I've spent; everything I owe. And I want you to know the facts. I'll have to start early.

I was born in 1913. Our family was one of modest circumstances and most of my early life was spent in a store out in East Whittier. It was a grocery store – one of those family enterprises. The only reason we were able to make it go was because my mother and dad had five boys and we all worked in the store.

I worked my way through college and to a great extent through law school. And then, in 1940, probably the best thing that ever happened

to me happened, I married Pat – who is sitting over here. We had a rather difficult time after we were married, like so many of the young couples who may be listening to us. I practiced law; she continued to teach school. Then in 1942 I went into the service.

Let me say that my service record was not a particularly unusual one. I went to the South Pacific. I guess I'm entitled to a couple of battle stars. I got a couple of letters of commendation but I was just there when the bombs were falling and then I returned. I returned to the United States and in 1946 I ran for the Congress.

When we came out of the war, Pat and I – Pat during the war had worked as a stenographer and in a bank and as an economist for Government agency – and when we came out the total of our saving from both my law practice, her teaching and all the time that I as in the war – the total for that entire period was just a little less than $10,000. Every cent of that, incidentally, was in Government bonds.

Well, that's where we start when I go into politics. Now what have I earned since I went into politics? Well, here it is – I jotted it down, let me read the notes. First of all I've had my salary as a Congressman and as a Senator. Second, I have received a total in this past six years of $1,600 from estates which were in my law firm the time that I severed my connection with it.

And, incidentally, as I said before, I have not engaged in any legal practice and have not accepted any fees from business that came to the firm after I went into politics. I have made an average of approximately $1,500 a year from nonpolitical speaking engagements and lectures. And then, fortunately, we've inherited a little money. Pat sold her interest in her father's estate for $3,000 and I inherited $1,500 from my grandfather.

We live rather modestly. For four years we lived in an apartment in Park Fairfax, in Alexandria, Virginia. The rent was $80 a month. And we saved for the time that we could buy a house.

Now, that was what we took in. What did we do with this money? What do we have today to show for it? This will surprise you, because it is so little, I suppose, as standards generally go, of people in public life. First of all, we've got a house in Washington which cost $41,000 and on which we owe $20,000. We have a house in Whittier, California, which cost $13,000 and on which we owe $3,000*. My folks are living there at the present time.

I have just $4,000 in life insurance, plus my G.I. policy which I've never been able to convert and which will run out in two years. I have no insurance whatever on Pat. I have no life insurance on our youngsters, Patricia and Julie. I own a 1950 Oldsmobile car. We have our furniture. We have no stocks and bonds of any type. We have no interest of any kind, direct or indirect, in any business.

Now, that's what we have. What do we owe? Well, in addition to the mortgage, the $20,000 mortgage on the house in Washington, the $10,000 one on the house in Whittier, I owe $4,500 to the Riggs Bank in Washington, D.C. with interest 4 ½ percent.

I owe $3,500 to my parents and the interest on that loan which I pay regularly, because it's the part of the savings they made through the years they were working so hard, I pay regularly 4 per cent interest. And then I have a $500 loan which I have on my life insurance.

Well, that's about it. That's what we have and that's what we owe. It isn't very much but Pat and I have the satisfaction that every dime that we've got is honestly ours. I should say this – that Pat doesn't have a mink coat. But she does have a respectable Republican cloth coat. And I always tell her that she'd look good in anything.

One other thing I probably should tell you because if we don't they'll probably be saying this about me too, we did get something – a

Nixon addresses a large gathering of potential voters from the back of an open truck.

And I just want to make my position clear. I don't agree with Mr. Mitchell when he says that only a rich man should serve his Government in the United States Senate or in the Congress. I don't believe that represents the thinking of the Democratic Party, and I know that it doesn't represent the thinking of the Republican Party.

I believe that it's fine that a man like Governor Stevenson who inherited a fortune from his father can run for President. But I also feel that it's essential in this country of ours that a man of modest means can also run for President. Because, you know, remember Abraham Lincoln, you remember what he said: "God must have loved the common people – he made so many of them."

And now I'm going to suggest some courses of conduct. First of all, you have read in the papers about other funds now. Mr. Stevenson, apparently, had a couple. One of them in which a group of business people paid and helped to supplement the salaries of state employees. Here is where the money went directly into their pockets.

And I think that what Mr. Stevenson should do is come before the American people as I have, give the names of the people that have contributed to that fund; give the names of the people who put this money into their pockets at the same time that they were receiving money from their state government, and see what favors, if any, they have out for that.

I don't condemn Mr. Stevenson for what he did. But until the facts are in there is a doubt that will be raised.

And as far as Mr. Sparkman is concerned, I would suggest the same thing. He's had his wife on the payroll. I don't condemn him for that. But I think that he should come before the American people and indicate what outside sources of income he has had.

I would suggest that under the circumstances both Mr. Sparkman and Mr. Stevenson should come before the American people as I have and make a complete financial statement as to their financial history. And if they don't, it will be an admission that they have something to hide. And I think that you will agree with me.

Because, folks, remember, a man that's to be President of the United States, a man that's to be Vice President of the United States must have the confidence of all the people. And that's why I'm doing what I'm doing, and that's why I suggest that Mr. Stevenson and Mr. Sparkman since they are under attack should do what I am doing.

Now, let me say this: I know that this is not the last of the smears. In spite of my explanation tonight other smears will be made; others have been made in the past. And the purpose of the smears, I know, is this – to silence me, to make me let up.

gift – after the election. A man down in Texas heard Pat on the radio mention the fact that our two youngsters would like to have a dog. And, believe it or not, the day before we left on this campaign trip we got a message from Union Station in Baltimore saying they had a package for us. We went down to get it. You know what it was.

It was a little cocker spaniel dog in a crate that he'd sent all the way from Texas. Black and white spotted. And our little girl – Tricia, the 6-year old – named it Checkers. And you know, the kids, like all kids, love the dog and I just want to say this right now, that regardless of what they say about it, we're gonna keep it.

It isn't easy to come before a nationwide audience and air your life as I've done. But I want to say some things before I conclude that I think most of you will agree on. Mr. Mitchell, the chairman of the Democratic National Committee, made the statement that if a man couldn't afford to be in the United States Senate he shouldn't run for the Senate.

Well, they just don't know who they're dealing with. I'm going l tell you this: I remember in the dark days of the Hiss case some of the same columnists, some of the same radio commentators who are attacking me now and misrepresenting my position were violently opposing me at the time I was after Alger Hiss.

But I continued the fight because I knew I was right. And I say to this great television and radio audience that I have no apologies to the American people for my part in putting Alger Hiss where he is today.

And as far as this is concerned, I intend to continue the fight.

Why do I feel so deeply? Why do I feel that in spite of the smears, the misunderstandings, the necessity for a man to come up here and bare his soul as I have? Why is it necessary for me to continue this fight?

And I want to tell you why. Because, you see, I love my country. And I think my country is in danger. And I think that the only man that can save America at this time is the man that's running for President on my ticket – Dwight Eisenhower.

You say, "Why do I think it's in danger?" and I say look at the record. Seven years of the Truman-Acheson Administration and what's happened? Six hundred million people lost to the Communists, and a war in Korea in which we have lost 117,000 American casualties.

And I say to all of you that a policy that results in a loss of six hundred million people to the Communists and a war which costs us 117,000 American casualties isn't good enough for America.

And I say that those in the State Department that made the mistakes which caused that war and which resulted in those losses should be kicked out of the State Department just as fast as we can get 'em out of there.

And let me say that I know Mr. Stevenson won't do that. Because he defends the Truman policy and I know that Dwight Eisenhower will do that, and that he will give America the leadership that it needs.

Take the problem of corruption. You've read about the mess in Washington. Mr. Stevenson can't clean it up because he was picked by the man, Truman, under whose Administration the mess was made. You wouldn't trust a man who made the mess to clean it up – that's Truman.

President Eisenhower (left) and Vice-President Nixon (right) watch the Inaugural parade.

And by the same token you can't trust the man who was picked by the man that made the mess to clean it up – and that's Stevenson.

And so I say, Eisenhower, who owes nothing to Truman, nothing to the big city bosses, he is the man that can clean up the mess in Washington.

Take Communism. I say that as far as that subject is concerned, the danger is great to America. In the Hiss case they got the secrets which enabled them to break the American secret State Department code. They got secrets in the atomic bomb case which enabled them to get the secret of the atomic bomb, five years before they would have gotten it by their own devices.

And I say that any man who called the Alger Hiss case a "red herring" isn't fit to be President of the United States. I say that a man who like Mr. Stevenson has pooh-poohed and ridiculed the Communist threat in the United States – he said that they are phantoms among ourselves; he's accused us that have attempted to expose the Communists of looking for Communists in the Bureau of Fisheries and Wildlife – I say that a man who says that isn't qualified to be President of the United States.

And I say that the only man who can lead us in this fight to rid the Government of both those who are Communists and those who have corrupted this Government is Eisenhower, because Eisenhower, you can be sure, recognizes the problem and he knows how to deal with it.

Now let me say that, finally, this evening I want to read to you just briefly excerpts from a letter which I received, a letter which, after all this is over, no one can take away from us. It reads as follows:

"Dear Senator Nixon:

Since I'm only 19 years of age I can't vote in this Presidential election but believe me if I could you and General Eisenhower would certainly get my vote. My husband is in the Fleet Marines in Korea. He's a corpsman on the front lines and we have a two-month-old son he's never seen. And I feel confident that with great Americans like you and General Eisenhower in the White House, lonely Americans like myself will be united with their loved ones now in Korea.

"I only pray to God that you won't be too late. Enclosed is a small check to help you in your campaign. Living on $85 a month it is all I can afford at present. But let me know what else I can do."

Folks, it's a check for $10, and it's one that I will never cash.

And just let me say this. We hear a lot about prosperity these days but I say, why can't we have prosperity built on peace rather than prosperity built on war? Why can't we have prosperity and an honest government in Washington, D.C., at the same time. Believe me, we can.

Richard Nixon with his wife and two daughters take the family dog for a walk on the beach.

And Eisenhower is the man that can lead this crusade to bring us that kind of prosperity.

And, now, finally, I know that you wonder whether or not I am going to stay on the Republican ticket or resign.

Let me say this: I don't believe that I ought to quit because I'm not a quitter. And, incidentally, Pat's not a quitter. After all, her name was Patricia Ryan and she was born on St. Patrick's Day, and you know the Irish never quit.

But the decision, my friends, is not mine. I would do nothing that would harm the possibilities of Dwight Eisenhower to become President of the United States. And for that reason I am submitting to the Republican National Committee tonight through this television broadcast the decision which is theirs to make.

Let them decide whether my position on the ticket will help or hurt. And I am going to ask you to help them decide. Wire and write the Republican National Committee whether you think I should stay on or whether I should get off. And whatever their decision is, I will abide by it.

But just let me say this last word. Regardless of what happens I'm going to continue this fight. I'm going to campaign up and down America until we drive the crooks and the Communists and those that defend them out of Washington. And remember, folks, Eisenhower is a great man. Believe me. He's a great man. And a vote for Eisenhower is a vote for what's good for America.

* Nixon meant to say $10,000.

Analysis

Nixon spoke from the stage of the deserted El Capitan Theatre in Los Angeles, on a set containing two chairs and a desk. His wife, Pat, sat silently in one of the chairs. Nixon opened the speech sitting at the desk and looking directly into the camera. He usually preferred to speak from a script, which he habitually memorized, but this time he spoke from notes. Stenographers were standing by to take an accurate transcript – not necessarily a good thing, because without a script Nixon was not a terribly articulate man, and sometimes bordered on the incoherent. That is clear in the transcript. Neither was his performance particularly adept. On television, the humorless demeanor and awkward body language that the world came to know were on full display.

Nevertheless, the same un-telegenic style that lost Nixon the debates with John F. Kennedy eight years later carried the day in this instance. He opened the speech with a straightforward defense of "The Fund", explaining its uses and the fact that it was needed because he was not rich, and did not put his wife on his payroll as his opponent for Vice-

President, Alabama Senator John Sparkman, did. He used the occasion to call attention, again rather awkwardly, to his wife Pat.

Nixon then took the brave step of complete disclosure of all his finances. He started with his own personal history from childhood, laying it out simply and effectively. A speaker is almost always effectual – and frequently compelling – when telling personal stories in a speech, because they elicit honest emotion and are likely to resonate with the audience, as they did in this case. Nixon's emotions were on display during the portions of the address in which he recounted his humble origins, his rise to the Senate, and the straitened circumstances of him and his family that led to the creation of the fund. The section on his finances and the references to his wife and family have been mocked ever since as strained and tacky, but they served to humanize Nixon, and he was at his most genuine when delivering them.

The evocation of Pat Nixon's "good Republican cloth coat" has taken its place in American political lore but, of course, the most famous anecdote, and the one that has given the speech its name, is the story of the Nixon children's dog, Checkers. The anecdote was a disingenuous tearjerker but, in the simpler times of 1952, remarkably effective. Reportedly, at least one of the cameramen and several stenographers were moved to tears.

Nixon's strategy included many rhetorical questions, which he asked and answered throughout. What did you use the fund for, Senator? Do you think public money should be used for political purposes? Should only a rich man be allowed to run for office (pointing out that Stevenson had inherited wealth)? The technique of framing the questions and giving the answers he wanted was quite persuasive for the lawyerly Nixon.

In the last segment of the speech, Nixon went on the attack. Stevenson had his own fund, he said, and should give a full accounting. Sparkman, whose wife was on the payroll, should detail his outside income. He jumped out from behind the desk and became more animated as he warned that more smears would be made against him, but that "they don't know who they're dealing with"; that Stevenson had downplayed the threat of Communism and that the country was in danger from "crooks and communists" infesting Washington.

He made one last foray into pathos, telling the story of a woman who had sent him a check for $10 because she knew he was fighting to protect her husband and all the other soldiers in Korea. Then he addressed the big question: would he resign as candidate for Vice-President. He would leave that to the Republican National Committee and the people, but he delivered one other statement that has become the stuff of Nixonian legend: "I'm not a quitter," followed by an allusion to Pat Nixon's Irish heritage and "you know the Irish never quit."

He asked people to call or write the RNC and tell them whether he deserved to remain on the ticket, ending with a call for viewers and listeners to support Eisenhower.

The speech was a unique performance: quirky, hokey, clumsy, but – ultimately – successful. More than four million postcards, letters, and phone calls poured into Republican headquarters, running about 75 to one in Nixon's favor. Eisenhower was greeted by crowds shouting, "We want Nixon." The RNC announced that it had voted unanimously to retain Nixon and the Republicans won the election in a landslide. The victory was largely due, of course, to Eisenhower's personal popularity, but political experts acknowledged that the Checkers Speech gave the ticket "a bounce." At any rate, it preserved Nixon's political career for all the drama to come.

Nixon was not considered a particularly articulate orator without a script.

October 14, 1890	David Dwight Eisenhower is born in Denison, Texas, and nicknamed "Ike". (He later reversed the order of his given names when he enrolled at West Point Military Academy.)
1911–1915	Attends the United States Military Academy at West Point and is commissioned a Second Lieutenant. Serves with the infantry at various camps in Texas and Georgia until 1918.
July 1, 1916	Marries Mamie Geneva Doud.
1922–1924	Serves as Executive Officer to General Conner in the Panama Canal Zone and then as a Battalion Commander at Fort Benning, Georgia.
1925–1926	Attends the Command and General Staff School at Fort Leavenworth, Kansas.
1927–1928	Attends the Army War College in Washington, D.C.
February 20, 1933	Becomes Chief Military Aide to General Douglas MacArthur while MacArthur serves as Chief of Staff of the War Department General Staff and military adviser to the Philippine Commonwealth.
1941	Eisenhower is promoted to Colonel, then to Brigadier General.
June 1942	Designated Commanding General of U.S. Army forces in the European Theater of Operations.
November 1941	Named Commander-in-Chief of Allied Forces in North Africa.
December 1943	Eisenhower is named Supreme Commander of the Allied Expeditionary Force in Europe.
June 6, 1944	Carries out the Allied invasion of Europe with the D-Day landing in Normandy.
December 20, 1944	Promoted to General of the Army
1945–1948	Serves as Chief of Staff of the U.S. Army.
1948	Resigns from the Army (February) and becomes President of Columbia University in New York City (June).
December 1950	Takes leave of absence from Columbia to become Supreme Commander of NATO forces in Europe.
November 4, 1952	Eisenhower is elected President of the United States and Richard Nixon is elected Vice-President. They are both re-elected on November 6, 1956.
September 24, 1955	Suffers a heart attack in Denver.
September 24, 1957	Orders Federal troops to Little Rock, Arkansas, to uphold court-ordered integration of Little Rock High School.
April 2, 1958	Recommends the creation of the National Aeronautics and Space Administration.
January 17, 1961	In his farewell speech, President Eisenhower warns of the "Military-Industrial Complex".
January 1961	Retires to his farm in Gettysburg, Pennsylvania.
March 28, 1969	Eisenhower dies at Walter Reed Army Hospital in Washington, D.C.

President Dwight D. Eisenhower

"In the councils of government, we must guard against the acquisition of unwarranted influence, whether sought or unsought, by the military-industrial complex."

THE EIGHT YEARS OF DWIGHT D. Eisenhower's Presidency were marked by an escalation in arms capability unprecedented in human history, in peacetime or war. By the end of the Cold War, each of the superpowers would have a large enough nuclear arsenal to obliterate all life on the planet many times over. At the same time, the U.S. was frenetically engaged in making alliances around the globe, sometimes with unsavoury dictators, in an attempt to contain international Communism. The Soviets were equally active in trying to convert countries small and great to their ideology. The constant threat of nuclear war became an anxious backdrop of all aspects of American life.

During Eisenhower's Presidency, every Soviet feint or thrust anywhere in the world – the Middle East, Southeast Asia, Cuba, or even into space via *Sputnik* – required some sort of American response. The air of apprehension was palpable: what would be next, and would it be the beginning of the end?

Yet, life went on. The decade was one of considerable prosperity for America. The nation continued its ascension toward unparalleled industrial and economic power.

Eisenhower presided over all this with an avuncular, smiling presence that belied his tough, strategic military mind. He has come to be dismissed as a President who

Dwight D. Eisenhower speaking shortly before President John F. Kennedy's Inauguration in January 1961.

was safe and sane, but who did not do much of anything except play golf. This image persists in part because Ike was, at heart, an old-line conservative – strongly opposed to unnecessary government intrusions into society. Nevertheless, he ended the Korean War, kept pressure on the Soviets, oversaw the start of the interstate highway system, initiated the Space Race as well as the scientific and technological capabilities needed to run it, greatly expanded Social Security, supported racial equality, and generally held things together during a difficult period.

Eisenhower was not a very visible President by today's standards, so when he took the opportunity to unburden himself of some final thoughts on national radio and television just before leaving office, his words carried considerable weight.

FAREWELL ADDRESS TO THE AMERICAN PEOPLE

JANUARY 17, 1961
WHITE HOUSE, WASHINGTON, D.C.

My fellow Americans:

Three days from now, after half a century in the service of our country, I shall lay down the responsibilities of office as, in traditional and solemn ceremony, the authority of the Presidency is vested in my successor.

This evening I come to you with a message of leave-taking and farewell, and to share a few final thoughts with you, my countrymen.

Crowds in the streets of Washington, D.C. welcome General Dwight D. Eisenhower home from World War II on 21 June, 1945.

Like every other citizen, I wish the new President, and all who will labor with him, Godspeed. I pray that the coming years will be blessed with peace and prosperity for all. Our people expect their President and the Congress to find essential agreement on issues of great moment, the wise resolution of which will better shape the future of the Nation.

My own relations with the Congress, which began on a remote and tenuous basis when, long ago, a member of the Senate appointed me to West Point, have since ranged to the intimate during the war and immediate post-war period, and, finally, to the mutually interdependent during these past eight years.

In this final relationship, the Congress and the Administration have, on most vital issues, cooperated well, to serve the national good rather than mere partisanship, and so have assured that the business of the Nation should go forward. So, my official relationship with the Congress ends in a feeling, on my part, of gratitude that we have been able to do so much together.

II.

We now stand ten years past the midpoint of a century that has witnessed four major wars among great nations. Three of these involved our own country. Despite these holocausts America is today the strongest, the most influential and most productive nation in the world. Understandably proud of this pre-eminence, we yet realize that America's leadership and prestige depend, not

merely upon our unmatched material progress, riches and military strength, but on how we use our power in the interests of world peace and human betterment.

III.

Throughout America's adventure in free government, our basic purposes have been to keep the peace; to foster progress in human achievement, and to enhance liberty, dignity and integrity among people and among nations. To strive for less would be unworthy of a free and religious people. Any failure traceable to arrogance, or our lack of comprehension or readiness to sacrifice would inflict upon us grievous hurt both at home and abroad.

Progress toward these noble goals is persistently threatened by the conflict now engulfing the world. It commands our whole attention, absorbs our very beings. We face a hostile ideology – global in scope, atheistic in character, ruthless in purpose, and insidious in method. Unhappily the danger it poses promises to be of indefinite duration. To meet it successfully, there is called for, not so much the emotional and transitory sacrifices of crisis, but rather those which enable us to carry forward steadily, surely, and without complaint the burdens of a prolonged and complex struggle – with liberty the stake. Only thus shall we remain, despite every provocation, on our charted course toward permanent peace and human betterment.

Crises there will continue to be. In meeting them, whether foreign or domestic, great or small, there is a recurring temptation to feel that some spectacular and costly action could become the miraculous solution to all current difficulties. A huge increase in newer elements of our defense; development of unrealistic programs to cure every ill in agriculture; a dramatic expansion in basic and applied research – these and many other possibilities, each possibly promising in itself, may be suggested as the only way to the road we wish to travel.

But each proposal must be weighed in the light of a broader consideration: the need to maintain balance in and among national programs – balance between the private and the public economy, balance between cost and hoped for advantage – balance between the clearly necessary and the comfortably desirable; balance between our essential requirements as a nation and the duties imposed by the nation upon the individual; balance between actions of the moment and the national welfare of the future. Good judgment seeks balance and progress; lack of it eventually finds imbalance and frustration.

The record of many decades stands as proof that our people and their government have, in the main, understood these truths and have responded to them well, in the face of stress and threat. But threats, new in kind or degree, constantly arise. I mention two only.

Dwight D. Eisenhower speaks during a 1958 Presidential press conference.

IV.

A vital element in keeping the peace is our military establishment. Our arms must be mighty, ready for instant action, so that no potential aggressor may be tempted to risk his own destruction. Our military organization today bears little relation to that known by any of my predecessors in peacetime, or indeed by the fighting men of World War II or Korea. Until the latest of our world conflicts, the United States had no armaments industry. American makers of plowshares could, with time and as required, make swords as well. But now we can no longer risk emergency improvisation of national defense; we have been compelled to create a permanent armaments industry of vast proportions. Added to this, three and a half million men and women are directly engaged in the defense establishment. We annually spend on military security more than the net income of all United States corporations.

This conjunction of an immense military establishment and a large arms industry is new in the American experience. The total influence – economic, political, even spiritual – is felt in every city, every State house, every office of the Federal government. We recognize the imperative need for this development. Yet we must not fail to comprehend its grave implications. Our toil, resources and livelihood are all involved; so is the very structure of our society.

In the councils of government, we must guard against the acquisition of unwarranted influence, whether sought or unsought, by the military-industrial complex. The potential for the disastrous rise of misplaced power exists and will persist.

We must never let the weight of this combination endanger our liberties or democratic processes. We should take nothing for granted. Only an alert and knowledgeable citizenry can compel the proper meshing of the huge industrial and military machinery of defense with our peaceful methods and goals, so that security and liberty may prosper together.

Akin to, and largely responsible for the sweeping changes in our industrial-military posture, has been the technological revolution during recent decades. In this revolution, research has become central; it also becomes more formalized, complex, and costly. A steadily increasing share is conducted for, by, or at the direction of, the Federal government.

Today, the solitary inventor, tinkering in his shop, has been overshadowed by task forces of scientists in laboratories and testing fields. In the same fashion, the free university, historically the fountainhead of free ideas and scientific discovery, has experienced a revolution in the conduct of research. Partly because of the huge costs involved, a government contract becomes virtually a substitute for intellectual curiosity. For every old blackboard there are now hundreds of new electronic computers.

The prospect of domination of the nation's scholars by Federal employment, project allocations, and the power of money is ever present – and is gravely to be regarded. Yet, in holding scientific research and discovery in respect, as we should, we must also be alert to the equal and opposite danger that public policy could itself become the captive of a scientific-technological elite.

It is the task of statesmanship to mold, to balance, and to integrate these and other forces, new and old, within the principles of our democratic system – ever aiming toward the supreme goals of our free society.

V.

Another factor in maintaining balance involves the element of time. As we peer into society's future, we – you and I, and our government – must avoid the impulse to live only for today, plundering, for our own ease and convenience, the precious resources of tomorrow. We cannot mortgage the material assets of our grandchildren without risking the loss also of their political and spiritual heritage. We want democracy to survive for all generations to come, not to become the insolvent phantom of tomorrow.

VI.

Down the long lane of the history yet to be written America knows that this world of ours, ever growing smaller, must avoid becoming a community of dreadful fear and hate, and be, instead, a proud confederation of mutual trust and respect.

Such a confederation must be one of equals. The weakest must come to the conference table with the same confidence as do we, protected as we are by our moral, economic, and military strength. That table, though scarred by many past frustrations, cannot be abandoned for the certain agony of the battlefield.

Disarmament, with mutual honor and confidence, is a continuing imperative. Together we must learn how to compose differences, not with arms, but with intellect and decent purpose. Because this need is so sharp and apparent I confess that I lay down my official responsibilities in this field with a definite sense of disappointment. As one who has witnessed the horror and the lingering sadness of war – as one who knows that another war could utterly destroy this civilization which has been so slowly and painfully built over thousands of years – I wish I could say tonight that a lasting peace is in sight.

Happily, I can say that war has been avoided. Steady progress toward our ultimate goal has been made. But, so much remains to be done. As a private citizen, I shall never cease to do what little I can to help the world advance along that road.

VII.

So – in this my last good night to you as your President – I thank you for the many opportunities you have given me for public service in war and peace. I trust that in that service you find some things worthy; as for the rest of it, I know you will find ways to improve performance in the future.

You and I – my fellow citizens – need to be strong in our faith that all nations, under God, will reach the goal of peace with justice. May we be ever unswerving in devotion to principle, confident but humble with power, diligent in pursuit of the Nation's great goals.

To all the peoples of the world, I once more give expression to America's prayerful and continuing aspiration:

We pray that peoples of all faiths, all races, all nations, may have their great human needs satisfied; that those now denied opportunity shall come to enjoy it to the full; that all who yearn for freedom may experience its spiritual blessings; that those who have freedom will understand, also, its heavy responsibilities; that all who are insensitive to the needs of others will learn charity; that the scourges of poverty, disease, and ignorance will be made to disappear from the earth, and that, in the goodness of time, all peoples will come to live together in a peace guaranteed by the binding force of mutual respect and love.

Analysis

Eisenhower was not a dynamic speaker. His flat, mid-American twang and low-key delivery did little to excite an audience. However, excitement was not what the fraught 1950s demanded. His long military career had gained him an effortlessly commanding presence and an air of control. The country was comfortable with his finger on the nuclear trigger.

He looked Presidential and, when he spoke seriously, he was taken seriously. In his final speech as President, Eisenhower was sober, but not grave. His language was relatively simple, embellished by the efforts of two speechwriters: Ralph E. Williams and Malcolm Moos. It was one of them who coined the term by which the speech has become known: the "military-industrial complex."

Interestingly, scholarly students of the speech have found that an early draft warned of the "military-industrial-congressional complex" and of the potential influence of that triangular power structure. However,

Dwight D. Eisenhower passes some fans while on the way home after President John F. Kennedy's Inauguration ceremony on January 20, 1961.

Eisenhower worried about offending Congress and eliminated references to the Congressional appropriations process as an element of the "potential for the disastrous rise of misplaced power." In fact, he began with a statement of appreciation for his good relationship with Congress and how much they had been able to achieve together.

Although the speech is remembered almost entirely for the military-industrial complex warnings, the first point Eisenhower wanted to make was one that stemmed from his Republican ideological leanings: America had faced crises, and would continue to face them, but it was important not to overreact. This section, in all likelihood, had its roots in his dislike for and distrust of John F. Kennedy, whom Eisenhower regarded as a dangerous, activist liberal.

Ike decried the "recurring temptation to feel that some spectacular and costly action could become the miraculous solution to all current difficulties." Let us retain a balanced approach, he said, with "balance" becoming the key word in his use of the rhetorical technique of repetition to hammer home the point. "Good judgment seeks balance and progress; lack of it eventually finds imbalance and frustration," he concluded. One could readily draw the conclusion that Eisenhower regarded this argument as of equal importance with his more famous warning.

Following that admonition, Eisenhower turned to his principal argument, explaining that prior to World War II, "American makers of plowshares could … make swords as well" (one of the few metaphors the speech contains). The times, he continued, demanded a strong industry dedicated to the production of weaponry, but America must guard against the "acquisition of unwarranted influence" by the military-industrial complex. Having been a top officer during World War II, Eisenhower was uniquely qualified both to understand the need for an arms industry and the danger of its untrammelled growth. As a master of strategic planning, Eisenhower was well aware of the great love

military men have always had for bigger and better armaments, and the fact that they could easily fall into cozy relationships with those who have vested interests in selling them more elaborate and advanced – and more expensive – war machines.

Interestingly, Eisenhower also warned of the dangers of "Big Science" – the replacement of "the solitary inventor, tinkering in his shop" with enormous corporate projects and the rise of what he called a "scientific-technological elite" that could usurp the public policy process. That warning of Eisenhower's has been often debated in the years since his speech, with "small science" advocates alleging that America has embraced the incremental applied science practiced by corporations at the expense of potentially more valuable pure science.

Eisenhower's final point was a rather plaintive and, in retrospect, poignant plea to consider future generations and to forego "plundering for our own ease and convenience, the precious resources of tomorrow." "We want democracy to survive for all generations to come, not to become the insolvent phantom of tomorrow." This was perhaps his most eloquent, and least heeded, warning.

The most heeded, and the one that gives this speech its name, was the "military-industrial complex" caution. It was particularly prominent during the Vietnam War, when opponents of the war used the term as a pejorative. Now, decades after Eisenhower spoke, the U.S. accounts for more than half of the total world military expenditures of more than $1 trillion a year. The temptation is to say that Eisenhower's warning was fruitless. Who is to say, however, what the situation would be if he had not spoken out? He certainly played a large role in framing a continuing debate, and that, in itself, has had a significant impact. The warning could not have come from a more authoritative figure and it has resonated ever since with critics of militarism, perhaps serving as a check to those engaged in the arms trade, either as vendors or consumers.

May 29, 1917	John Fitzgerald Kennedy is born in Brookline, Massachusetts, to Joseph P. Kennedy, Sr. and his wife Rose Kennedy (Fitzgerald).
June 1940	Graduates *cum laude* from Harvard University. Kennedy's college thesis, "Appeasement in Munich", details Britain's failure to prepare itself against Nazi Germany and is published as a book titled *Why England Slept*.
August 3, 1943	While on active duty in the Pacific, *PT-109* – under his command – is sunk by the Japanese.
June 11, 1944	Kennedy is awarded the Navy and Marine Corps Medal and Purple Heart for his heroic actions while in command of *PT-109*.
November 5, 1946	Kennedy is elected to the U.S. House of Representatives. He is re-elected in 1948 and 1950.
November 4, 1952	Elected Senator from Massachusetts. Re-elected in 1958.
September 12, 1953	Marries Jacqueline Lee Bouvier in Newport, Rhode Island.
1953–1955	Undergoes two spinal surgeries for a back injury he received during the *PT-109* incident. During his convalescence, Kennedy writes *Profiles in Courage*.
1957	Wins Pulitzer Prize for *Profiles in Courage*.
November 8, 1960	Defeats Richard M. Nixon to become the 35th President of the United States. Lyndon B. Johnson is elected Vice-President.
April 17, 1961	The U.S.-backed invasion of Cuba ends disastrously at the Bay of Pigs.
October 1962	After photos show Soviet missile emplacements being built in Cuba, Kennedy orders a naval quarantine. The Soviet Union agrees to remove its missiles, avoiding an armed conflict.
June 11, 1963	Kennedy sends the Alabama National Guard to the University of Alabama to protect two African-American students.
October 7, 1963	Signs the Nuclear Test Ban Treaty in Washington, D.C. The treaty bans nuclear weapon tests in the atmosphere, in outer space, and under water.
November 22, 1963	John Fitzgerald Kennedy is shot at 12:30 p.m. while riding in an open-top limousine in a motorcade through downtown Dallas. He is pronounced dead at 1 p.m. at Parkland Memorial Hospital.
November 23–25, 1963	Lies in state at the U.S. Capitol and is buried at Arlington National Cemetery.

President John F. Kennedy

"Ask not what your country can do for you – ask what you can do for your country."

THE MORNING OF JANUARY 20, 1961, was bitterly cold – so cold that officials had given thought to cancelling the outdoor Presidential Inauguration ceremony. But despite the temperature in Washington, D.C., the world was hot with conflict. Communist expansionism was nearing its peak, supporting insurgencies everywhere from Africa to Southeast Asia to the Middle East and cozying up to the brand new dictatorship of Fidel Castro just 90 miles from the coast of Florida. The domestic situation was heating up, too: the Montgomery, Alabama, bus boycott and rioting over school integration in Little Rock, Arkansas, had begun to push the issue of race under the nation's collective nose.

Despite the cold, the ceremony went on as planned, and the newly sworn-in President approached the podium to a mixture of doubt and anticipation. Kennedy was the youngest elected President in U.S. history, just 43 years old. He was also the first Roman Catholic to be elected in a country where, in some areas, the Ku Klux Klan still conducted anti-Catholic demonstrations. He had won a razor-thin margin of victory amid allegations of electoral improprieties. Many wondered whether he was up to the task of leading the nation against the implacable Soviets and the Communist Chinese. His legislative record during his brief Senate tenure had been unexceptional, but he was exceptionally handsome, charismatic, and articulate. Could those qualities translate into effective control of the executive branch of government?

Kennedy's performance on that frigid day answered many questions and removed many doubts. He set a hopeful, high-minded tone for his Administration that inspired many to national service and sustained it through the dark days of the Cuban Missile Crisis, right up to the even darker day of November 22, 1963.

John F. Kennedy gives his first, and only, Inaugural Address in front of the newly-extended East Front of the Capitol.

INAUGURAL ADDRESS

JANUARY 20, 1961

UNITED STATES CAPITOL, WASHINGTON, D.C.

Vice President Johnson, Mr. Speaker, Mr. Chief Justice, President Eisenhower, Vice President Nixon, President Truman, Reverend Clergy, fellow citizens:

We observe today not a victory of party but a celebration of freedom – symbolizing an end as well as a beginning – signifying renewal as well as change. For I have sworn before you and Almighty God the same solemn oath our forbears prescribed nearly a century and three-quarters ago.

The world is very different now. For man holds in his mortal hands the power to abolish all forms of human poverty and all forms of human life. And yet the same revolutionary beliefs for which our forebears fought are still at issue around the globe – the belief that the rights of man come not from the generosity of the state but from the hand of God.

We dare not forget today that we are the heirs of that first revolution. Let the word go forth from this time and place, to friend and foe alike, that the torch has been passed to a new generation of Americans – born in this century, tempered by war, disciplined by a hard and bitter peace, proud of our ancient heritage – and unwilling to witness or permit the slow undoing of those human rights to which this nation has always been committed, and to which we are committed today at home and around the world.

Let every nation know, whether it wishes us well or ill, that we shall pay any price, bear any burden, meet any hardship, support any friend, oppose any foe to assure the survival and the success of liberty.

This much we pledge – and more.

To those old allies whose cultural and spiritual origins we share, we pledge the loyalty of faithful friends. United there is little we cannot do in a host of cooperative ventures. Divided there is little we can do – for we dare not meet a powerful challenge at odds and split asunder.

To those new states whom we welcome to the ranks of the free, we pledge our word that one form of colonial control shall not have passed away merely to be replaced by a far more iron tyranny. We shall not always expect to find them supporting our view. But we shall always hope to find them strongly supporting their own freedom – and to remember that, in the past, those who foolishly sought power by riding the back of the tiger ended up inside.

To those people in the huts and villages of half the globe struggling to break the bonds of mass misery, we pledge our best efforts to help

them help themselves, for whatever period is required – not because the communists may be doing it, not because we seek their votes, but because it is right. If a free society cannot help the many who are poor, it cannot save the few who are rich.

To our sister republics south of our border, we offer a special pledge – to convert our good words into good deeds – in a new alliance for progress – to assist free men and free governments in casting off the chains of poverty. But this peaceful revolution of hope cannot become the prey of hostile powers. Let all our neighbors know that we shall join with them to oppose aggression or subversion anywhere in the Americas. And let every other power know that this Hemisphere intends to remain the master of its own house.

To that world assembly of sovereign states, the United Nations, our last best hope in an age where the instruments of war have far

President John F. Kennedy is driven through crowded streets with his wife Jackie on the day of his inauguration.

72

John F. Kennedy is given a rousing ovation by voters.

outpaced the instruments of peace, we renew our pledge of support – to prevent it from becoming merely a forum for invective – to strengthen its shield of the new and the weak – and to enlarge the area in which its writ may run.

Finally, to those nations who would make themselves our adversary, we offer not a pledge but a request: that both sides begin anew the quest for peace, before the dark powers of destruction unleashed by science engulf all humanity in planned or accidental self-destruction.

We dare not tempt them with weakness. For only when our arms are sufficient beyond doubt can we be certain beyond doubt that they will never be employed.

But neither can two great and powerful groups of nations take comfort from our present course – both sides overburdened by the cost of modern weapons, both rightly alarmed by the steady spread of the deadly atom, yet both racing to alter that uncertain balance of terror that stays the hand of mankind's final war.

So let us begin anew – remembering on both sides that civility is not a sign of weakness, and sincerity is always subject to proof. Let us never negotiate out of fear. But let us never fear to negotiate.

Let both sides explore what problems unite us instead of belaboring those problems which divide us.

Let both sides, for the first time, formulate serious and precise proposals for the inspection and control of arms – and bring the absolute

power to destroy other nations under the absolute control of all nations.

Let both sides seek to invoke the wonders of science instead of its terrors. Together let us explore the stars, conquer the deserts, eradicate disease, tap the ocean depths, and encourage the arts and commerce.

Let both sides unite to heed in all corners of the earth the command of Isaiah – to "undo the heavy burdens ... (and) let the oppressed go free."

And if a beachhead of cooperation may push back the jungle of suspicion, let both sides join in creating a new endeavor, not a new balance of power, but a new world of law, where the strong are just and the weak secure and the peace preserved.

All this will not be finished in the first one hundred days. Nor will it be finished in the first one thousand days, nor in the life of this Administration, nor even perhaps in our lifetime on this planet. But let us begin.

In your hands, my fellow citizens, more than mine, will rest the final success or failure of our course. Since this country was founded, each generation of Americans has been summoned to give testimony to its national loyalty. The graves of young Americans who answered the call to service surround the globe.

Now the trumpet summons us again – not as a call to bear arms, though arms we need – not as a call to battle, though embattled we are – but a call to bear the burden of a long twilight struggle, year in and year out, "rejoicing in hope, patient in tribulation" – a struggle against the common enemies of man: tyranny, poverty, disease, and war itself.

Can we forge against these enemies a grand and global alliance, North and South, East and West, that can assure a more fruitful life for all mankind? Will you join in that historic effort?

In the long history of the world, only a few generations have been granted the role of defending freedom in its hour of maximum danger. I do not shrink from this responsibility – I welcome it. I do not believe that any of us would exchange places with any other people or any other generation. The energy, the faith, the devotion which we bring to this endeavor will light our country and all who serve it – and the glow from that fire can truly light the world.

And so, my fellow Americans: ask not what your country can do for you – ask what you can do for your country.

My fellow citizens of the world: ask not what America will do for you, but what together we can do for the freedom of man.

Finally, whether you are citizens of America or citizens of the world, ask of us here the same high standards of strength and sacrifice which we ask of you. With a good conscience our only sure reward, with history the final judge of our deeds, let us go forth to lead the land we love, asking His blessing and His help, but knowing that here on earth God's work must truly be our own.

Analysis

Kennedy's Inaugural speech was just 1,364 words in length and took less than 14 minutes to deliver. It was the fourth shortest inaugural address in history and the shortest of the 20th Century, except for FDR's fourth, which was kept minimal because of wartime conditions. Nevertheless, Kennedy's ranks among the greatest Inaugural speeches ever delivered, and one of the best speeches of any kind in the 20th Century, almost by acclamation. Indeed, the great poet Carl Sandburg told speechwriter Ted Sorenson that it was the greatest Inaugural speech since Lincoln, with the possible exception of FDR's first (see page 8). Most observers agreed.

Kennedy, of course, had help. Sorenson had been his speechwriter in the Senate and during the campaign, and books have been written concerning his contribution to Kennedy's eloquence, including two devoted entirely to the Inaugural speech. Significantly, the two authors come to opposite conclusions as to which – Kennedy or Sorenson – contributed more. Sorenson himself acknowledges that he assisted Kennedy, but discounts the evidence of his handwritten copy of the first draft, claiming that he only recopied and consolidated earlier work from the campaign and other material he had taken from Kennedy. Sorenson also says that Kennedy took ideas from Adlai Stevenson, economist John Kenneth Galbraith, and others, but concludes that "it is less important who wrote those words than that the principles live on."

Kennedy expended great effort in preparing the speech, knowing that it would help to put a stamp on his Administration, for better or for worse, and that a boring or poor speech would encourage his critics. The speech itself deals almost exclusively with foreign policy, on the grounds that domestic issues were either too complex or too humdrum to cover in a short address. The only reference to domestic conditions in the U.S. is in the fourth paragraph when Kennedy, significantly, gave a commitment to human rights "at home and around the world."

For such a brief speech, it has contributed a number of unforgettable phrases to American political history. Perhaps the most famous is, "And so, my fellow Americans: ask not what your country can do for you – ask what you can do for your country." That was, and still is, effective both as a call to public service and as an encouragement to conservatives concerned about a possible slide toward the welfare state. The line is even more effective, though, in context, as the following line was addressed to "My fellow citizens of the world: ask not what America will do for you, but what together we can do for the freedom of man."

The whole speech is a remarkable journey from one phrase to another, many of which rank alongside the very best ever uttered by an American politician, beginning with the powerful observation, "… man holds in his mortal hands the power to abolish all forms of human poverty and all forms of human life."

Other notable phrases, include:

"the torch has been passed to a new generation of Americans …"

"Let every nation know… that we shall pay any price, bear any burden, meet any hardship, support any friend, oppose any foe to assure the survival and the success of liberty."

"Let us never negotiate out of fear. But let us never fear to negotiate."

"… the belief that the rights of man come not from the generosity of the state, but from the hand of God."

"For only when our arms are sufficient beyond doubt can we be certain beyond doubt that they will never be used."

"All this will not be finished in the first 100 days. Nor will it be finished in the first one thousand days, nor in the life of this Administration, nor even perhaps in our lifetime on this planet. But let us begin."

Scattered between those highlights are graceful reminders of the best qualities of the statesman – both the warrior and the peacemaker – that any other politician might have been glad to make the centerpiece of an address. One such example is the warning to "any nation who would make themselves our adversary [to seek peace] … before the dark powers of destruction unleashed by science engulf all humanity in planned or accidental self-destruction."

Overall, the speech itself is simply a jewel, from beginning to end, and Kennedy's delivery exuded dynamism. The combination of words and performance did exactly what the new President intended. It transformed him in the minds of the American people and leaders around the world from an untried young man to a confident leader. He would build on that first impression, surviving debacles such as the Bay of Pigs and cementing his reputation during the Cuban Missile Crisis, until tragedy intervened.

President John F. Kennedy answers questions at a press conference on April 14, 1961, just three days before the failed "Bay of Pigs" invasion of Cuba.

General Douglas MacArthur

"Yours is the profession of arms, the will to win, the sure knowledge that in war there is no substitute for victory, that if you lose, the Nation will be destroyed, that the very obsession of your public service must be Duty, Honor, Country."

GENERAL DOUGLAS MACARTHUR WAS ONE of the most important, controversial, and enigmatic figures of the 20th Century. He lived his entire life in the U.S. military, from his earliest childhood as the son of Lieutenant General Arthur MacArthur to his last days, which he spent polishing his legacy through a series of memoirs and memorable addresses such as the one below. He delivered this speech – his last major public address – to the Corps of Cadets at West Point upon receiving the Sylvanus Thayer Award for outstanding service to America from the U.S. Military Academy, where he had once served as Commandant.

MacArthur possessed an undeniably brilliant mind, finishing first in his class at West Point and demonstrating great strategic skills throughout his military career. He was also physically courageous: during World War I he led his troops into battle and became the second most decorated soldier in the war, with awards including the Medal of Honor. Interestingly, before the U.S. entered the war, MacArthur had become the U.S. Army's first public relations officer, beginning a career that his critics charged was built on self-promotion.

FOR DOUGLAUS MACARTHUR TIMELINE, PLEASE SEE PAGE 36

A statue of General Douglas MacArthur overlooks a plaza at the United States Military Academy at West Point, New York.

MacArthur's career between the wars included a stint as Army Chief of Staff. He was asked to build an army for the Philippines in the late 1930s, serving as its Field Marshal while retaining the rank of Major General in the U.S. Army. General, later President, Dwight Eisenhower served as his assistant in the Philippines. Eisenhower summed up the attitude of many when asked later whether he knew MacArthur. "Know him," Ike responded, "I studied dramatics under him for seven years."

During World War II, MacArthur served as Supreme Allied Commander in the Pacific, famously vowing "I shall return" when his forces were defeated in the Philippines, and then making good on the promise. After the war, he was a virtual dictator as commander of the occupation forces in Japan, receiving credit for helping rebuild that nation. He commanded allied forces in Korea before being relieved of his command in 1951 by President Truman as the Chinese entered the war. Addressing a joint session of the U.S. Congress after his dismissal, he delivered another famous line, "old soldiers never die; they just fade away."

Eleven years later, 82 years old and ill, he gave what would truly be his valedictory.

CORPS OF CADETS AT WEST POINT

MAY 12, 1962

UNITED STATES MILITARY ACADEMY AT WEST POINT, NEW YORK

General Westmoreland, General Groves, distinguished guests, and gentlemen of the Corps. As I was leaving the hotel this morning, a doorman asked me, "Where are you bound for, General?" and when I replied, "West Point," he remarked, "Beautiful place, have you ever been there before?"

No human being could fail to be deeply moved by such a tribute as this, coming from a profession I have served so long and a people I have loved so well. It fills me with an emotion I cannot express. But this award is not intended primarily for a personality, but to symbolize a great moral code – the code of conduct and chivalry of those who guard this beloved land of culture and ancient descent. That is the meaning of this medallion. For all eyes and for all time, it is an expression of the ethics of the American soldier. That I should be integrated in this way with so noble an ideal arouses a sense of pride and yet of humility which will be with me always.

Duty, Honor, Country: Those three hallowed words reverently dictate what you ought to be, what you can be, what you will be. They are your rallying points: to build courage when courage seems to fail; to regain faith when there seems to be little cause for faith; to create hope when hope becomes forlorn. Unhappily, I possess neither that eloquence of diction, that poetry of imagination, nor that brilliance of metaphor to tell you all that they mean.

The unbelievers will say they are but words, but a slogan, but a flamboyant phrase. Every pedant, every demagogue, every cynic, every hypocrite, every troublemaker, and, I am sorry to say, some others of an entirely different character, will try to downgrade them even to the extent of mockery and ridicule.

But these are some of the things they do. They build your basic character. They mold you for your future roles as the custodians of the nation's defense. They make you strong enough to know when you are weak, and brave enough to face yourself when you are afraid.

General Douglas MacArthur speaks in the Philippines.

MacArthur proudly displays the Congressional Citation he received from Speaker McCormick and Vice-President Lyndon Johnson.

MacArthur receives tributes from cadets on his 84th birthday.

They teach you to be proud and unbending in honest failure, but humble and gentle in success; not to substitute words for action; not to seek the path of comfort, but to face the stress and spur of difficulty and challenge; to learn to stand up in the storm, but to have compassion on those who fall; to master yourself before you seek to master others; to have a heart that is clean, a goal that is high; to learn to laugh, yet never forget how to weep; to reach into the future, yet never neglect the past; to be serious, yet never take yourself too seriously; to be modest so that you will remember the simplicity of true greatness; the open mind of true wisdom, the meekness of true strength.

They give you a temperate will, a quality of imagination, a vigor of the emotions, a freshness of the deep springs of life, a temperamental predominance of courage over timidity, an appetite for adventure over love of ease. They create in your heart the sense of wonder, the unfailing hope of what next, and the joy and inspiration of life. They teach you in this way to be an officer and a gentleman.

And what sort of soldiers are those you are to lead? Are they reliable? Are they brave? Are they capable of victory?

Their story is known to all of you. It is the story of the American man at arms. My estimate of him was formed on the battlefields many, many years ago, and has never changed. I regarded him then, as I regard him now, as one of the world's noblest figures; not only as one of the finest military characters, but also as one of the most stainless.

His name and fame are the birthright of every American citizen. In his youth and strength, his love and loyalty, he gave all that mortality can give. He needs no eulogy from me, or from any other man. He has written his own history and written it in red on his enemy's breast.

But when I think of his patience under adversity, of his courage under fire, and of his modesty in victory, I am filled with an emotion of admiration I cannot put into words. He belongs to history as furnishing one of the greatest examples of successful patriotism. He belongs to posterity as the instructor of future generations in the principles of liberty and freedom. He belongs to the present, to us, by his virtues and by his achievements.

In twenty campaigns, on a hundred battlefields, around a thousand campfires, I have witnessed that enduring fortitude, that patriotic self-abnegation, and that invincible determination which have carved his statue in the hearts of his people.

From one end of the world to the other, he has drained deep the chalice of courage. As I listened to those songs of the glee club, in memory's eye I could see those staggering columns of the First World War, bending under soggy packs on many a weary march, from dripping dusk to drizzling dawn, slogging ankle deep through mire of shell-pocked roads; to form grimly for the attack, blue-lipped, covered with sludge and mud, chilled by the wind and rain, driving home to their objective, and for many, to the judgment seat of God.

I do not know the dignity of their birth, but I do know the glory of their death. They died unquestioning, uncomplaining, with faith in their hearts, and on their lips the hope that we would go on to victory. Always for them: Duty, Honor, Country. Always their blood, and sweat, and tears, as they saw the way and the light.

And twenty years after, on the other side of the globe, against the filth of dirty foxholes, the stench of ghostly trenches, the slime of dripping dugouts, those boiling suns of the relentless heat, those torrential rains of devastating storms, the loneliness and utter desolation of jungle trails, the bitterness of long separation of those they loved and cherished, the deadly pestilence of tropic disease, the horror of stricken areas of war.

Their resolute and determined defense, their swift and sure attack, their indomitable purpose, their complete and decisive victory – always victory, always through the bloody haze of their last reverberating shot,

the vision of gaunt, ghastly men, reverently following your password of Duty, Honor, Country.

The code which those words perpetuate embraces the highest moral laws and will stand the test of any ethics or philosophies ever promulgated for the uplift of mankind. Its requirements are for the things that are right, and its restraints are from the things that are wrong. The soldier, above all other men, is required to practice the greatest act of religious training – sacrifice. In battle and in the face of danger and death, he discloses those divine attributes which his Maker gave when he created man in his own image. No physical courage and no brute instinct can take the place of the Divine help which alone can sustain him. However horrible the incidents of war may be, the soldier who is called upon to offer and to give his life for his country, is the noblest development of mankind.

You now face a new world, a world of change. The thrust into outer space of the satellite, spheres and missiles marked the beginning of another epoch in the long story of mankind – the chapter of the space age. In the five or more billions of years the scientists tell us it has taken to form the earth, in the three or more billion years of development of the human race, there has never been a greater, a more abrupt or staggering evolution. We deal now not with things of this world alone, but with the illimitable distances and as yet unfathomed mysteries of the universe. We are reaching out for a new and boundless frontier. We speak in strange terms: of harnessing the cosmic energy; of making winds and tides work for us; of creating unheard synthetic materials to supplement or even replace our old standard basics; of purifying sea water for our drink; of mining ocean floors for new fields of wealth and food; of disease preventatives to expand life into the hundred of years; of controlling the weather for a more equitable distribution of heat and cold, of rain and shine; of space ships to the moon; of the primary target in war, no longer limited to the armed forces of an enemy, but instead to include his civil populations; of ultimate conflict between a united human race and the sinister forces of some other planetary galaxy; of such dreams and fantasies as to make life the most exciting of all time.

And through all this welter of change and development your mission remains fixed, determined, inviolable. It is to win our wars. Everything else in your professional career is but corollary to this vital dedication. All other public purpose, all other public projects, all other public needs, great or small, will find others for their accomplishments; but you are the ones who are trained to fight.

Yours is the profession of arms, the will to win, the sure knowledge that in war there is no substitute for victory, that if you lose, the Nation will be destroyed, that the very obsession of your public service must be Duty, Honor, Country.

Others will debate the controversial issues, national and international, which divide men's minds. But serene, calm, aloof, you stand as the Nation's war guardians, as its lifeguards from the raging tides of international conflict, as its gladiators in the arena of battle. For a century and a half you have defended, guarded and protected its hallowed traditions of liberty and freedom, of right and justice.

Let civilian voices argue the merits or demerits of our processes of government. Whether our strength is being sapped by deficit financing indulged in too long, by federal paternalism grown too mighty, by power groups grown too arrogant, by politics grown too corrupt, by crime grown too rampant, by morals grown too low, by taxes grown too high, by extremists grown too violent; whether our personal liberties are as firm and complete as they should be.

These great national problems are not for your professional participation or military solution. Your guidepost stands out like a tenfold beacon in the night: Duty, Honor, Country.

You are the leaven which binds together the entire fabric of our national system of defense. From your ranks come the great captains who hold the Nation's destiny in their hands the moment the war tocsin sounds.

American soldiers read a Douglas MacArthur quote cut into a Vietnamese bunker.

The long gray line has never failed us. Were you to do so, a million ghosts in olive drab, in brown khaki, in blue and gray, would rise from their white crosses, thundering those magic words: Duty, Honor, Country.

This does not mean that you are warmongers. On the contrary, the soldier above all other people prays for peace, for he must suffer and bear the deepest wounds and scars of war. But always in our ears ring the ominous words of Plato, that wisest of all philosophers: "Only the dead have seen the end of war."

The shadows are lengthening for me. The twilight is here. My days of old have vanished – tone and tints. They have gone glimmering through the dreams of things that were. Their memory is one of wondrous beauty, watered by tears and coaxed and caressed by the smiles of yesterday. I listen then, but with thirsty ear, for the witching melody of faint bugles blowing reveille, of far drums beating the long roll.

In my dreams I hear again the crash of guns, the rattle of musketry, the strange, mournful mutter of the battlefield. But in the evening of my memory I come back to West Point. Always there echoes and re-echoes: Duty, Honor, Country.

Today marks my final roll call with you. But I want you to know that when I cross the river, my last conscious thoughts will be of the Corps, and the Corps, and the Corps.

I bid you farewell.

Analysis

When a renowned speaker such as MacArthur belittles his own oratorical abilities, as he did at the beginning of this speech, he is almost always indulging in false modesty – in effect saying to the audience, "Stay tuned for some verbal fireworks." In this case, MacArthur delivered. The speech is full to bursting with brilliant turns of phrase and sophisticated rhetorical devices. MacArthur was particularly fond of "the Rule of Three"; a basic rhetorical technique in which the speaker strings together three related items to build to a heightened impact. To cite just one example, "… to be modest so that you will remember the simplicity of true greatness; the open mind of true wisdom, the meekness of true strength." MacArthur employed the rule a number of times, along with many other techniques calculated to hold the attention of an audience. The result was a speech that remains a gem of its kind; a lofty, spiritual panegyric (formal speech of praise) to the American soldier and to the deeds and sacrifices he has made to build a great nation.

MacArthur's putative message was that duty, honor, country had been the guiding principles of the forebears of the cadets he was addressing, and of the men they had led to great feats on the battlefield. In fact, though, MacArthur's subliminal message was that he had, himself, played pivotal roles in many of those historic battles and that he was a great man who had devoted his life to the service of his country, and now could do no more. He regretted that, was the implication, and so should the country. The fact that it was all true, based on an indisputable record of towering accomplishment, lent even more poignancy to the occasion. MacArthur's lifelong reputation was one of a man who had been an enthusiastic steward of his own legend, but who had rarely – if ever – had to embellish or inflate his very real record of achievement. If his aim in this speech was to further secure his place in history, as it surely was, he accomplished that admirably.

"Duty, Honor, Country", is the motto of the U.S. Military Academy. MacArthur began and closed the speech with those words, and repeatedly intoned them at key moments to heighten the impacts of his rhetorical flights. Early in the speech, he rebuked the "unbelievers" who disparage the motto as "just words." Some of those are cynics, hypocrites, or otherwise unsavoury, he said, but some are "of an entirely different character." That was a reference to President Kennedy, who had said the previous year that the future would place a different set of demands on the American soldier than the past had. Nonsense, replied MacArthur in his speech and telling the cadets that they might face a new world, but that their virtues and qualities of character are timeless and will carry them into the future. "These great national problems are not for your professional participation or military solution. Your guidepost stands out like a tenfold beacon in the night: Duty, Honor, Country."

MacArthur, from all accounts, spoke without a script, and his audience must have been in awe of this frail old man, striding around the platform, and tossing off phrases such as "he has written his own history and written it in red on his enemy's breast," and dozens more like it, apparently *ex tempore*. However, MacArthur was known as a consummate actor, who wrote, rewrote, polished, and rehearsed his speeches, then committed them to memory. A contemporary account has him "… pacing like a brooding hawk through his ten-room apartment, puffing a corncob as he rehearsed." Others have pointed out that many of the key phrases and images had appeared in other speeches, sometimes repeatedly.

Polished, honed, recycled as they may have been, even on the page the words still soar. In performance, given the fact that virtually everyone in the audience knew that this was probably his last major public address, the impact was immeasurably heightened. MacArthur was clearly failing – he spoke slowly and the audience could hear age in his voice, though his delivery was strong. This knowledge lent enormous veracity, and power, to his beautifully rendered closing words.

President John F. Kennedy

"We choose to go to the moon."

T HE RACE TO SPACE WAS one of the highest-profile aspects of the Cold War. Starting with its launch of *Sputnik 1* in 1957, the Soviet Union grabbed and held the lead, while the U.S. stumbled in its efforts to catch up – as evidenced by the highly public failure of the first U.S. satellite launch, *Vanguard*. The U.S. eventually began to put satellites into orbit, but the Soviets greeted President Kennedy with their first manned orbital flight, by Cosmonaut Yuri Gagarin, less than three months after he took office. The U.S. countered weakly with the sub-orbital flight of Astronaut Alan Shepard, and it was nearly a year before the world saw the first orbiting American, John Glenn.

Superiority in space grabbed worldwide headlines and conveyed great prestige on the Soviets. The behind-the-scenes stakes were even higher. Satellites offered a new dimension in spying. Moreover, rockets that could put a man in orbit could also easily reach enemy territory – or place weapons into those same orbits. The U.S. was desperately fearful of Soviet military occupation of space, and vice versa.

Kennedy responded with public announcements that he was according space a high priority and, behind the scenes, with orders to catch the Soviets and get ahead of them. Kennedy's advisors told him that the Soviets had bigger, heavier rockets more adapted to placing large objects, such as manned space capsules, in orbit. Thus, they would likely continue to score firsts. Moving to outflank the other superpower, Kennedy set his sights on the moon. While seeking money from Congress for an expanded space program in mid-1961, he first pledged that America would reach the moon by the end of the decade, and reach it before the Soviet Union.

One of the initiatives accelerated under the new commitment was the Manned Space Center. In September 1961, the Center (now called the Johnson Space Center) was begun on 1,000 acres donated by Rice University in Houston, Texas. The following year Kennedy visited and, in a speech at Rice University, fully articulated his goals for space exploration, and their rationale.

FOR JOHN F. KENNEDY TIMELINE, PLEASE SEE PAGE 70

Kennedy speaking in front of a full-size model of the projected design for a lunar landing module at the Manned Spacecraft Center.

ADDRESS AT RICE UNIVERSITY ON THE NATION'S SPACE EFFORT

SEPTEMBER 12, 1962

RICE UNIVERSITY, HOUSTON, TEXAS

President Pitzer, Mr. Vice President, Governor, Congressman Thomas, Senator Wiley, and Congressman Miller, Mr. Webb, Mr. Bell, scientists, distinguished guests, and ladies and gentlemen:

I appreciate your president having made me an honorary visiting professor, and I will assure you that my first lecture will be very brief.

I am delighted to be here and I'm particularly delighted to be here on this occasion.

We meet at a college noted for knowledge, in a city noted for progress, in a State noted for strength, and we stand in need of all three, for we meet in an hour of change and challenge, in a decade of hope and fear, in an age of both knowledge and ignorance. The greater our knowledge increases, the greater our ignorance unfolds.

Despite the striking fact that most of the scientists that the world has ever known are alive and working today, despite the fact that this

President John F. Kennedy presents astronaut Alan Shepard with a medal for the successful *Freedom 7* spaceflight that made him the first American in space on May 5, 1961.

Nation's own scientific manpower is doubling every 12 years in a rate of growth more than three times that of our population as a whole, despite that, the vast stretches of the unknown and the unanswered and the unfinished still far outstrip our collective comprehension.

No man can fully grasp how far and how fast we have come, but condense, if you will, the 50,000 years of man's recorded history in a time span of but a half a century. Stated in these terms, we know very little about the first 40 years, except at the end of them advanced man had learned to use the skins of animals to cover them. Then about 10 years ago, under this standard, man emerged from his caves to construct other kinds of shelter. Only five years ago man learned to write and use a cart with wheels. Christianity began less than two years ago. The printing press came this year, and then less than two months ago, during this whole 50-year span of human history, the steam engine provided a new source of power.

Newton explored the meaning of gravity. Last month electric lights and telephones and automobiles and airplanes became available. Only last week did we develop penicillin and television and nuclear power, and now if America's new spacecraft succeeds in reaching Venus, we will have literally reached the stars before midnight tonight.

This is a breathtaking pace, and such a pace cannot help but create new ills as it dispels old, new ignorance, new problems, new dangers. Surely the opening vistas of space promise high costs and hardships, as well as high reward.

So it is not surprising that some would have us stay where we are a little longer to rest, to wait. But this city of Houston, this State of Texas, this country of the United States was not built by those who waited and rested and wished to look behind them. This country was conquered by those who moved forward – and so will space.

William Bradford, speaking in 1630 of the founding of the Plymouth Bay Colony, said that all great and honorable actions are accompanied with great difficulties, and both must be enterprised and overcome with answerable courage.

If this capsule history of our progress teaches us anything, it is that man, in his quest for knowledge and progress, is determined and cannot be deterred. The exploration of space will go ahead, whether we join in it or not, and it is one of the great adventures of all time, and no nation which expects to be the leader of other nations can expect to stay behind in the race for space.

Those who came before us made certain that this country rode the first waves of the industrial revolutions, the first waves of modern invention, and the first wave of nuclear power, and this generation does not intend to founder in the backwash of the coming age of space. We mean to be a part of it – we mean to lead it. For the eyes of the world

President Kennedy is shown scale models of booster rockets and missiles on September 12, 1962.

now look into space, to the moon and to the planets beyond, and we have vowed that we shall not see it governed by a hostile flag of conquest, but by a banner of freedom and peace. We have vowed that we shall not see space filled with weapons of mass destruction, but with instruments of knowledge and understanding.

Yet the vows of this Nation can only be fulfilled if we in this Nation are first, and, therefore, we intend to be first. In short, our leadership in science and in industry, our hopes for peace and security, our obligations to ourselves as well as others, all require us to make this effort, to solve these mysteries, to solve them for the good of all men, and to become the world's leading space-faring nation.

We set sail on this new sea because there is new knowledge to be gained, and new rights to be won, and they must be won and used for the progress of all people. For space science, like nuclear science and all technology, has no conscience of its own. Whether it will become a force for good or ill depends on man, and only if the United States occupies a position of pre-eminence can we help decide whether this new ocean will be a sea of peace or a new terrifying theater of war. I do not say that we should or will go unprotected against the hostile misuse of space any more than we go unprotected against the hostile use of land or sea, but I do say that space can be explored and mastered without feeding the fires of war, without repeating the mistakes that man has made in extending his writ around this globe of ours.

There is no strife, no prejudice, no national conflict in outer space as yet. Its hazards are hostile to us all. Its conquest deserves the best of all mankind, and its opportunity for peaceful cooperation many never come again. But why, some say, the moon? Why choose this as our goal? And they may well ask why climb the highest mountain? Why, 35 years ago, fly the Atlantic? Why does Rice play Texas?

We choose to go to the moon. We choose to go to the moon in this decade and do the other things, not because they are easy, but because they are hard, because that goal will serve to organize and measure the best of our energies and skills, because that challenge is one that we are willing to accept, one we are unwilling to postpone, and one which we intend to win, and the others, too.

It is for these reasons that I regard the decision last year to shift our efforts in space from low to high gear as among the most important decisions that will be made during my incumbency in the office of the Presidency.

In the last 24 hours we have seen facilities now being created for the

President Kennedy with astronaut John Glenn, the first American to orbit the Earth.

greatest and most complex exploration in man's history. We have felt the ground shake and the air shattered by the testing of a *Saturn* C-1 booster rocket, many times as powerful as the *Atlas* which launched John Glenn, generating power equivalent to 10,000 automobiles with their accelerators on the floor. We have seen the site where five F-1 rocket engines, each one as powerful as all eight engines of the *Saturn* combined, will be clustered together to make the advanced *Saturn* missile, assembled in a new building to be built at Cape Canaveral as tall as a 48 story structure, as wide as a city block, and as long as two lengths of this field.

Within these last 19 months at least 45 satellites have circled the earth. Some 40 of them were "made in the United States of America" and they were far more sophisticated and supplied far more knowledge to the people of the world than those of the Soviet Union.

Kennedy tries out the Apollo space capsule to see for himself the conditions astronauts will have to work in.

The *Mariner* spacecraft now on its way to Venus is the most intricate instrument in the history of space science. The accuracy of that shot is comparable to firing a missile from Cape Canaveral and dropping it in this stadium between the 40-yard lines.

Transit satellites are helping our ships at sea to steer a safer course. Tiros satellites have given us unprecedented warnings of hurricanes and storms, and will do the same for forest fires and icebergs.

We have had our failures, but so have others, even if they do not admit them. And they may be less public.

To be sure, we are behind, and will be behind for some time in manned flight. But we do not intend to stay behind, and in this decade, we shall make up and move ahead.

The growth of our science and education will be enriched by new knowledge of our universe and environment, by new techniques of learning and mapping and observation, by new tools and computers for industry, medicine, the home as well as the school. Technical institutions, such as Rice, will reap the harvest of these gains.

And finally, the space effort itself, while still in its infancy, has already created a great number of new companies, and tens of thousands of new jobs. Space and related industries are generating new demands in investment and skilled personnel, and this city and this State, and this region, will share greatly in this growth. What was once the furthest outpost on the old frontier of the West will be the furthest outpost on the new frontier of science and space. Houston, your City of Houston, with its Manned Spacecraft Center, will become the heart of a large scientific and engineering community. During the next 5 years the National Aeronautics and Space Administration expects to double the number of scientists and engineers in this area, to increase its outlays for salaries and expenses to $60 million a year; to invest some $200 million in plant and laboratory facilities; and to direct or contract for new space efforts over $1 billion from this Center in this City.

To be sure, all this costs us all a good deal of money. This year's space budget is three times what it was in January 1961, and it is greater than the space budget of the previous eight years combined. That budget now stands at $5,400 million a year – a staggering sum, though somewhat less than we pay for cigarettes and cigars every year. Space expenditures will soon rise some more, from 40 cents per person per week to more than 50 cents a week for every man, woman and child in the United States, for we have given this program a high national priority – even though I realize that this is in some measure an act of faith and vision, for we do not now know what benefits await us. But if I were to say, my fellow citizens, that we shall send to the moon, 240,000 miles away from the control station in Houston, a giant rocket more than 300 feet tall, the length of this football field, made of new metal alloys, some of which have not yet been invented, capable of standing heat and stresses several times more than have ever been experienced, fitted together with a precision better than the finest watch, carrying all the equipment needed for propulsion, guidance, control, communications, food and survival, on an untried mission, to an unknown celestial body, and then return it safely to earth, re-entering the atmosphere at speeds of over 25,000 miles per hour, causing heat about half that of the temperature of the sun – almost as hot as it is here today – and do all this, and do it right, and do it first before this decade is out – then we must be bold.

I'm the one who is doing all the work, so we just want you to stay cool for a minute. [laughter]

However, I think we're going to do it, and I think that we must pay what needs to be paid. I don't think we ought to waste any money, but I think we ought to do the job. And this will be done in the decade of the sixties. It may be done while some of you are still here at school at this college and university. It will be done during the term of office of some of the people who sit here on this platform. But it will be done. And it will be done before the end of this decade.

I am delighted that this university is playing a part in putting a man on the moon as part of a great national effort of the United States of America.

Many years ago the great British explorer George Mallory, who was to die on Mount Everest, was asked why did he want to climb it. He said, "Because it is there."

Well, space is there, and we're going to climb it, and the moon and the planets are there, and new hopes for knowledge and peace are there. And, therefore, as we set sail we ask God's blessing on the most hazardous and dangerous and greatest adventure on which man has ever embarked.

Thank you.

Analysis

Texas had always been somewhat hostile to Kennedy – owing in part to his primary fight with Lyndon Johnson for the 1960 Democratic nomination, and in part to the state's inherent conservatism. Thus, his trip to Houston to tour the new Manned Space Center was in part to draw attention to the space program and in part with an eye to the 1964 election. The same political considerations, regrettably, led to his fatal trip to Dallas the following year.

Kennedy was – as indeed he was in Dallas – greeted by large and enthusiastic crowds during his visit, and fattened his speech with positive references to the state and its people, and with local inside jokes. Rhetoricians call this "consubstantiation," the process of establishing identification with the audience – a difficult chore for a Northeastern "elitist" liberal in the Southwest. However, it was a technique at which Kennedy excelled, and he used it effectively in this speech. In one of the most famous segments, he exercised the Kennedy wit with the biggest laugh line in the speech. In explaining why the nation should set its sights on the moon, he set up the line by asking, rhetorically, why climb the highest mountain, and why (referring to Lindbergh's solo flight) fly the Atlantic. He followed that by asking, "Why does Rice play Texas?" Tumultuous laughter and applause followed, because the audience knew that the chronically weak Rice football team was trounced annually by powerful Texas.

Kennedy followed up the laughter with the most famous line of the speech, "We choose to go to the moon … and do the other things … not because they are easy, but because they are hard." That was an example of the Kennedy ability to make historic phrases, and is a "sound bite" heard countless times since in news accounts and documentaries on space.

However, the speech as a whole is much more substantive than his Inaugural Address, which attempted only to set the tone and direction of his Administration. Here was a working executive selling a costly program that proposed an outlandishly ambitious goal to a less-than-friendly audience.

Kennedy began with the familiar rhetorical technique of compressing a timeline to dramatize it. How many times have we heard a speaker say that if the history of the world were expressed as 24 hours, man would occupy only the last few seconds? Kennedy did the same with human history, expressing it in terms of half a century. He used that compression as a way of saying we are moving fast, but it is necessary and not unprecedented when cast in terms of recent versus ancient history. And again, he alluded to Texas in his argument, "This city of Houston, this State of Texas, this country of the United States was not built by those who waited and rested and wished to look behind them. This country was conquered by those who moved forward – and so will space [be]."

While President Kennedy did not live to see his dream realized, America did win the race to the moon. In this photograph, astronauts Neil Armstrong and Buzz Aldrin plant an American flag on the lunar surface on July 16, 1969.

Both the transcript and the recording of the speech show that the fastidiousness that marked some of Kennedy's earlier efforts was missing, as evidenced by the grammatical lapse in the above quote. He followed that with an obscure and confusing quote from Plymouth Colony Governor William Bradford in 1630, to the effect that difficult undertakings must be "enterprised and overcome with answerable courage." The quote was perhaps included because the occasion for Kennedy's presence at Rice was his having been made an honorary visiting professor. Kennedy was a history buff who liked to show off his knowledge in his speeches. Nevertheless, the quote was labored, and in using it, Kennedy committed the orator's cardinal sin of forcing the audience to stop and puzzle over what he meant by that. Some speech communications scholars call these "stop signs" and claim that they reduce the audience's absorption of the message. Kennedy rarely made such mistakes, but this was one.

In the speech, Kennedy extensively raised the spectre of the military competition for space as justification for going forward. He pointed to American progress, and explained away American failures as a result of the country's open society, compared to the Soviets who conducted their program in secret. Kennedy also talked about the considerable cost of the program – a major sticking point both with fiscal conservatives and with liberals who thought the money could be used more effectively to alleviate poverty. Before this audience, as an astute politician, Kennedy made sure to recount the positive economic impact of the new space center on the city and state. Another puzzling gaffe in the official transcript as provided by the Kennedy Library is the reference to the "$5,400 million" NASA budget. The usual American style would be to refer to $5.4 billion.

Nevertheless, the speech as delivered showcased Kennedy at his charismatic best and effectively highlighted U.S. commitment to the space program. NASA got most of its money and, of course, did begin to put men on the moon by the date promised, though Kennedy sadly did not live to see it.

President John F. Kennedy

"Ich bin ein Berliner."

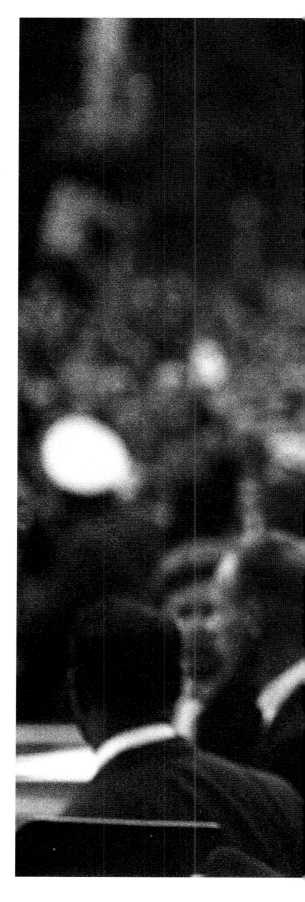

NO PLACE IN THE WORLD better symbolized the struggle between democracy and Communism after World War II than Berlin. The defeat of Nazi Germany had left the country in the charge of the four major powers – the United States, Great Britain, France, and the Soviet Union. The capital city of Berlin, which was located within the Soviet controlled region, was also divided in this way. As relations among the Western and Soviet blocs deteriorated after the war, the Soviets sealed the border between their sector, which became East Germany, and the West. The Western powers refused to relinquish control of their sectors of Berlin to East Germany, maintaining their military occupation and effectively making West Berlin an enclave of West Germany deep within East Germany.

In June 1948, the Soviets cut off all land access to Berlin, to try to force the Allies to cede control of Berlin to them, and thus absorb it into the new Communist state of East Germany. The Allies countered with the Berlin Airlift. For nearly a year, West Berlin was completely supplied by air. The success of the Airlift was a humiliating defeat for the Soviets, and they ended their blockade. Thereafter, Berlin became the major crossing point for East Germans, with 3.5 million people using the route to escape to the West until the Soviets and East Germans blocked the transit point in August 1961 by surrounding West Berlin with the famous wall. The erection of the Berlin Wall heightened tensions between East and West and was just one of a series of confrontational situations that spiked fears of impending nuclear war during the early '60s.

The Berlin Wall was built at about the time of the Bay of Pigs fiasco, in which the U.S. backed an ill-fated invasion of Cuba, and the embarrassed Kennedy Administration did not make a strong response at the time. However, with the West Berlin and West German governments increasingly fearful that the Communists would take over the rest of the city, President Kennedy decided to visit Berlin in June 1963 to underscore his support for Berlin as part of the West.

FOR JOHN F. KENNEDY TIMELINE, PLEASE SEE PAGE 70

President John F. Kennedy prepares to give his famous "Ich bin ein Berliner" speech. The square where he stood would be renamed John F. Kennedy-Platz three days after his assassination.

SPEECH GIVEN DURING GOOD WILL VISIT TO WESTERN EUROPE

JUNE 26, 1963

RATHAUS SCHÖNEBERG, BERLIN

I am proud to come to this city as the guest of your distinguished Mayor, who has symbolized throughout the world the fighting spirit of West Berlin. And I am proud to visit the Federal Republic with your distinguished Chancellor who for so many years has committed Germany to democracy and freedom and progress, and to come here in the company of my fellow American, General Clay, who has been in this city during its great moments of crisis and will come again if ever needed.

Two thousand years ago the proudest boast was "civis Romanus sum." Today, in the world of freedom, the proudest boast is "Ich bin ein Berliner."

I appreciate my interpreter translating my German!

There are many people in the world who really don't understand, or say they don't, what is the great issue between the free world and the Communist world. Let them come to Berlin. There are some who say that communism is the wave of the future. Let them come to Berlin. And there are some who say in Europe and elsewhere we can work with the Communists. Let them come to Berlin. And there are even a few who say that it is true that communism is an evil system, but it permits us to make economic progress. Lass' sie nach Berlin kommen. Let them come to Berlin.

Freedom has many difficulties and democracy is not perfect, but we have never had to put a wall up to keep our people in, to prevent them from leaving us. I want to say, on behalf of my countrymen, who live many miles away on the other side of the Atlantic, who are far distant from you, that they take the greatest pride that they have been able to share with you, even from a distance, the story of the last 18 years. I know of no town, no city, that has been besieged for 18 years that still lives with the vitality and the force, and the hope and the determination of the city of West Berlin. While the wall is the most obvious and vivid demonstration of the failures of the Communist system, for all the world to see, we take no satisfaction in it, for it is, as your Mayor has said, an offense not only against history but an offense against humanity, separating families, dividing husbands and wives and brothers and sisters, and dividing a people who wish to be joined together.

What is true of this city is true of Germany – real, lasting peace in Europe can never be assured as long as one German out of four is denied the elementary right of free men, and that is to make a free choice. In 18 years of peace and good faith, this generation of Germans has earned the right to be free, including the right to unite their families and their nation in lasting peace, with good will to all people. You live in a defended island of freedom, but your life is part of the main. So let me ask you as I close, to lift your eyes beyond the dangers of today, to the hopes of tomorrow,

President Kennedy disembarks from *Air Force One*. His visit to West Germany was designed to demonstrate Western unity against Soviet oppression.

beyond the freedom merely of this city of Berlin, or your country of Germany, to the advance of freedom everywhere, beyond the wall to the day of peace with justice, beyond yourselves and ourselves to all mankind.

Freedom is indivisible, and when one man is enslaved, all are not free. When all are free, then we can look forward to that day when this city will be joined as one and this country and this great Continent of Europe in a peaceful and hopeful globe. When that day finally comes, as it will, the people of West Berlin can take sober satisfaction in the fact that they were in the front lines for almost two decades.

All free men, wherever they may live, are citizens of Berlin, and, therefore, as a free man, I take pride in the words "Ich bin ein Berliner."

Analysis

The speech is considered one of Kennedy's finest, and struck a deep chord of support both within Germany and around the world. Its success was more a matter of who he was and where he was speaking than the words he used. Kennedy had enormously increased his stature in the world by facing down the Soviets during the Cuban Missile Crisis and was now going on the offensive, telling the Soviets that the U.S. would stay the course in West Berlin, and West Germany. By this time, his charisma and oratorical abilities were well known and a high level of quality was expected. Kennedy fulfilled those expectations.

The speech was a brief but powerful indictment of Communism, pointedly linking freedom and democracy, and juxtaposing them against Communism. No democracy, Kennedy pointed out, ever had to build a wall to keep its people from leaving. He also criticized Communism using the rhetorical technique of repetition. To anyone who does not understand the issues between Communism and the free world, or who in one way or another supports Communism, Kennedy said, "Let them come to Berlin." He repeated that line three times, and – even more effectively – ended the fourth repetition by repeating the phrase in German. His use of the German language was intended to, and succeeded in, heightening his identification with the audience.

His most famous use of German in the speech is "Ich bin ein Berliner," which he repeated in the second paragraph and with which he closed the speech. His foray into the German language thrilled the crowd, as is plain in filmed coverage of the speech, conveying as it did the depth of Kennedy's, and America's, commitment to the city.

"Ich bin ein Berliner" has gone down in history, but not entirely for the right reasons. An "urban legend" has grown up that Kennedy committed a major gaffe through a mistranslation of the phrase. "Berliner," goes the story, is a local name for a jelly doughnut. Any native German would have said, "Ich bin Berliner," and Kennedy's verbal construction actually translates as, "I am a jelly doughnut."

It is a funny story, but not strictly true. The jelly doughnuts in question are known as "Berliners" elsewhere in Germany, but not in Berlin, where they are known as "Pfannkuchen." In other words, German listeners elsewhere in the country might have perceived a verbal error, but as Presidential speechwriter Ted Sorenson says, "I believe that everyone in that vast audience knew exactly what Kennedy meant by that phrase." Sorenson recalls that West Berlin Mayor Willy Brandt had rehearsed the line with him the previous evening and adds that "I do not … believe that he would have permitted such an error."

One other noteworthy aspect of the speech that drew criticism was Kennedy's acknowledgement of East Berlin's status as part of the Soviet bloc. Until then, official U.S. policy had been that Berlin was under the joint military control of the four powers. Some diplomats were unhappy that he had undermined the official story, though the pragmatic Kennedy was merely accepting the reality of the situation.

In the end, his whirlwind eight-hour visit to West Berlin did much more good than harm, putting the Soviets on notice that the West would fight for the city, and the country. The visit was a triumph, and Sorenson reports that a tired but elated Kennedy said to him once they were seated on *Air Force One*, "We will never have another day like this one."

"Sadly," says Sorenson, "that was true. But the day, the speech, and its inspiring (though erroneous) last line are still remembered."

The speech and the gauntlet Kennedy threw down helped to preserve an uneasy but lasting place for West Berlin for the next 27 years, until the Soviet Union, East Germany, and the rest of the Communist Bloc imploded in 1989, and the Berlin Wall came down.

Construction work on the Berlin Wall in August 1961. The wall was begun after more than 3.5 million people fled from East to West Germany.

January 15, 1929	Born in Atlanta, Georgia, and named Michael King Jr. Several years later, his father changes both his and his son's names to Martin Luther King.
1944	Graduates from Booker T. Washington High School in Atlanta and is admitted to Morehouse College, also in Atlanta.
February 25, 1948	Ordained to the Baptist ministry.
1948	Graduates from Morehouse and is admitted to Crozer Theological Seminary in Chester, Pennsylvania.
1951	Graduates from Crozer.
June 18, 1953	Marries Coretta Scott.
June 5, 1955	Graduates from Boston University with a Doctor of Philosophy degree.
December 1955	Dr. King joins the Montgomery bus boycott after Rosa Parks is arrested for sitting at the front of a segregated bus.
1957	Dr. King and others form the Southern Christian Leadership Conference (SCLC) to fight segregation and achieve civil rights.
1958	Publishes his first book, *Stride Toward Freedom*.
1961	Dr. King becomes co-pastor, with his father, of the Ebenezer Baptist Church in Atlanta.
July 27, 1962	Arrested and jailed in Albany, Georgia. Sentenced to 45 days in jail, he is released after three days.
April 12, 1963	Arrested by Birmingham, Alabama, Police Commissioner Eugene "Bull" Conner for demonstrating without a permit. During his 11 days in jail he writes the famous "Letter from Birmingham Jail".
May 10, 1963	The Birmingham city government announces an agreement that stores, restaurants, and schools will be desegregated, hiring of blacks increased, and charges against Dr. King dropped.
June 23, 1963	Leads 125,000 people on a Freedom Walk in Detroit.
August 28, 1963	Dr. King leads the March on Washington and delivers his "I Have a Dream" speech.
1964	Dr. King becomes the youngest person in history to be awarded the Nobel Peace Prize.
June 1966	Begins The March Against Fear through the South.
November 27, 1967	Announces the beginning of the Poor People's Campaign for jobs and economic equality for the poor.
April 4, 1968	Dr. King is assassinated while standing on the balcony of his room at the Lorraine Motel in Memphis.
November 2, 1983	President Ronald Reagan signs a bill designating Martin Luther King Day a national holiday.

Dr. Martin Luther King

"I have a dream."

DURING THE SUMMER OF 1963, legions of African-Americans and their white supporters intensified their non-violent protests of segregation and civil rights abuses, and were met with an equally intense – and violent – response throughout the American South. Despite his relative youth, Dr. Martin Luther King was fast becoming the acknowledged leader of the Civil Rights movement, propelled into the spotlight by his organization of sit-ins and other protests in Birmingham, Alabama. The demonstrators – some high school students or younger – were met with police dogs and high-pressure water cannons. Many were injured and some, including Dr. King, were jailed.

Scenes of marchers attacked by dogs and beaten by police became a nightly staple of television news, and many Americans were appalled and outraged. Support for the Civil Rights movement built rapidly and dramatically, particularly among the young. Events in Birmingham, and elsewhere, prompted President John F. Kennedy to deliver a major televised address in June of that year underscoring his support of racial equality, and to introduce civil rights legislation.

The movement gained momentum throughout the summer, and on August 28, enormous crowds descended on Washington, D.C., via special buses, trains, and private vehicles for the culminating event of the demonstrations, the March on Washington for Jobs and Freedom. Organized by a group of labor, civil rights, and religious organizations, the march drew more than 200,000 people. The huge crowd surged from the Washington Monument grounds to the Lincoln Memorial. Most in attendance were African-American, but an estimated 20 percent were white. A parade of prominent civil rights and labor leaders, black and white, spoke. Entertainers included Joan Baez and Bob Dylan.

The media gave the march national exposure, with a reported 500 cameras filming, live coverage, and huge numbers of print reporters in attendance. The speech by Dr. King, from the steps of the Lincoln Memorial, was carried live on network television, and became instant history. His opening words proved prophetic.

Dr. Martin Luther King delivers his famous "I Have a Dream" speech at the Lincoln Memorial in Washington, D.C. on August 28, 1963.

SPEECH MADE DURING THE MARCH ON WASHINGTON FOR JOBS AND FREEDOM

AUGUST 28, 1963

LINCOLN MEMORIAL, WASHINGTON, D.C.

I am happy to join with you today in what will go down in history as the greatest demonstration for freedom in the history of our nation.

Five score years ago, a great American, in whose symbolic shadow we stand, signed the Emancipation Proclamation. This momentous decree came as a great beacon light of hope to millions of Negro slaves who had been seared in the flames of withering injustice. It came as a joyous daybreak to end the long night of captivity.

But one hundred years later, we must face the tragic fact that the Negro is still not free. One hundred years later, the life of the Negro is still sadly crippled by the manacles of segregation and the chains of discrimination. One hundred years later, the Negro lives on a lonely island of poverty in the midst of a vast ocean of material prosperity.

One hundred years later, the Negro is still languishing in the corners of American society and finds himself an exile in his own land. So we have come here today to dramatize an appalling condition.

In a sense we have come to our nation's capital to cash a check. When the architects of our republic wrote the magnificent words of the Constitution and the Declaration of Independence, they were signing a promissory note to which every American was to fall heir. This note was a promise that all men would be guaranteed the inalienable rights of life, liberty, and the pursuit of happiness.

It is obvious today that America has defaulted on this promissory note insofar as her citizens of color are concerned. Instead of honoring this sacred obligation, America has given the Negro people a bad check which has come back marked "insufficient funds." But we refuse to believe that the bank of justice is bankrupt. We refuse to believe that there are insufficient funds in the great vaults of opportunity of this nation. So we have come to cash this check – a check that will give us upon demand the riches of freedom and the security of justice. We have also come to this hallowed spot to remind America of the fierce urgency of now. This is no time to engage in the luxury of cooling off or to take the tranquilizing drug of gradualism. Now is the time to rise from the dark and desolate valley of segregation to the sunlit path of racial justice. Now is the time to open the doors of opportunity to all of God's children. Now is the time to lift our nation from the quicksands of racial injustice to the solid rock of brotherhood.

It would be fatal for the nation to overlook the urgency of the moment and to underestimate the determination of the Negro. This sweltering summer of the Negro's legitimate discontent will not pass until there is an invigorating autumn of freedom and equality. Nineteen sixty-three is not an end, but a beginning. Those who hope that the Negro needed to blow off steam and will now be content will have a rude awakening if the nation returns to business as usual. There will be neither rest nor tranquility in America until the Negro is granted his citizenship rights. The whirlwinds of revolt will continue to shake the foundations of our nation until the bright day of justice emerges.

But there is something that I must say to my people who stand on the warm threshold which leads into the palace of justice. In the process of gaining our rightful place we must not be guilty of wrongful deeds. Let us not seek to satisfy our thirst for freedom by drinking from the cup of bitterness and hatred.

We must forever conduct our struggle on the high plane of dignity and discipline. We must not allow our creative protest to degenerate into physical violence. Again and again we must rise to the majestic heights of meeting physical force with soul force. The marvelous new militancy which has engulfed the Negro community must not lead us to distrust of all white people, for many of our white brothers, as evidenced by their presence here today, have come to realize that their destiny is tied up with our destiny and their freedom is inextricably bound to our freedom. We cannot walk alone.

And as we walk, we must make the pledge that we shall march ahead. We cannot turn back. There are those who are asking the

Martin Luther King and fellow protestors photographed during the March on Washington For Jobs and Freedom.

Dr. Martin Luther King (center) shakes hands with President Lyndon Johnson (left) during the ceremonies for the signing of the Civil Rights Bill at the White House in July 1964.

devotees of civil rights, "When will you be satisfied?" We can never be satisfied as long as our bodies, heavy with the fatigue of travel, cannot gain lodging in the motels of the highways and the hotels of the cities. We cannot be satisfied as long as the Negro's basic mobility is from a smaller ghetto to a larger one. We can never be satisfied as long as a Negro in Mississippi cannot vote and a Negro in New York believes he has nothing for which to vote. No, no, we are not satisfied, and we will not be satisfied until justice rolls down like waters and righteousness like a mighty stream.

I am not unmindful that some of you have come here out of great trials and tribulations. Some of you have come fresh from narrow cells. Some of you have come from areas where your quest for freedom left you battered by the storms of persecution and staggered by the winds of police brutality. You have been the veterans of creative suffering. Continue to work with the faith that unearned suffering is redemptive.

Go back to Mississippi, go back to Alabama, go back to Georgia, go back to Louisiana, go back to the slums and ghettos of our northern cities, knowing that somehow this situation can and will be changed. Let us not wallow in the valley of despair.

I say to you today, my friends, that in spite of the difficulties and frustrations of the moment, I still have a dream. It is a dream deeply rooted in the American dream.

I have a dream that one day this nation will rise up and live out the true meaning of its creed: "We hold these truths to be self-evident: that all men are created equal."

I have a dream that one day on the red hills of Georgia the sons of former slaves and the sons of former slave owners will be able to sit down together at a table of brotherhood.

I have a dream that one day even the state of Mississippi, a desert state, sweltering with the heat of injustice and oppression, will be transformed into an oasis of freedom and justice.

I have a dream that my four children will one day live in a nation where they will not be judged by the color of their skin but by the content of their character.

I have a dream today.

I have a dream that one day the state of Alabama, whose governor's lips are presently dripping with the words of interposition and nullification, will be transformed into a situation where little black boys and black girls will be able to join hands with little white boys and white girls and walk together as sisters and brothers.

I have a dream today.

I have a dream that one day every valley shall be exalted, every hill and mountain shall be made low, the rough places will be made plain, and the crooked places will be made straight, and the glory of the Lord shall be revealed, and all flesh shall see it together.

This is our hope. This is the faith with which I return to the South. With this faith we will be able to hew out of the mountain of despair a stone of hope. With this faith we will be able to transform the jangling discords of our nation into a beautiful symphony of brotherhood. With this faith we will be able to work together, to pray together, to struggle together, to go to jail together, to stand up for freedom together, knowing that we will be free one day.

This will be the day when all of God's children will be able to sing with a new meaning, "My country, 'tis of thee, sweet land of liberty, of thee I sing. Land where my fathers died, land of the pilgrim's pride, from every mountainside, let freedom ring."

And if America is to be a great nation this must become true. So let freedom ring from the prodigious hilltops of New Hampshire. Let freedom ring from the mighty mountains of New York. Let freedom ring from the heightening Alleghenies of Pennsylvania!

Let freedom ring from the snowcapped Rockies of Colorado!

Let freedom ring from the curvaceous peaks of California!

But not only that; let freedom ring from Stone Mountain of Georgia!

Let freedom ring from Lookout Mountain of Tennessee!

Let freedom ring from every hill and every molehill of Mississippi. From every mountainside, let freedom ring.

When we let freedom ring, when we let it ring from every village and every hamlet, from every state and every city, we will be able to speed up that day when all of God's children, black men and white men, Jews and Gentiles, Protestants and Catholics, will be able to join hands and sing in the words of the old Negro spiritual, "Free at last! Free at last! Thank God Almighty, we are free at last!"

Analysis

Rhetoric – the art of public speaking – has been defined as "situated speech": the right person saying the right things in the right place at the right time to impart a message. In the case of Dr. Martin Luther King's "I Have a Dream" speech, all four elements came together in near perfection. His words that day have been judged the greatest speech of the 20th Century by scholars in the field of public address.

Dr. King was clearly the right person to deliver the message. Many other people, some prominent, spoke that day, just as a number of people spoke the day Lincoln delivered his Gettysburg Address. But only King's words, like Lincoln's, are remembered. Dr. King spoke from a height of moral authority earned by putting his body on the line, and behind bars, in Birmingham and other flashpoints in the South. He had met vicious racism with calm dignity and he carried his experiences and dignity to the podium that August day.

King's words matched his personal stature. He was a preacher, and had learned his style from his preacher father, then honed it in the pulpits of African-American Baptist churches. His was an emotional, inspirational style of the sort that in lesser hands can and does move toward self-parody. In Dr. King's case, his innate dignity kept his sometimes-florid language from going over the top.

In addition, the organizers of the march could not have chosen a more symbolically appropriate place for the day's speeches than the Lincoln Memorial. The connection between the Great Emancipator and those who were emancipated, but not yet equal, underlay every word he spoke. Early in the speech, Dr. King explicitly acknowledged the connection through his "Five-score years ago" reference to the Emancipation Proclamation.

The fourth element – timing – was equally propitious. As previously noted, the American people had watched televised brutality against black demonstrators during what Dr. King characterized as "the sweltering summer of the Negro's legitimate discontent" and for months and even years before that. They were ready and willing to be moved, and Dr. King's words met their needs admirably.

The speech is full to bursting with imagery, metaphor, and all of the techniques of a great orator and preacher – principally repetition and alliteration – that hammer home his points.

It, essentially, has two parts. At the beginning, Dr. King eloquently and movingly made the case for equality for his people. In doing so, he used the curiously everyday metaphor of "a promissory note" and "a bad check which has come back marked insufficient funds" to illustrate the denial of equal rights to African-Americans. The imagery seems ordinary on the printed page, but his performance made it work.

After firmly establishing the justice of his people's cause, and calling on his people to forego the violence that could justifiably rise from their frustration, Dr. King entered the second part of the speech. There, he abandoned the substantive argument of his case in favor of a purely emotional appeal but, with his exceptional voice and body language, King transformed his words, in the words of one scholar, "from cliché to commandment."

It is only in the second half of the speech that he introduced his "I have a dream" theme, using repetition to hammer home his aspiration of a better world of the future. The imagery of slavery and oppression, and his hopes for his "four little children" remain immensely powerful. The finish was pure Southern Baptist preaching of the highest order, the rolling cadences building to the final, almost musical crescendo of "Thank God Almighty we are free at last." In the end, the massive crowd – and the audience viewing the speech on television – were moved, motivated, and convinced.

It is impossible to get the feeling of the moment from a reading of the text. Some of the language, such as the "bad check" metaphor and the reference to "the curvaceous peaks of California" are less successful than others. However, Dr. King carried the speech off with the bravura performance of a skilled and polished orator that lifted even the most ordinary imagery to soaring heights.

Martin Luther King displays his Nobel Peace Prize medal, awarded for his fight against racism in America.

As with any other public address, the final test was the impact. Dr. King's words may well have been the decisive factor in his being named *Time* magazine's Man of the Year for 1963 and, the following year, becoming the youngest person ever to receive the Nobel Peace Prize. The groundswell of support that followed the speech was a significant factor in the passage of the Civil Rights Act of 1964, the most sweeping civil rights legislation in nearly a century. To this day, Dr. Martin Luther King's "I Have a Dream" speech endures as an inspirational example of the power of the spoken word.

February 6, 1911	Ronald Wilson Reagan is born in Tampico, Illinois.
1920	After moving several times, the Reagan family settles in Dixon, Illinois.
1928–1932	Attends Eureka College where he majors in economics and sociology while pursuing an interest in drama. He is also very active in sports, including football.
January 26, 1940	Marries actress Jane Wyman. They divorce in 1948.
April 18, 1942	An Army reservist since 1937, Reagan is called up to active service. He spends most of his active service in the Motion Picture Army Unit in Culver City, making training and propaganda films.
March 1947	Reagan is elected President of the Screen Actors Guild for the first of five consecutive terms.
March 4, 1952	Reagan and movie actress Nancy Davis are married.
1954	Reagan is hired as a spokesman for General Electric and to host the *General Electric Theater* television weekly drama, a job he holds for eight years.
October 27, 1964	Reagan gives a television address supporting Republican Presidential candidate Barry Goldwater. The speech launches his political career.
November 8, 1966	Reagan defeats California incumbent governor Edmund G. ("Pat") Brown by a landslide. He is re-elected in 1970.
November 4, 1980	Reagan is elected President in a landslide victory. George H.W. Bush is elected as Vice-President.
March 30, 1981	John Hinckley, Jr. attempts to assassinate Reagan, who is seriously wounded. His press secretary, James Brady, and two others are also shot.
Spring 1983	Reagan gives a series of speeches including "We Will Not Be Turned Back" and the "Evil Empire" speech, and also unveils his proposal for a Strategic Defense Initiative, later dubbed "Star Wars", in a nationally televised speech.
November 4, 1984	Reagan is re-elected, defeating Walter Mondale in a landslide.
January 28, 1986	U.S. Space Shuttle *Challenger* disintegrates just after takeoff. Six astronauts and the first civilian passenger, teacher Christa McAuliffe, are killed. That evening Reagan delivers a speech to the nation.
June 12, 1987	In a speech at Berlin's Brandenburg Gate, Reagan demands "Mr. Gorbachev, tear down this wall."
November 5, 1994	Reagan discloses in a letter to the American public that he has Alzheimer's disease.
June 5, 2004	Ronald Reagan dies at his home in California.

Ronald Reagan

"You and I have a rendezvous with destiny."

I N 1964, RONALD REAGAN WAS mainly known to the American public as a minor movie actor who had moved to television as host of a series called *GE Theater*. Along with his hosting chores, the sponsor, General Electric, sent him out to towns where GE had plants to deliver motivational speeches to local civic groups. Gradually, the subject matter of Reagan's speeches moved beyond a pro-business company message to espousal of conservative ideological positions. Reagan, and his message, began getting wide attention. Speaking of those times, he later said "I was told that I was the most popular speaker in the country after President Kennedy." However, despite his popularity, Reagan was becoming too controversial for GE and the relationship ended.

The 1964 Republican Presidential campaign saw a bitter battle between moderate "Eisenhower" Republicans, who had long held control of the party, and a new, more conservative, insurgency led by Arizona Senator Barry Goldwater. Goldwater defeated New York Governor Nelson Rockefeller for the nomination and, during the campaign, he was savaged by the Democratic incumbent, Lyndon Johnson, as a dangerous man who would lead the country into nuclear war.

Reagan, a lifelong Democrat, had switched parties in 1962 and now began campaigning for Goldwater, traveling the country to deliver a well-received stump speech. One evening, he was speaking in California when he was approached by prominent Republicans who asked him to deliver the message on national television. The private group bought a half-hour of prime time on NBC, hence the reference to a "sponsor" at the beginning. Goldwater was dubious, because Reagan intended to discuss social security and other issues on which Goldwater was being attacked, but he agreed to the appearance after viewing a tape of the speech, which had been filmed in advance before a studio audience.

The speech proved a sensation, raising $8 million for Goldwater's campaign, and launching Reagan's political career.

Ronald Reagan stands among the crowd during the Republican National Convention at the Cow Palace, San Francisco, California, in July 1964.

TELEVISED SPEECH ON BEHALF OF REPUBLICAN BARRY GOLDWATER'S 1964 PRESIDENTIAL CAMPAIGN (KNOWN AS "A TIME FOR CHOOSING" OR "THE SPEECH")

OCTOBER 27, 1964

LOS ANGELES, CALIFORNIA

Thank you very much. Thank you and good evening. The sponsor has been identified, but unlike most television programs, the performer hasn't been provided with a script. As a matter of fact, I have been permitted to choose my own ideas regarding the choice that we face in the next few weeks.

I have spent most of my life as a Democrat. I recently have seen fit to follow another course. I believe that the issues confronting us cross party lines. Now, one side in this campaign has been telling us that the issues of this election are the maintenance of peace and prosperity. The line has been used "We've never had it so good."

But I have an uncomfortable feeling that this prosperity isn't something on which we can base our hopes for the future. No nation in history has ever survived a tax burden that reached a third of its national income. Today, 37 cents of every dollar earned in this country is the tax collector's share, and yet our government continues to spend $17 million a day more than the government takes in. We haven't balanced our budget 28 out of the last 34 years. We have raised our debt limit

Reagan's "Time for Choosing" speech was given on behalf of Presidential hopeful Barry Goldwater, but is credited with launching his own political career.

three times in the last twelve months, and now our national debt is one and a half times bigger than all the combined debts of all the nations in the world. We have $15 billion in gold in our treasury – we don't own an ounce. Foreign dollar claims are $27.3 billion, and we have just had announced that the dollar of 1939 will now purchase 45 cents in its total value.

As for the peace that we would preserve, I wonder who among us would like to approach the wife or mother whose husband or son has died in South Vietnam and ask them if they think this is a peace that should be maintained indefinitely. Do they mean peace, or do they mean we just want to be left in peace? There can be no real peace while one American is dying some place in the world for the rest of us. We are at war with the most dangerous enemy that has ever faced mankind in his long climb from the swamp to the stars, and it has been said if we lose that war, and in doing so lose this way of freedom of ours, history

will record with the greatest astonishment that those who had the most to lose did the least to prevent its happening. Well, I think it's time we ask ourselves if we still know the freedoms that were intended for us by the Founding Fathers.

Not too long ago two friends of mine were talking to a Cuban refugee, a businessman who had escaped from Castro, and in the midst of his story one of my friends turned to the other and said, "We don't know how lucky we are." And the Cuban stopped and said, "How lucky you are! I had someplace to escape to." In that sentence he told us the entire story. If we lose freedom here, there is no place to escape to. This is the last stand on Earth. And this idea that government is beholden to the people, that it has no other source of power except to sovereign people, is still the newest and most unique idea in all the long history of man's relation to man. This is the issue of this election. Whether we believe in our capacity for self-government or whether we abandon the American revolution and confess that a little intellectual elite in a far-distant capital can plan our lives for us better than we can plan them ourselves.

You and I are told increasingly that we have to choose between a left or right, but I would like to suggest that there is no such thing as a left or right. There is only an up or down – up to a man's age-old dream, the ultimate in individual freedom consistent with law and order – or down to the ant heap totalitarianism, and regardless of their sincerity, their humanitarian motives, those who would trade our freedom for security have embarked on this downward course.

In this vote-harvesting time, they use terms like the "Great Society," or as we were told a few days ago by the President, we must accept a "greater government activity in the affairs of the people." But they have been a little more explicit in the past and among themselves – and all of the things that I now will quote have appeared in print. These are not Republican accusations. For example, they have voices that say "the cold war will end through acceptance of a not undemocratic socialism." Another voice says that the profit motive has become outmoded, it must be replaced by the incentives of the welfare state; or our traditional system of individual freedom is incapable of solving the complex problems of the 20th century. Senator Fulbright has said at Stanford University that the Constitution is outmoded. He referred to the President as our moral teacher and our leader, and he said he is hobbled in his task by the restrictions in power imposed on him by this antiquated document. He must be freed so that he can do for us what he knows is best. And Senator Clark of Pennsylvania, another articulate spokesman, defines liberalism as "meeting the material needs of the masses through the full power of centralized government." Well, I for one resent it when a representative of the people refers to you and me – the free man and woman of this country – as "the masses." This is a term we haven't applied to ourselves in America. But beyond that, "the full power of centralized government" – this was the very thing the Founding Fathers sought to minimize. They knew that governments don't control things. A government can't control the economy without controlling people. And they know when a government sets out to do that, it must use force and coercion to achieve its purpose. They also knew, those Founding Fathers, that outside of its legitimate functions, government does nothing as well or as economically as the private sector of the economy.

Now, we have no better example of this than the government's involvement in the farm economy over the last 30 years. Since 1955, the cost of this program has nearly doubled. One-fourth of farming in America is responsible for 85% of the farm surplus. Three-fourths of farming is out on the free market and has known a 21% increase in the per capita consumption of all its produce. You see, that one-fourth of farming is regulated and controlled by the federal government. In the last three years we have spent $43 in feed grain program for every bushel of corn we don't grow.

Senator Humphrey last week charged that Barry Goldwater as President would seek to eliminate farmers. He should do his homework a little better, because he will find out that we have had a decline of 5 million in the farm population under these government programs. He will also find that the Democratic administration has sought to get from Congress an extension of the farm program to include that three-fourths that is now free. He will find that they have also asked for the right to imprison farmers who wouldn't keep books as prescribed by the federal government. The Secretary of Agriculture asked for the right to seize farms through condemnation and resell them to other individuals. And contained in that same program was a provision that would have allowed the federal government to remove 2 million farmers from the soil.

At the same time, there has been an increase in the Department of Agriculture employees. There is now one for every 30 farms in the United States, and still they can't tell us how 66 shiploads of grain headed for Austria disappeared without a trace and Billie Sol Estes never left shore.

Ronald Reagan sits in front of a bank of microphones with his wife, Nancy.

Every responsible farmer and farm organization has repeatedly asked the government to free the farm economy, but who are farmers to know what is best for them? The wheat farmers voted against a wheat program. The government passed it anyway. Now the price of bread goes up; the price of wheat to the farmer goes down.

Meanwhile, back in the city, under urban renewal the assault on freedom carries on. Private property rights are so diluted that public interest is almost anything that a few government planners decide it should be. In a program that takes for the needy and gives to the greedy, we see such spectacles as in Cleveland, Ohio, a million-and-a-half-dollar building completed only three years ago must be destroyed to make way for what government officials call a "more compatible use of the land." The President tells us he is now going to start building public housing units in the thousands where heretofore we have only built them in the hundreds. But FHA and the Veterans Administration tell us that they have 120,000 housing units they've taken back through mortgage foreclosures. For three decades, we have sought to solve the problems of unemployment through government planning, and the more the plans fail, the more the planners plan. The latest is the Area Redevelopment Agency. They have just declared Rice County, Kansas, a depressed area. Rice County, Kansas, has two hundred oil wells, and the 14,000 people there have over $30 million on deposit in personal savings in their banks. When the government tells you you're depressed, lie down and be depressed.

We have so many people who can't see a fat man standing beside a thin one without coming to the conclusion that the fat man got that way by taking advantage of the thin one. So they are going to solve all the problems of human misery through government and government planning. Well, now, if government planning and welfare had the answer and they've had almost 30 years of it, shouldn't we expect government to almost read the score to us once in a while? Shouldn't they be telling us about the decline each year in the number of people needing help? The reduction in the need for public housing?

But the reverse is true. Each year the need grows greater, the program grows greater. We were told four years ago that 17 million people went to bed hungry each night. Well, that was probably true. They were all on a diet. But now we are told that 9.3 million families in this country are poverty-stricken on the basis of earning less than $3,000 a year. Welfare spending is 10 times greater than in the dark depths of the Depression. We are spending $45 billion on welfare. Now do a little arithmetic, and you will find that if we divided the $45 billion

As a former actor and motivational speaker, performing in front of a crowd held no fears for Ronald Reagan.

up equally among those 9 million poor families, we would be able to give each family $4,600 a year, and this added to their present income should eliminate poverty! Direct aid to the poor, however, is running only about $600 per family. It would seem that someplace there must be some overhead.

So now we declare "war on poverty," or "you, too, can be a Bobby Baker!" Now, do they honestly expect us to believe that if we add $1 billion to the $45 million we are spending... one more program to the 30-odd we have – and remember, this new program doesn't replace any, it just duplicates existing programs – do they believe that poverty is suddenly going to disappear by magic? Well, in all fairness I should explain that there is one part of the new program that isn't duplicated. This is the youth feature. We are now going to solve the dropout problem, juvenile delinquency, by reinstituting something like the old CCC camps, and we are going to put our young people in camps, but again we do some arithmetic, and we find that we are going to spend each year just on room and board for each young person that we help $4,700 a year! We can send them to Harvard for $2,700! Don't get me wrong. I'm not suggesting that Harvard is the answer to juvenile delinquency.

But seriously, what are we doing to those we seek to help? Not too long ago, a judge called me here in Los Angeles. He told me of a young woman who had come before him for a divorce. She had six children, was pregnant with her seventh. Under his questioning, she revealed her husband was a laborer earning $250 a month. She wanted a divorce so that she could get an $80 raise. She is eligible for $330 a month in the Aid to Dependent Children Program. She got the idea from two women in her neighborhood who had already done that very thing.

Yet anytime you and I question the schemes of the do-gooders, we are denounced as being against their humanitarian goals. They say we are always "against" things, never "for" anything. Well, the trouble with our liberal friends is not that they are ignorant, but that they know so much that isn't so. We are for a provision that destitution should not follow unemployment by reason of old age, and to that end we have accepted Social Security as a step toward meeting the problem.

But we are against those entrusted with this program when they practice deception regarding its fiscal shortcomings, when they charge that any criticism of the program means that we want to end payments to those who depend on them for livelihood. They have called it insurance to us in a hundred million pieces of literature. But then they appeared before the Supreme Court and they testified that it was a welfare program. They only use the term "insurance" to sell it to the people. And they said Social Security dues are a tax for the general use of the government, and the government has used that tax. There is no fund, because Robert Byers, the actuarial head, appeared before a congressional committee and admitted that Social Security as of this moment is $298 billion in the hole. But he said there should be no cause for worry because as long as they have the power to tax, they could always take away from the people whatever they needed to bail them out of trouble! And they are doing just that.

A young man, 21 years of age, working at an average salary... his Social Security contribution would, in the open market, buy him an insurance policy that would guarantee $220 a month at age 65. The government promises $127. He could live it up until he is 31 and then take out a policy that would pay more than Social Security. Now, are we so lacking in business sense that we can't put this program on a sound basis so that people who do require those payments will find that they can get them when they are due... that the cupboard isn't bare? Barry Goldwater thinks we can.

At the same time, can't we introduce voluntary features that would permit a citizen who can do better on his own to be excused upon presentation of evidence that he had made provisions for the non-earning years? Should we allow a widow with children to work, and not lose the benefits supposedly paid for by her deceased husband? Shouldn't you and I be allowed to declare who our beneficiaries will be under these programs, which we cannot do? I think we are for telling our senior citizens that no one in this country should be denied medical care because of a lack of funds. But I think we are against forcing all citizens, regardless of need, into a compulsory government program, especially when we have such examples, as announced last week, when France admitted that their Medicare program was now bankrupt. They've come to the end of the road.

In addition, was Barry Goldwater so irresponsible when he suggested that our government give up its program of deliberate planned inflation so that when you do get your Social Security pension, a dollar will buy a dollar's worth, and not 45 cents' worth?

I think we are for an international organization, where the nations of the world can seek peace. But I think we are against subordinating American interests to an organization that has become so structurally unsound that today you can muster a two-thirds vote on the floor of the General Assembly among the nations that represent less than 10 percent of the world's population. I think we are against the hypocrisy of assailing our allies because here and there they cling to a colony, while we engage in a conspiracy of silence and never open our mouths about the millions of people enslaved in Soviet colonies in the satellite nation.

I think we are for aiding our allies by sharing of our material blessings with those nations which share in our fundamental beliefs, but we are against doling out money government to government, creating bureaucracy, if not socialism, all over the world. We set out to help 19 countries. We are helping 107. We spent $146 billion. With that money, we bought a $2 million yacht for Haile Selassie. We bought dress suits for Greek undertakers, extra wives for Kenyan government officials. We bought a thousand TV sets for a place where they have no electricity. In the last six years, 52 nations have bought $7 billion worth of our gold, and all 52 are receiving foreign aid from this country.

No government ever voluntarily reduces itself in size. Government programs, once launched, never disappear. Actually, a government bureau is the nearest thing to eternal life we'll ever see on this Earth. Federal employees number 2.5 million, and federal, state, and local, one out of six of the nation's work force is employed by the government. These proliferating bureaus with their thousands of regulations have cost us many of our constitutional safeguards. How many of us realize that today federal agents can invade a man's property without a warrant? They can impose a fine without a formal hearing, let alone a trial by jury, and they can seize and sell his property in auction to enforce the payment of that fine. In Chico County, Arkansas, James Wier overplanted his rice allotment. The government obtained a $17,000 judgment, and a U.S. marshal sold his 950-acre farm at auction. The government said it was necessary as a warning to others to make the system work. Last February 19 at the University of Minnesota, Norman Thomas, six-time candidate for President on the Socialist Party ticket, said, "If Barry Goldwater became President, he would stop the advance of socialism in the United States." I think that's exactly what he will do.

As a former Democrat, I can tell you Norman Thomas isn't the only man who has drawn this parallel to socialism with the present administration. Back in 1936, Mr. Democrat himself, Al Smith, the great American, came before the American people and charged that the leadership of his party was taking the party of Jefferson, Jackson, and Cleveland down the road under the banners of Marx, Lenin, and Stalin. And he walked away from his party, and he never returned to the day he died, because to this day, the leadership of that party has been taking that party, that honorable party, down the road in the image of the Labour socialist party of England. Now it doesn't require expropriation or confiscation of private property or business to impose socialism on a people. What does it mean whether you hold the deed or the title to your business or property if the government holds the power of life and death over that business or property? Such machinery already exists. The government can find some charge to bring against any concern it chooses to prosecute. Every businessman has his own tale of harassment. Somewhere a perversion has taken place. Our natural, inalienable rights are now considered to be a dispensation of government, and freedom has never been so fragile, so close to slipping from our grasp as it is at this moment. Our Democratic opponents seem unwilling to debate these issues. They want to make you and I believe that this is a contest between two men... that we are to choose just between two personalities.

Well, what of this man that they would destroy? And in destroying, they would destroy that which he represents, the ideas that you and I hold dear. Is he the brash and shallow and trigger-happy man they say he is? Well, I have been privileged to know him "when." I knew him long before he ever dreamed of trying for high office, and I can tell you personally I have never known a man in my life I believe so incapable of doing a dishonest or dishonorable thing.

This is a man who in his own business, before he entered politics, instituted a profit-sharing plan, before unions had ever thought of it. He put in health and medical insurance for all his employees. He took 50 percent of the profits before taxes and set up a retirement program, a pension plan for all his employees. He sent checks for life to an employee who was ill and couldn't work. He provided nursing care for the children of mothers who work in the stores. When Mexico was ravaged by floods from the Rio Grande, he climbed in his airplane and flew medicine and supplies down there.

An ex-GI told me how he met him. It was the week before Christmas during the Korean War, and he was at the Los Angeles airport trying to get a ride home to Arizona for Christmas, and he said that there were a lot of servicemen there and no seats available on the planes. Then a voice came over the loudspeaker and said, "Any men in uniform wanting a ride to Arizona, go to runway such-and-such," and they went down there, and there was this fellow named Barry Goldwater sitting in his plane. Every day in the weeks before Christmas, all day long, he would load up the plane, fly to Arizona, fly them to their homes, then fly back over to get another load.

During the hectic split-second timing of a campaign, this is a man who took time out to sit beside an old friend who was dying of cancer. His campaign managers were understandably impatient, but he said, "There aren't many left who care what happens to her. I'd like her to know I care." This is a man who said to his 19-year-old son, "There is no foundation like the rock of honesty and fairness, and when you begin to build your life upon that rock, with the cement of the faith in God that you have, then you have a real start." This is not a man who could carelessly send other people's sons to war. And that is the issue of this campaign that makes all of the other problems I have discussed academic, unless we realize that we are in a war that must be won.

Those who would trade our freedom for the soup kitchen of the welfare state have told us that they have a utopian solution of peace without victory. They call their policy "accommodation." And they say if we only avoid any direct confrontation with the enemy, he will forget his evil ways and learn to love us. All who oppose them are indicted as warmongers. They say we offer simple answers to complex problems. Well, perhaps there is a simple answer – not an easy answer – but simple.

If you and I have the courage to tell our elected officials that we want our national policy based upon what we know in our hearts is morally right. We cannot buy our security, our freedom from the threat of the bomb by committing an immorality so great as saying to a billion now in slavery behind the Iron Curtain, "Give up your dreams of freedom because to save our own skin, we are willing to make a deal with your slave masters." Alexander Hamilton said, "A nation which can prefer

Reagan waves to spectators during a motorcade.

disgrace to danger is prepared for a master, and deserves one." Let's set the record straight. There is no argument over the choice between peace and war, but there is only one guaranteed way you can have peace – and you can have it in the next second – surrender.

Admittedly there is a risk in any course we follow other than this, but every lesson in history tells us that the greater risk lies in appeasement, and this is the specter our well-meaning liberal friends refuse to face – that their policy of accommodation is appeasement, and it gives no choice between peace and war, only between fight and surrender. If we continue to accommodate, continue to back and retreat, eventually we have to face the final demand – the ultimatum. And what then? When Nikita Khrushchev has told his people he knows what our answer will be? He has told them that we are retreating under the pressure of the Cold War, and someday when the time comes to deliver the ultimatum, our surrender will be voluntary because by that time we will have weakened from within spiritually, morally, and economically. He believes this because from our side he has heard voices pleading for "peace at any price" or "better Red than dead," or as one commentator put it, he would rather "live on his knees than die on his feet." And therein lies the road to war, because those voices don't speak for the rest of us. You and I know and do not believe that life is so dear and peace so sweet as to be purchased at the price of chains and slavery. If nothing in life is worth dying for, when did this begin – just in the face of this enemy? Or should Moses have told the children of Israel to live

in slavery under the pharaohs? Should Christ have refused the cross? Should the patriots at Concord Bridge have thrown down their guns and refused to fire the shot heard 'round the world? The martyrs of history were not fools, and our honored dead who gave their lives to stop the advance of the Nazis didn't die in vain. Where, then, is the road to peace? Well, it's a simple answer after all.

You and I have the courage to say to our enemies, "There is a price we will not pay." There is a point beyond which they must not advance. This is the meaning in the phrase of Barry Goldwater's "peace through strength." Winston Churchill said that "the destiny of man is not measured by material computation. When great forces are on the move in the world, we learn we are spirits – not animals." And he said, "There is something going on in time and space, and beyond time and space, which, whether we like it or not, spells duty."

You and I have a rendezvous with destiny. We will preserve for our children this, the last best hope of man on Earth, or we will sentence them to take the last step into a thousand years of darkness.

We will keep in mind and remember that Barry Goldwater has faith in us. He has faith that you and I have the ability and the dignity and the right to make our own decisions and determine our own destiny.

Thank you very much.

Ronald Reagan takes his oath as the new Governor of California: the first step in his political career.

Analysis

Today, the sort of "red-meat conservatism" Ronald Reagan presented that night in 1964 is heard every night on American television from countless conservative commentators, who find enough of a receptive audience to sustain their ratings. Nearly 50 years ago, however, it was revelatory to a portion of the American public that had been raised in an era of ever-expanding government and had spent its formative years practicing "duck-and-cover" in the classroom and knowing the location of the nearest fallout shelter.

Barry Goldwater was proposing in his campaign to roll back the incursions of government begun by Franklin Roosevelt and to draw a line in the sand against international Communism, but he had rarely – if ever – articulated his brand of conservatism as persuasively as Ronald Reagan did. Goldwater bristled that "extremism in defense of liberty is no vice," but Reagan came across as more reasonable and more hopeful, in part because of his practiced, measured delivery. There were people in America who felt disenfranchised, overwhelmed, and powerless and Reagan, in this speech and those to follow, gave them a voice and a cause.

The speech itself is filled with rebuttable premises and sections that do not bear much analysis; but Reagan skated from one to the next without filling in the blanks or even completing some arguments. Instead, he built an unstoppable rhetorical momentum so that the speech, taken as a whole, was remarkably persuasive to those ready to be persuaded. The well-rehearsed delivery of a master public speaker carried the message in waves of words, the sheer density of the language producing a whole that was infinitely more inspirational to portions of his audience than the individual parts.

A careful reading of the speech, in the absence of Reagan's oratorical prowess, leads to some puzzles. In his opening section is he taking an anti-Vietnam position, or advocating a heightening of the war against international Communism beyond simply trying to contain the Communists in that country? It's not really clear.

The speech continues to make a number of statements that might not stand up under analysis, such as "No nation in history has ever survived a tax burden that reached a third of its national income." Is that true? Is it provable? It sounds good, and doubtless has been quoted as gospel many times since.

Reagan speaks to the audience at a Republican National Convention in Miami, Florida.

Reagan's words attribute statements to the Democrats such as "the cold war will end through acceptance of a not undemocratic socialism," "the profit motive has become outmoded," and "our traditional system of individual freedom is incapable of solving the complex problems of the 20th century." Who was he quoting, and did those people hold responsible positions? Were they representative of the views of the Democratic Party? Reagan did not say, but those socialist-sounding sentiments were pinned on the government in power anyway.

Reagan continued in that same vein throughout the speech, with plausible but poorly sourced statements and numbers attacking the "big government" that is taking the country down the road to totalitarianism.

He began with taxes, and then moved on to examples from the farm program and urban renewal and welfare programs. These programs are in place, he said, but are they doing any good? "Well now," he continued, "if government planning and welfare had the answer and they've had almost 30 years of it, shouldn't we expect government to read the score to us once in a while? Shouldn't they be telling us about the decline each year in the number of people needing help? The

reduction in the need for public housing?"

The technique of asking these questions and not answering – which is known as asking rhetorical questions – is a familiar one in public speaking and Reagan used it throughout this speech, allowing listeners to supply their own answers. He attacked social welfare programs, not even shying away from the sacrosanct topic of social security, in effect laying out the areas that would become central to the Republican counterrevolution over the next 50 years against Democratic programs ranging from the New Deal to Lyndon Johnson's Great Society.

Reagan conflated these programs with appeasement of Communism and the surrender of individual liberties. The speech is littered with unusually harsh one-liners to this effect:

"A government can't control the economy without controlling the people."

"Well, I for one resent it when a representative of the people refers to you and me – the free man and woman of this country – as 'the masses.' This is a term we haven't applied to ourselves in America."

"[a] program that takes for the needy and gives to the greedy."

"The problem with our liberal friends is not that they are ignorant, but that they know so much that isn't so." [an unattributed paraphrase of Will Rogers]

"Actually, a government bureau is the nearest thing to eternal life we'll ever see on this Earth."

"Those who would trade our freedom for the soup kitchen of the welfare state have told us that they have a utopian solution of peace without victory."

Those are among the many hard-edged statements that were somehow softened by Reagan's folksy delivery. They may seem mild compared to the Rush Limbaughs of today, but they were biting during an era of relative civility.

In Reagan's stirring climax he shamelessly appropriated Franklin Delano Roosevelt's 1936 phrase "rendezvous with destiny," again without attribution. He was perhaps signalling that he and his fellow conservatives intended to appropriate the destiny of the country.

The aftermath of the speech is well known. Goldwater suffered a defeat of historic proportions in the election. Reagan, a more palatable version of Goldwater, assumed the mantle of conservative leadership, won the governorship of California two years later, and went on to the Presidency. That 1964 speech was the first shot of the Reagan Revolution that shapes U.S. politics to this day.

August 27, 1908	Lyndon Baines Johnson is born on a farm near Stonewall, Texas, the eldest of five children of Sam Ealy Johnson and Rebekah Baines. His father served five terms in the Texas State Legislature.
1926–August 19, 1930	Johnson works his way through Southwest Texas State Teachers' College, dropping out between his second and third year to serve as principal and teach at a Mexican-American school.
November 29, 1931	Becomes legislative assistant to newly elected Congressman Richard Kleberg.
November 17, 1934	Marries Claudia Alta ("Lady Bird") Taylor.
July 25, 1935	Appointed by President Roosevelt as Texas Director of the National Youth Administration.
April 10, 1937	Johnson wins a special election to become a U.S. Representative. He is re-elected to a full term in 1938.
June 21, 1940	While serving in Congress, Johnson is appointed a Lieutenant Commander in the U.S. Naval Reserve.
December 9, 1941 –July 16, 1942	Serves on active duty in the U.S. Navy in the South Pacific, essentially as President Roosevelt's representative in the region.
November 2, 1948	Elected to the U.S. Senate.
January 2, 1951	Elected Majority Whip of the U.S. Senate. Later he becomes Senate Minority Leader (1953) and Senate Majority Leader (1955). In that capacity he guides legislation through the Senate including the Civil Rights Act of 1957.
November 8, 1960	John F. Kennedy is elected U.S. President, with Johnson as Vice-President.
November 22, 1963	John F. Kennedy is assassinated. Johnson is sworn in as President at 2:32pm while onboard the Presidential plane, *Air Force One*.
November 27, 1963	In an address before a joint session of Congress, Johnson pledges to support President Kennedy's legislative agenda including a new civil rights bill and a tax cut.
November 3, 1964	Johnson is elected President of the United States with the greatest percentage of the total popular vote ever attained by a Presidential candidate. Hubert Humphrey is Vice-President.
1965–1969	Johnson's major legislative victories during his second Administration include Medicare and the Voting Rights Act. His Presidency is dominated by controversy surrounding the Vietnam War.
March 3, 1968	Johnson announces that he will not run for re-election.
January 1969	Upon completion of his term, Johnson retires to his ranch in Johnson City, Texas.
January 22, 1973	Lyndon Baines Johnson dies of a heart attack at his ranch.

President Lyndon Baines Johnson

"We shall overcome."

LYNDON JOHNSON BEGAN HIS PRESIDENCY amid the tragedy of the Kennedy assassination and ended it in frustration over the Vietnam War, which caused him not to run for re-election in 1968. In the five years between those two low points, he amassed some great and lasting accomplishments through his boundlessly ambitious Great Society program, which aimed to end poverty and discrimination. Before becoming John F. Kennedy's Vice-President, and then his successor, Johnson had been a skilled arm-twister as Majority Leader of the Senate. As President, he used the same legislative talents to push through major civil rights and education legislation, along with the establishment of Medicare and other social and economic advances.

When he became President, many doubted the sincerity of this Texan in advancing civil rights legislation, even though he had promoted and expanded JFK's initiatives from the outset. However, no one doubted his commitment after his strong and sincere condemnation of the horrific events in Selma, Alabama, in March of 1965. The previous year, Johnson had initiated work on a tough voting rights bill, and had asked Congress to approve the bill in his State of the Union Message in January 1965. Nevertheless, the bill went nowhere until the Reverend Martin Luther King and other black leaders led a series of marches to call attention to a longstanding effort to register black voters in Selma. Alabama state troopers brutally attacked the marchers with nightsticks, and many were beaten bloody and tear gassed. A white minister was killed. The pictures of the attacks sickened and appalled the nation. After the first march, thousands of volunteers headed to Selma to join in two later marches, which also resulted in violent confrontations.

With the pictures of the Selma carnage still fresh in the minds of the nation, President Johnson addressed the Congress with a special message decrying the violence, asking for immediate passage of his voting rights legislation, and, beyond that, requesting a national commitment to racial equality and equal economic opportunity.

President Lyndon B. Johnson addresses the U.S. Congress.

ADDRESS TO A JOINT SESSION OF CONGRESS ON VOTING LEGISLATION

MARCH 15, 1965

UNITED STATES CAPITOL, WASHINGTON, D.C.

Mr. Speaker, Mr. President, Members of the Congress:

I speak tonight for the dignity of man and the destiny of democracy.

I urge every member of both parties, Americans of all religions and of all colors, from every section of this country, to join me in that cause.

At times history and fate meet at a single time in a single place to shape a turning point in man's unending search for freedom. So it was at

Lexington and Concord. So it was a century ago at Appomattox. So it was last week in Selma, Alabama.

There, long-suffering men and women peacefully protested the denial of their rights as Americans. Many were brutally assaulted. One good man, a man of God, was killed.

There is no cause for pride in what has happened in Selma. There is no cause for self-satisfaction in the long denial of equal rights of millions of Americans. But there is cause for hope and for faith in our democracy in what is happening here tonight.

For the cries of pain and the hymns and protests of oppressed people have summoned into convocation all the majesty of this

American Civil Rights campaigner Martin Luther King and his wife Coretta Scott King lead a black voting rights march from Selma, Alabama, to the State Capitol in Montgomery on March 30, 1965.

great Government – the Government of the greatest Nation on earth.

Our mission is at once the oldest and the most basic of this country: to right wrong, to do justice, to serve man.

In our time we have come to live with moments of great crisis. Our lives have been marked with debate about great issues; issues of war and peace, issues of prosperity and depression. But rarely in any time does

an issue lay bare the secret heart of America itself. Rarely are we met with a challenge, not to our growth or abundance, our welfare or our security, but rather to the values and the purposes and the meaning of our beloved Nation.

The issue of equal rights for American Negroes is such an issue. And should we defeat every enemy, should we double our wealth and conquer the stars, and still be unequal to this issue, then we will have failed as a people and as a nation.

For with a country as with a person, "What is a man profited, if he shall gain the whole world, and lose his own soul?"

There is no Negro problem. There is no Southern problem. There is no Northern problem. There is only an American problem. And we are met here tonight as Americans – not as Democrats or Republicans – we are met here as Americans to solve that problem.

This was the first nation in the history of the world to be founded with a purpose. The great phrases of that purpose still sound in every American heart, North and South: "All men are created equal" –

"government by consent of the governed" – "give me liberty or give me death." Well, those are not just clever words, or those are not just empty theories. In their name Americans have fought and died for two centuries, and tonight around the world they stand there as guardians of our liberty, risking their lives.

Those words are a promise to every citizen that he shall share in the dignity of man. This dignity cannot be found in a man's possessions; it cannot be found in his power, or in his position. It really rests on his right to be treated as a man equal in opportunity to all others. It says that he shall share in freedom, he shall choose his leaders, educate his

President Lyndon B. Johnson discusses the Voting Rights Act with Martin Luther King.

children, and provide for his family according to his ability and his merits as a human being.

To apply any other test – to deny a man his hopes because of his color or race, his religion or the place of his birth – is not only to do injustice, it is to deny America and to dishonor the dead who gave their lives for American freedom.

THE RIGHT TO VOTE

Our fathers believed that if this noble view of the rights of man was to flourish, it must be rooted in democracy. The most basic right of all was the right to choose your own leaders. The history of this country, in large measure, is the history of the expansion of that right to all of our people.

Many of the issues of civil rights are very complex and most difficult. But about this there can and should be no argument. Every American citizen must have an equal right to vote. There is no reason which can excuse the denial of that right. There is no duty which weighs more heavily on us than the duty we have to ensure that right.

Yet the harsh fact is that in many places in this country men and women are kept from voting simply because they are Negroes.

Every device of which human ingenuity is capable has been used to deny this right. The Negro citizen may go to register only to be told that the day is wrong, or the hour is late, or the official in charge is absent. And if he persists, and if he manages to present himself to the registrar, he may be disqualified because he did not spell out his middle name or because he abbreviated a word on the application.

And if he manages to fill out an application he is given a test. The registrar is the sole judge of whether he passes this test. He may be asked to recite the entire Constitution, or explain the most complex provisions of State law. And even a college degree cannot be used to prove that he can read and write.

For the fact is that the only way to pass these barriers is to show a white skin.

Experience has clearly shown that the existing process of law cannot overcome systematic and ingenious discrimination. No law that we now have on the books – and I have helped to put three of them there – can ensure the right to vote when local officials are determined to deny it.

In such a case our duty must be clear to all of us. The Constitution says that no person shall be kept from voting because of his race or his color. We have all sworn an oath before God to support and to defend that Constitution. We must now act in obedience to that oath.

GUARANTEEING THE RIGHT TO VOTE

Wednesday I will send to Congress a law designed to eliminate illegal barriers to the right to vote.

The broad principles of that bill will be in the hands of the Democratic and Republican leaders tomorrow. After they have reviewed it, it will come here formally as a bill. I am grateful for this opportunity to come here tonight at the invitation of the leadership to reason with my friends, to give them my views, and to visit with my former colleagues.

I have had prepared a more comprehensive analysis of the legislation which I had intended to transmit to the clerk tomorrow but which I will submit to the clerks tonight. But I want to really discuss with you now briefly the main proposals of this legislation,

This bill will strike down restrictions to voting in all elections – Federal, State, and local – which have been used to deny Negroes the right to vote.

This bill will establish a simple, uniform standard which cannot be used, however ingenious the effort, to flout our Constitution.

It will provide for citizens to be registered by officials of the United States Government if the State officials refuse to register them.

It will eliminate tedious, unnecessary lawsuits which delay the right to vote.

Finally, this legislation will ensure that properly registered individuals are not prohibited from voting.

I will welcome the suggestions from all of the Members of Congress – I have no doubt that I will get some – on ways and means to strengthen this law and to make it effective. But experience has plainly shown that this is the only path to carry out the command of the Constitution.

To those who seek to avoid action by their National Government in their own communities; who want to and who seek to maintain purely local control over elections, the answer is simple:

President Lyndon B. Johnson greets a multi-racial group of American troops at Cam Ranh Bay, Vietnam, in early 1966.

Open your polling places to all your people.

Allow men and women to register and vote whatever the color of their skin.

Extend the rights of citizenship to every citizen of this land.

THE NEED FOR ACTION

There is no constitutional issue here. The command of the Constitution is plain.

There is no moral issue. It is wrong – deadly wrong – to deny any of your fellow Americans the right to vote in this country.

There is no issue of States rights or national rights. There is only the struggle for human rights.

I have not the slightest doubt what will be your answer.

The last time a President sent a civil rights bill to the Congress it contained a provision to protect voting rights in Federal elections. That

Lyndon Johnson's oratory skills were consistently compared to those of his predecessor in the Oval Office, John F. Kennedy.

civil rights bill was passed after 8 long months of debate. And when that bill came to my desk from the Congress for my signature, the heart of the voting provision had been eliminated.

This time, on this issue, there must be no delay, no hesitation and no compromise with our purpose.

We cannot, we must not, refuse to protect the right of every American to vote in every election that he may desire to participate in. And we ought not and we cannot and we must not wait another 8 months before we get a bill. We have already waited a hundred years and more, and the time for waiting is gone.

So I ask you to join me in working long hours – nights and weekends, if necessary – to pass this bill. And I don't make that request lightly. For from the window where I sit with the problems of our country I recognize that outside this chamber is the outraged conscience of a nation, the grave concern of many nations, and the harsh judgment of history on our acts.

WE SHALL OVERCOME

But even if we pass this bill, the battle will not be over. What happened in Selma is part of a far larger movement which reaches into every section and State of America. It is the effort of American Negroes to secure for themselves the full blessings of American life.

Their cause must be our cause too. Because it is not just Negroes, but really it is all of us, who must overcome the crippling legacy of bigotry and injustice.

And we shall overcome.

As a man whose roots go deeply into Southern soil I know how agonizing racial feelings are. I know how difficult it is to reshape the attitudes and the structure of our society.

But a century has passed, more than a hundred years, since the Negro was freed. And he is not fully free tonight.

It was more than a hundred years ago that Abraham Lincoln, a great President of another party, signed the Emancipation Proclamation, but emancipation is a proclamation and not a fact.

A century has passed, more than a hundred years, since equality was promised. And yet the Negro is not equal.

A century has passed since the day of promise. And the promise is unkept.

The time of justice has now come. I tell you that I believe sincerely that no force can hold it back. It is right in the eyes of man and God that it should come. And when it does, I think that day will brighten the lives of every American.

For Negroes are not the only victims. How many white children have gone uneducated, how many white families have lived in stark poverty, how many white lives have been scarred by fear, because we have wasted our energy and our substance to maintain the barriers of hatred and terror?

So I say to all of you here, and to all in the Nation tonight, that those who appeal to you to hold on to the past do so at the cost of denying you your future.

This great, rich, restless country can offer opportunity and education and hope to all: black and white, North and South, sharecropper and city dweller. These are the enemies: poverty, ignorance, disease. They are the enemies and not our fellow man, not our neighbor. And these enemies too, poverty, disease and ignorance, we shall overcome.

AN AMERICAN PROBLEM

Now let none of us in any sections look with prideful righteousness on the troubles in another section, or on the problems of our neighbors. There is really no part of America where the promise of equality has been fully kept. In Buffalo as well as in Birmingham, in Philadelphia as well as in Selma, Americans are struggling for the fruits of freedom.

This is one Nation. What happens in Selma or in Cincinnati is a matter of legitimate concern to every American. But let each of us look within our own hearts and our own communities, and let each of us put our shoulder to the wheel to root out injustice wherever it exists.

As we meet here in this peaceful, historic chamber tonight, men from the South, some of whom were at Iwo Jima, men from the North who have carried Old Glory to far corners of the world and brought it back without a stain on it, men from the East and from the West, are all fighting together without regard to religion, or color, or region, in Viet-Nam. Men from every region fought for us across the world 20 years ago.

And in these common dangers and these common sacrifices the South made its contribution of honor and gallantry no less than any other region of the great Republic – and in some instances, a great many of them, more.

And I have not the slightest doubt that good men from everywhere in this country, from the Great Lakes to the Gulf of Mexico, from the Golden Gate to the harbors along the Atlantic, will rally together now in this cause to vindicate the freedom of all Americans. For all of us owe this duty; and I believe that all of us will respond to it.

Your President makes that request of every American.

PROGRESS THROUGH THE DEMOCRATIC PROCESS

The real hero of this struggle is the American Negro. His actions and protests, his courage to risk safety and even to risk his life, have awakened the conscience of this Nation. His demonstrations have been designed to call attention to injustice, designed to provoke change, designed to stir reform.

He has called upon us to make good the promise of America. And who among us can say that we would have made the same progress were it not for his persistent bravery, and his faith in American democracy.

For at the real heart of battle for equality is a deep-seated belief in the democratic process. Equality depends not on the force of arms or tear gas but upon the force of moral right; not on recourse to violence but on respect for law and order.

There have been many pressures upon your President and there will be others as the days come and go. But I pledge you tonight that we intend to fight this battle where it should be fought: in the courts, and in the Congress, and in the hearts of men.

We must preserve the right of free speech and the right of free assembly. But the right of free speech does not carry with it, as has been said, the right to holler fire in a crowded theater. We must preserve the right to free assembly, but free assembly does not carry with it the right to block public thoroughfares to traffic.

We do have a right to protest, and a right to march under conditions that do not infringe the constitutional rights of our neighbors. And I intend to protect all those rights as long as I am permitted to serve in this office.

We will guard against violence, knowing it strikes from our hands the very weapons which we seek – progress, obedience to law, and belief in American values.

In Selma as elsewhere we seek and pray for peace. We seek order. We seek unity. But we will not accept the peace of stifled rights, or the order imposed by fear, or the unity that stifles protest. For peace cannot be purchased at the cost of liberty.

In Selma tonight, as in every – and we had a good day there – as in every city, we are working for just and peaceful settlement. We must all remember that after this speech I am making tonight, after the police and the FBI and the Marshals have all gone, and after you have promptly passed this bill, the people of Selma and the other cities of the Nation must still live and work together. And when the attention of the Nation has gone elsewhere they must try to heal the wounds and to build a new community.

This cannot be easily done on a battleground of violence, as the history of the South itself shows. It is in recognition of this that men of both races have shown such an outstandingly impressive responsibility in recent days – last Tuesday, again today,

RIGHTS MUST BE OPPORTUNITIES

The bill that I am presenting to you will be known as a civil rights bill. But, in a larger sense, most of the program I am recommending is a civil rights program. Its object is to open the city of hope to all people of all races.

Because all Americans just must have the right to vote. And we are going to give them that right.

All Americans must have the privileges of citizenship regardless of race. And they are going to have those privileges of citizenship regardless of race.

But I would like to caution you and remind you that to exercise these privileges takes much more than just legal right. It requires a trained mind and a healthy body. It requires a decent home, and the chance to find a job, and the opportunity to escape from the clutches of poverty.

Of course, people cannot contribute to the Nation if they are never taught to read or write, if their bodies are stunted from hunger, if their sickness goes untended, if their life is spent in hopeless poverty just drawing a welfare check.

So we want to open the gates to opportunity. But we are also going to give all our people, black and white, the help that they need to walk through those gates.

THE PURPOSE OF THIS GOVERNMENT

My first job after college was as a teacher in Cotulla, Texas, in a small Mexican-American school. Few of them could speak English, and I couldn't speak much Spanish. My students were poor and they often came to class without breakfast, hungry. They knew even in their youth the pain of prejudice. They never seemed to know why people disliked them. But they knew it was so, because I saw it in their eyes. I often walked home late in the afternoon, after the classes were finished, wishing there was more that I could do. But all I knew was to teach them the little that I knew, hoping that it might help them against the hardships that lay ahead.

Somehow you never forget what poverty and hatred can do when you see its scars on the hopeful face of a young child.

I never thought then, in 1928, that I would be standing here in 1965. It never even occurred to me in my fondest dreams that I might have the chance to help the sons and daughters of those students and to help people like them all over this country.

But now I do have that chance – and I'll let you in on a secret – I mean to use it. And I hope that you will use it with me.

This is the richest and most powerful country which ever occupied the globe. The might of past empires is little compared to ours. But I do not want to be the President who built empires, or sought grandeur, or extended dominion.

I want to be the President who educated young children to the wonders of their world. I want to be the President who helped to feed the hungry and to prepare them to be taxpayers instead of taxeaters.

I want to be the President who helped the poor to find their own way and who protected the right of every citizen to vote in every election.

I want to be the President who helped to end hatred among his fellow men and who promoted love among the people of all races and all regions and all parties.

I want to be the President who helped to end war among the brothers of this earth.

And so at the request of your beloved Speaker and the Senator from Montana; the majority leader, the Senator from Illinois; the minority leader, Mr. McCulloch, and other Members of both parties, I came here tonight – not as President Roosevelt came down one time in person to veto a bonus bill, not as President Truman came down one time to urge the passage of a railroad bill – but I came down here to ask you to share this task with me and to share it with the people that we both work for. I want this to be the Congress, Republicans and Democrats alike, which did all these things for all these people.

Beyond this great chamber, out yonder in 50 States, are the people that we serve. Who can tell what deep and unspoken hopes are in their hearts tonight as they sit there and listen. We all can guess, from our own lives, how difficult they often find their own pursuit of happiness, how many problems each little family has. They look most of all to themselves for their futures. But I think that they also look to each of us.

Above the pyramid on the great seal of the United States it says – in Latin – "God has favored our undertaking."

God will not favor everything that we do. It is rather our duty to divine His will. But I cannot help believing that He truly understands and that He really favors the undertaking that we begin here tonight.

Analysis

Lyndon Johnson was not a notably effective public speaker, and he suffered by comparison to the incandescent Kennedy. In this instance, however, he was terrific. His words were simple but forceful, and the evident conviction with which he spoke was compelling. This is arguably his finest speech and he probably wrote at least some of it himself. Many reports have him speaking from rough notes, with the speech not being complete in time to be put on a teleprompter.

The speech title "The American Promise" denotes not only the potential of America but also the unkept promise of equality, and perhaps the most moving moment came when the President quoted the anthem of the Civil Rights movement, "We shall overcome." With those words, Johnson affirmed his identification with the movement and left no doubt as to his commitment to finally delivering on America's promise.

The speech contains a number of other memorable rhetorical constructions. Johnson used the device of repetition on two occasions, noting three times that "a century has passed" without full freedom for the Negro and, later, that "I want to be the President" who accomplishes various goals. It is also sprinkled with memorable phrases, such as "this great, rich, restless country."

One of the most effective aspects of the speech was that Johnson took the extraordinary step of addressing his remarks directly to Congress, a step rarely taken by previous Presidents. His seriousness of purpose was further emphasized by his eloquence and rhetoric. He spoke of the great issues the country had confronted, but noted that, "rarely in any time does an issue lay bare the secret heart of America itself." Economic or national security issues were held up as much different challenges from those pertaining to "the values and purposes and the meaning of our beloved Nation." With his words, Johnson cast discrimination

as antithetical to American ideals, and prejudice as – in effect – un-American. For the President to call conservative, ostentatiously patriotic Southerners "un-American" to their faces in his deep Texas drawl was a certain body blow to them.

Johnson spoke of the horrors of Selma, then cast them in a positive light, in that the beatings and indignities visited upon the marchers had "summoned into convocation all the majesty of this great Government." Thus, the events would result in action to redress historic wrongs. But, having castigated the actions of the attackers of the Selma marchers as barbaric and un-American, Johnson took care elsewhere in the speech to share the blame for discrimination with the North and to note the contributions of Southerners in building the country. For Johnson, the problem at hand was an American problem. Discrimination had to be rooted out in every region of the country.

It was a deeply personal speech, with a very powerful closing. One of the most effective ways for any speaker to convey conviction is through personal experience, and Johnson spoke movingly of his time as a teacher of poor Mexican-American children in rural Texas. He described how that experience had shaped his views with the poignant phrase, "Somehow you never forget what poverty and hatred can do when you see its scars on the hopeful face of a young child."

"I never thought then, in 1928," he continued, "that I … might have the chance to help the sons and daughters of those students … But now I do have that chance – and I'll let you in on a secret – I mean to use it."

In the speech, Johnson was asking specifically for voting rights legislation, which would bring an unprecedented Federal presence into local government, especially in the South. Essentially, if any jurisdiction failed to register at least half of the local population of voting age, the Justice Department would consider that evidence of discrimination and would take over the voter registration process. Congress had balked previously at such Federal pre-emption, but the speech helped to carry the day. The legislation passed within a matter of months.

The law worked. Most Southern states realized they were beaten and voluntarily opened voter rolls. Where they did not, as in Mississippi, the Justice Department took over, and within three years, enrolment of black voters jumped from six percent to 44 percent. Majority black districts began to elect mayors and other public officials and, not long after, even confirmed race baiters such as George Wallace of Alabama began actively campaigning for black votes.

Much of the credit for the progress belongs to the civil rights workers who put their lives on the line, but no small portion belongs to a man whose roots, in his own words, went "deeply into Southern soil," and who did use the chance he was offered, for the good of the country.

President Richard M. Nixon

"There can be no whitewash at the White House."

NEARLY 21 YEARS AFTER THE Checkers Speech, Richard Nixon went on television with his political fate in the balance once again. This time, the issue was not a slush fund, but Watergate. On June 17, 1972, five men were caught breaking into the Democratic National Committee's Headquarters. An FBI investigation connected the men to the Committee to Re-Elect the President: Nixon's campaign organization. Nixon's Press Secretary, Ron Ziegler, had initially dismissed the break-in at Democratic Headquarters as a "third-rate burglary" but the story would not go away. A steady stream of articles, principally in the *Washington Post*, brought the blame for the break-in closer and closer to the White House.

Nixon was handily re-elected in November 1972, but the scandal kept growing. Nixon's White House staff, led by H.R. Haldeman and John Ehrlichman, began orchestrating a cover-up, which started unraveling almost immediately. The central revelation was the existence of a secret Republican fund, controlled by Attorney General John Mitchell and used to collect intelligence on the Democrats. Shady dealings other than the burglary were also uncovered piece by piece, with the aid of a highly-placed informant dubbed "Deep Throat".

The actual Watergate burglars were tried and convicted in January 1973, but that did not end the investigation into potential crimes associated with the break-in and the cover-up of White House involvement. North Carolina Senator Sam Ervin set up a committee to investigate Watergate, and began issuing subpoenas to White House staffers. On April 30, Nixon went on television in an attempt to contain the problem. He announced that he had asked for the resignations of Haldeman and Ehrlichman, and replaced Attorney General Herbert Kleindienst with Eliot Richardson. He also announced the resignation of White House Counsel John Dean. In fact, Dean, who was giving damaging testimony to the Senate Watergate investigators, was fired.

FOR RICHARD NIXON TIMELINE, PLEASE SEE PAGE 52

White House reporters watch the President's television broadcast as he tells the nation of White House involvement in the Watergate scandal.

ADDRESS TO THE NATION

APRIL 30, 1973

WHITE HOUSE, WASHINGTON, D.C.

Good evening:

I want to talk to you tonight from my heart on a subject of deep concern to every American.

In recent months, members of my Administration and officials of the Committee for the Re-Election of the President – including some of my closest friends and most trusted aides – have been charged with involvement in what has come to he known as the Watergate affair. These include charges of illegal activity during and preceding the 1972 Presidential election and charges that responsible officials participated in efforts to cover up that illegal activity.

The inevitable result of these charges has been to raise serious questions about the integrity of the White House itself. Tonight I wish to address those questions.

Last June 17, while I was in Florida trying to get a few days rest after my visit to Moscow, I first learned from news reports of the Watergate break-in. I was appalled at this senseless, illegal action, and I was shocked to learn that employees of the Re-Election Committee were apparently among those guilty. I immediately ordered an investigation by appropriate Government authorities. On September 15, as you will recall, indictments were brought against seven defendants in the case.

As the investigations went forward, I repeatedly asked those conducting the investigation whether there was any reason to believe that members of my Administration were in any way involved. I received repeated assurances that there were not. Because of these continuing reassurances, because I believed the reports I was getting, because I had faith in the persons from whom I was getting them, I discounted the stories in the press that appeared to implicate members of my Administration or other officials of the campaign committee.

Until March of this year, I remained convinced that the denials were true and that the charges of involvement by members of the White House Staff were false. The comments I made during this period, and the comments made by my Press Secretary on my behalf, were based on the information provided to us at the time we made those comments. However, new information then came to me which persuaded me that there was a real possibility that some of these charges were true, and suggesting further that there had been an effort to conceal the facts both from the public, from you, and from me.

As a result, on March 21, I personally assumed the responsibility for coordinating intensive new inquiries into the matter, and I personally ordered those conducting the investigations to get all the facts and to report them directly to me, right here in this office.

I again ordered that all persons in the Government or at the Re-Election Committee should cooperate fully with the FBI, the prosecutors, and the grand jury. I also ordered that anyone who refused to cooperate in telling the truth would be asked to resign from Government service. And, with ground rules adopted that would preserve the basic constitutional separation of powers between the Congress and the Presidency, I directed that members of the White House Staff should appear and testify voluntarily under oath before the Senate committee which was investigating Watergate.

I was determined that we should get to the bottom of the matter, and that the truth should be fully brought out – no matter who was involved.

At the same time, I was determined not to take precipitate action and to avoid, if at all possible, any action that would appear to reflect on innocent people. I wanted to be fair. But I knew that in the final analysis, the integrity of this office – public faith in the integrity of this office – would have to take priority over all personal considerations.

Today, in one of the most difficult decisions of my Presidency, I accepted the resignations of two of my closest associates in the White House – Bob Haldeman, John Ehrlichman – two of the finest public servants it has been my privilege to know.

I want to stress that in accepting these resignations, I mean to leave no implication whatever of personal wrongdoing on their part, and I leave no implication tonight of implication on the part of others who have been charged in this matter. But in matters as sensitive as guarding the integrity of our democratic process, it is essential not only that rigorous legal and ethical standards be observed but also that the public, you, have total confidence that they are both being observed and enforced by those in authority and particularly by the President of the United States. They agreed with me that this move was necessary in order to restore that confidence.

Because Attorney General Kleindienst – though a distinguished public servant, my personal friend for 20 years, with no personal involvement whatever in this matter – has been a close personal and professional associate of some of those who are involved in this case, he and I both felt that it was also necessary to name a new Attorney General.

The Counsel to the President, John Dean, has also resigned.

As the new Attorney General, I have today named Elliot Richardson, a man of unimpeachable integrity and rigorously high principle. I have directed him to do everything necessary to ensure that the Department of Justice has the confidence and the trust of every law-abiding person in this country.

President Richard Nixon delivers his State of the Union Address to the Congress in January 1973.

WORDS THAT CHANGED THE WORLD

Demonstrators make their feelings known to President Nixon as he leaves the Expo 74 opening ceremonies.

I have given him absolute authority to make all decisions bearing upon the prosecution of the Watergate case and related matters. I have instructed him that if he should consider it appropriate, he has the authority to name a special supervising prosecutor for matters arising out of the case.

Whatever may appear to have been the case before, whatever improper activities may yet be discovered in connection with this whole sordid affair, I want the American people, I want you to know beyond the shadow of a doubt that during my term as President, justice will be pursued fairly, fully, and impartially, no matter who is involved. This office is a sacred trust and I am determined to be worthy of that trust.

Looking back at the history of this case, two questions arise:

• How could it have happened?

• Who is to blame?

Political commentators have correctly observed that during my 27 years in politics I have always previously insisted on running my own campaigns for office.

But 1972 presented a very different situation. In both domestic and foreign policy, 1972 was a year of crucially important decisions, of intense negotiations, of vital new directions, particularly in working toward the goal which has been my overriding concern throughout my political career – the goal of bringing peace to America, peace to the world.

That is why I decided, as the 1972 campaign approached, that the Presidency should come first and politics second. To the maximum extent possible, therefore, I sought to delegate campaign operations, to remove the day-to-day campaign decisions from the President's office and from the White House. I also, as you recall, severely limited the number of my own campaign appearances.

Who, then, is to blame for what happened in this case?

For specific criminal actions by specific individuals, those who committed those actions must, of course, bear the liability and pay the penalty.

For the fact that alleged improper actions took place within the White House or within my campaign organization, the easiest course would be for me to blame those to whom I delegated the responsibility to run the campaign. But that would be a cowardly thing to do.

I will not place the blame on subordinates – on people whose zeal exceeded their judgment and who may have done wrong in a cause they deeply believed to be right.

In any organization, the man at the top must bear the responsibility. That responsibility, therefore, belongs here, in this office. I accept it. And I pledge to you tonight, from this office, that I will do everything in my power to ensure that the guilty are brought to justice and that such abuses are purged from our political processes in the years to come, long after I have left this office.

Some people, quite properly appalled at the abuses that occurred, will say that Watergate demonstrates the bankruptcy of the American political system. I believe precisely the opposite is true. Watergate represented a series of illegal acts and bad judgments by a number of individuals. It was the system that has brought the facts to light and that will bring those guilty to justice – a system that in this case has included a determined grand jury, honest prosecutors, a courageous judge, John Sirica, and a vigorous free press.

It is essential now that we place our faith in that system – and especially in the judicial system. It is essential that we let the judicial process go forward, respecting those safeguards that are established to protect the innocent as well as to convict the guilty. It is essential that in reacting to the excesses of others, we not fall into excesses ourselves.

It is also essential that we not be so distracted by events such as this that we neglect the vital work before us, before this Nation, before America, at a time of critical importance to America and the world.

Since March, when I first learned that the Watergate affair might in fact be far more serious than I had been led to believe, it has claimed far too much of my time and my attention. Whatever may now transpire in the case, whatever the actions of the grand jury, whatever the outcome of any eventual trials, I must now turn my full attention – and I shall do so – once again to the larger duties of this office. I owe it to this great office that I hold, and I owe it to you – to my country.

I know that as Attorney General, Elliot Richardson will be both fair and he will be fearless in pursuing this case wherever it leads. I am confident that with him in charge, justice will be done.

There is vital work to be done toward our goal of a lasting structure of peace in the world – work that cannot wait, work that I must do.

Tomorrow, for example, Chancellor Brandt of West Germany will visit the White House for talks that are a vital element of "The Year of Europe," as 1973 has been called, We are already preparing for the next Soviet-American summit meeting later this year.

This is also a year in which we are seeking to negotiate a mutual and balanced reduction of armed forces in Europe, which will reduce our defense budget and allow us to have funds for other purposes at home so desperately needed. It is the year when the United States and Soviet negotiators will seek to work out the second and even more important round of our talks on limiting nuclear arms and of reducing the danger of a nuclear war that would destroy civilization as we know it. It is a year in which we confront the difficult tasks of maintaining peace in Southeast Asia and in the potentially explosive Middle East.

There is also vital work to be done right here in America: to ensure prosperity, and that means a good job for everyone who wants to work; to control inflation, that I know worries every housewife, everyone who tries to balance a family budget in America; to set in motion new and better ways of ensuring progress toward a better life for all Americans,

When I think of this office – of what it means – I think of all the things that I want to accomplish for this Nation, of all the things I want to accomplish for you.

On Christmas Eve, during my terrible personal ordeal of the renewed bombing of North Vietnam, which after 12 years of war finally helped to bring America peace with honor, I sat down just before midnight. I wrote out some of my goals for my second term as President.

Let me read them to you:

• To make it possible for our children, and for our children's children, to live in a world of peace.

• To make this country be more than ever a land of opportunity – of equal opportunity, full opportunity for every American.

• To provide jobs for all who can work, and generous help for those who cannot work.

• To establish a climate of decency and civility, in which each person respects the feelings and the dignity and the God-given rights of his neighbor.

• To make this a land in which each person can dare to dream, can live his dreams – not in fear, but in hope – proud of his community,

proud of his country, proud of what America has meant to himself and to the world.

These are great goals. I believe we can, we must work for them. We can achieve them. But we cannot achieve these goals unless we dedicate ourselves to another goal.

We must maintain the integrity of the White House, and that integrity must be real, not transparent. There can be no whitewash at the White House.

We must reform our political process – ridding it not only of the violations of the law but also of the ugly mob violence and other inexcusable campaign tactics that have been too often practiced and too readily accepted in the past, including those that may have been a response by one side to the excesses or expected excesses of the other side. Two wrongs do not make a right.

I have been in public life for more than a quarter of a century. Like any other calling, politics has good people and bad people. And let me tell you, the great majority in politics – in the Congress, in the Federal Government, in the State government – are good people. I know that it can be very easy, under the intensive pressures of a campaign, for even well-intentioned people to fall into shady tactics – to rationalize this on

the grounds that what is at stake is of such importance m the Nation that the end justifies the means. And both of our great parties have been guilty of such tactics in the past.

In recent years, however, the campaign excesses that have occurred on all sides have provided a sobering demonstration of how far this

false doctrine can take us. The lesson is clear: America, in its political campaigns, must not again fall into the trap of letting the end, however great that end is, justify the means.

I urge the leaders of both political parties, I urge citizens, all of you, everywhere, to join in working toward a new set of standards, new rules and procedures to ensure that future elections will be as nearly free of such abuses as they possibly can be made. This is my goal. I ask you to join in making it America's goal.

When I was inaugurated for a second time this past January 20, I gave each member of my Cabinet and each member of my senior White House staff a special 4-year calendar, with each day marked to show the number of days remaining to the Administration. In the inscription on each calendar, I wrote these words: "The Presidential term which begins today consists of 1,461 days – no more, no less. Each can be a day of strengthening and renewal for America; each can add depth and dimension to the American experience. If we strive together, if we make the most of the challenge and the opportunity that these days offer us, they can stand out as great days for America, and great moments in the history of the world."

I looked at my own calendar this morning up at Camp David as I was working on this speech. It showed exactly 1,361 days remaining in

President Richard Nixon conducts his final cabinet meeting prior to resigning from the Presidency.

my term. I want these to be the best days in America's history, because I love America. I deeply believe that America is the hope of the world. And I know that in the quality and wisdom of the leadership America gives lies the only hope for millions of people all over the world that they can live their lives in peace and freedom. We must be worthy of that hope, in every sense of the word. Tonight, I ask for your prayers to help me in everything that I do throughout the days of my Presidency to be worthy of their hopes and of yours.

God bless America and God bless each and every one of you.

Analysis

This speech is of interest mainly as an artifact of the Watergate scandal, and as an echo of the graceless Nixon oratorical style unveiled in the "Checkers" speech. Nixon started by averring that he would be talking "from my heart" and then offered an account of the situation as he would like the public to see it. In fact, subsequent revelations about Watergate have shown that he was lying throughout this speech. As one author once said about another, every word he said was a lie, including "and" and "the."

As has been noted elsewhere in this volume, a speech is composed of three elements: *logos*, the information provided; *ethos*, the speaker's own personality and authoritativeness; and *pathos*, emotional appeal. Nixon provided *logos* (though the account he gave was fallacious and disingenuous) and *pathos* in his ham-handed way, but his *ethos* sank the whole endeavor. Simply put, by this time few people liked Nixon, and even fewer believed him.

One of Nixon's rhetorical tactics was sprinkling unsubtle appeals for sympathy in his remarks, and he started early in this speech. Explaining his whereabouts on June 17, he noted that he was resting up after an arduous trip to Moscow, conducting the nation's business and presumably holding the treacherous Soviets at bay. As the world later discovered, he learned of the break-in much earlier than he admitted in this speech, and while he might have been appalled, fully approved the cover-up. His statement that, "Until March of this year, I remained convinced that the denials were true ..." was, as the Watergate tapes later proved, a flat lie: a lie that convinced few people.

Certainly, Nixon was genuine in regretting the resignations of Haldeman and Ehrlichman, who both served him well and who were falling on their swords to protect him, as indeed was Attorney General Kleindienst. Hindsight also provides some rich irony in his announcement of the appointment of Eliot Richardson as Attorney General. Nixon praised him as a man of "unimpeachable integrity and rigorously high principle." He was, as he proved by resigning after refusing to fire Watergate Special Prosecutor Archibald Cox later in the year.

After yet another protestation that "justice will be pursued fairly,

President Nixon announces his resignation on television in August 1974.

fully, and impartially, no matter who is involved ..." Nixon returned to one of his preferred debating tactics, the rhetorical question: How could it have happened? Who is to blame?

As in the Checkers speech so many years before, while manfully acknowledging that the ultimate responsibility was his, Nixon offloaded the blame. He had always run his own campaigns, he said, but in the 1972 election he was so overwhelmed with the task of doing the country's work as President that he delegated the job of running the campaign to others. If they were guilty of illegal acts, he would see them brought to justice. The fact that Watergate had come to light was an indicator that the system was working, he told his audience, adding words to the effect of "now let it work and let me get back to my job."

Nixon then launched into a truly awful section wherein he spoke of his goals for his second term, such as "to make it possible for our children, and for our children's children, to live in a world of peace" and "to establish a climate of decency and civility, in which each person respects the dignity and God-given rights of his neighbor," etc. The sight and sound of these vague, cotton-candy goals coming from the scowling, jowly Nixon was truly cringe-inducing at the time, and remains so when the performance is viewed on tape.

Finally, Nixon being Nixon, he could not resist one last attack. Both sides engage in "shady tactics" he said, and urged everyone to join with him in adopting a new, higher set of standards for politics.

The speech, of course, was wholly ineffective. The following day, the Watergate investigation resumed and broadened into hearings that transfixed the nation, revealing the existence of a secret taping system that captured the whole sordid affair and finally did him in. Nixon went on television again in August 1973 in an equally ineffectual attempt to limit damage and over the months thereafter presided over a number of futile attempts to stay in power until, finally, the disclosure of the "smoking gun" tape forced his resignation on August 9, 1974.

July 14, 1913	Born Leslie Lynch King, Jr. in Omaha, Nebraska to Leslie Lynch King and Dorothy King.
December 19, 1913	Mother divorces father.
February 1, 1917	Dorothy King marries Gerald Rudolph Ford, Sr., a Grand Rapids, Michigan, businessman. Although not formally adopted, Leslie Lynch King Jr. is renamed Gerald R. Ford, Jr.
1927–1931	Ford attends South High School in Grand Rapids where he excels at football, being named to All-City and All-State teams.
1931–1935	Ford attends the University of Michigan, graduating with a B.A. in Economics. He also plays center on the football team, earns three varsity letters, and is named Most Valuable Player on the 1934 team.
1937–1941	Attends Yale Law School, graduating in the top third of his class.
February 1942	Ford volunteers for the Navy, where he initially becomes an athletic training officer, then is assigned to sea duty on the aircraft carrier U.S.S. *Monterey*.
June 14, 1948	Ford announces his candidacy for the U.S. Congress, Fifth District of Michigan.
October 15, 1948	Marries Betty Bloomer Warren.
November 2, 1948	Wins the election with 60.5 percent of the vote.
October 12, 1973	Following the resignation of Spiro T. Agnew, Ford is nominated as Vice-President of the United States.
August 9, 1974	Following President Richard M. Nixon's resignation as a result of the Watergate scandal, Ford is sworn in as the 38th President of the United States.
September 8, 1974	Ford announces that he is pardoning Richard Nixon for any crimes he may have committed as President.
April 28, 1975	Ford orders the emergency evacuation of U.S. personnel as Saigon falls to Communist forces, marking the end of the Vietnam War.
September 5, 1975	Charles Manson follower Lynette "Squeaky" Fromme attempts to assassinate Ford in Sacramento, California.
September 22, 1975	Sara Jane Moore attempts to assassinate Ford in San Francisco, California.
November 2, 1976	Loses the Presidential election to Jimmy Carter.
August 11, 1999	Receives the Presidential Medal of Freedom, the nation's highest civilian award, from President Clinton.
May 21, 2001	The John F. Kennedy Foundation presents Ford with the Profiles in Courage Award for putting the nation's interest above his own political future with the pardon of Richard Nixon.
December 26, 2006	Ford dies at his California home at age 93.

President Gerald R. Ford

"I, Gerald R. Ford, President of the United States... do grant a full, free, and absolute pardon unto Richard Nixon."

GERALD R. FORD BECAME THE 38th President of the United States when Richard Nixon, facing impeachment over the cover-up of the Watergate burglary, resigned as President on August 9, 1974. The resignation capped a harrowing two-year period of revelations about White House involvement in Watergate, concluding in the appointment of a Special Prosecutor and in televised Congressional hearings that captivated the American people during the spring and summer of 1974. Nixon fought hard to retain his office and many worried that his efforts could lead to Constitutional crisis if he tried to extend the powers of the Executive branch at the expense of Congress.

Nearly four decades after Watergate, it is difficult to comprehend the rage against Richard Nixon that held sway over much of the country. As the devious and cynical atmosphere of the White House was revealed day by day on the pages of the *Washington Post* and other media outlets, people felt betrayed by their government. When Nixon resigned the mood was relief, but the rage persisted. The public wanted him punished.

Ford had become Vice-President after Spiro T. Agnew resigned the office the previous October in the midst of a bribery investigation, a scandal that further weakened Nixon's standing with the public. Ford had been a 25-year member of the U.S. House of Representatives, rising to the office of Republican Minority Leader. He was widely regarded by both political parties as an honest and decent man and, therefore, an excellent choice to replace the divisive and unsavory Agnew.

Less than a year later, as Watergate continued to unravel, Ford succeeded Nixon, becoming the first President of the United States to have been elected neither President

Gerald Ford signs Proclamation 4311 in the Oval Office of The White House on September 8, 1974, pardoning Richard Nixon..

nor Vice-President. In his initial remarks to the American people on the day of Nixon's departure, he proclaimed that "our long national nightmare is over" and promised "openness and candor," which seemed a welcome prospect after the secretive Nixon.

Ford's proclamation of the end of the "nightmare" proved premature, however. Public demand for Nixon's prosecution remained strong and investigations of his alleged crimes continued. A month after assuming office, on September 8, 1974, Ford appeared in a nationally televised prime time address to announce that he was pardoning Richard Nixon.

PROCLAMATION 4311 – THE PARDONING OF RICHARD NIXON

SEPTEMBER 8, 1974

WHITE HOUSE, WASHINGTON, D.C.

Ladies and gentlemen:

I have come to a decision which I felt I should tell you and all of my fellow American citizens, as soon as I was certain in my own mind and in my own conscience that it is the right thing to do.

Gerald Ford (left) shakes hands with President Richard Nixon (right) as James Eastland, President Pro Tempore of the Senate (rear) looks on, during Ford's Vice-Presidential Inauguration on December 6, 1973.

I have learned already in this office that the difficult decisions always come to this desk. I must admit that many of them do not look at all the same as the hypothetical questions that I have answered freely and perhaps too fast on previous occasions.

My customary policy is to try and get all the facts and to consider the opinions of my countrymen and to take counsel with my most valued friends. But these seldom agree and, in the end, the decision is mine. To procrastinate, to agonize, and to wait for a more favorable turn of events that may never come or more compelling external pressures that may as well be wrong as right, is itself a decision of sorts and a weak and potentially dangerous course for a President to follow.

I have promised to uphold the Constitution, to do what is right as God gives me to see the right, and to do the very best that I can for America.

I have asked your help and your prayers, not only when I became President but many times since. The Constitution is the supreme law of our land and it governs our actions as citizens. Only the laws of God, which govern our consciences, are superior to it.

As we are a nation under God, so I am sworn to uphold our laws with the help of God. And I have sought such guidance and searched my own conscience with special diligence to determine the right thing for me to do with respect to my predecessor in this place, Richard Nixon, and his loyal wife and family.

Theirs is an American tragedy in which we all have played a part. It could go on and on and on, or someone must write the end to it. I have concluded that only I can do that, and if I can, I must.

There are no historic or legal precedents to which I can turn in this matter, none that precisely fit the circumstances of a private citizen who has resigned the Presidency of the United States. But it is common knowledge that serious allegations and accusations hang like a sword over our former President's head, threatening his health as he tries to reshape his life, a great part of which was spent in the service of this country and by the mandate of its people.

After years of bitter controversy and divisive national debate, I have been advised, and I am compelled to conclude that many months and perhaps more years will have to pass before Richard Nixon could obtain a fair trial by jury in any jurisdiction of the United States under governing decisions of the Supreme Court.

I deeply believe in equal justice for all Americans, whatever their station or former station. The law, whether human or divine, is no respecter of persons; but the law is a respecter of reality.

The facts, as I see them, are that a former President of the United States, instead of enjoying equal treatment with any other citizen accused of violating the law, would be cruelly and excessively penalized either in preserving the presumption of his innocence or in obtaining a speedy determination of his guilt in order to repay a legal debt to society.

During this long period of delay and potential litigation, ugly passions would again be aroused. And our people would again be polarized in their opinions. And the credibility of our free institutions of government would again be challenged at home and abroad.

In the end, the courts might well hold that Richard Nixon had been denied due process, and the verdict of history would even more be inconclusive with respect to those charges arising out of the period of his Presidency, of which I am presently aware.

But it is not the ultimate fate of Richard Nixon that most concerns me, though surely it deeply troubles every decent and

A demonstration outside the White House calls for the impeachment of President Nixon following the Watergate revelations.

every compassionate person. My concern is the immediate future of this great country.

In this, I dare not depend upon my personal sympathy as a long-time friend of the former President, nor my professional judgment as a lawyer, and I do not.

As President, my primary concern must always be the greatest good of all the people of the United States whose servant I am. As a man, my first consideration is to be true to my own convictions and my own conscience.

My conscience tells me clearly and certainly that I cannot prolong the bad dreams that continue to reopen a chapter that is closed. My conscience tells me that only I, as President, have the constitutional power to firmly shut and seal this book. My conscience tells me it is my duty, not merely to proclaim domestic tranquillity but to use every means that I have to insure it.

I do believe that the buck stops here, that I cannot rely upon public opinion polls to tell me what is right.

I do believe that right makes might and that if I am wrong, 10 angels swearing I was right would make no difference.

I do believe, with all my heart and mind and spirit, that I, not as President but as a humble servant of God, will receive justice without mercy if I fail to show mercy.

Finally, I feel that Richard Nixon and his loved ones have suffered enough and will continue to suffer, no matter what I do, no matter what we, as a great and good nation, can do together to make his goal of peace come true.

At this point, the President began reading from the proclamation granting the pardon.

"Now, therefore, I, Gerald R. Ford, President of the United States, pursuant to the pardon power conferred upon me by Article II, Section 2, of the Constitution, have granted and by these presents do grant a full, free, and absolute pardon unto Richard Nixon for all offenses against the United States which he, Richard Nixon, has committed or may have committed or taken part in during the period from July (January) 20, 1969 through August 9, 1974."

The President signed the proclamation and then resumed reading.

"In witness whereof, I have hereunto set my hand this eighth day of September, in the year of our Lord nineteen hundred and seventy-four, and of the Independence of the United States of America the one hundred and ninety-ninth."

Analysis

The Nixon pardon speech itself is unremarkable, either for eloquence or delivery. Gerald Ford was never known as a great orator. He spoke with a flat, Mid-western twang, in a voice curiously high-pitched for such a big man – a former All-American football player. Ford produced no other memorable speeches during his long public career, aside from his initial remarks upon assuming the Presidency. His single most significant quote is the "long national nightmare" reference – other than a gaffe during a 1976 debate with Jimmy Carter, when he strangely asserted that there was no Soviet domination of Eastern Europe.

The significance of the speech rests principally in its subject – a momentous event unprecedented in U.S. history. To some degree, the significance rests with the speaker, as well.

The address, about 1,100 words in length, took Ford less than 10 minutes to deliver in his slow, careful style. Sitting, he directed his unwavering gaze at the audience through the television screen. His words were adorned with few rhetorical flourishes, effectively conveying the simple, direct meaning of a plainspoken man. Of the rhetorical devices that were used, the evocation of Abraham Lincoln and Harry Truman were the most prominent. The phrase "as God gives me to see the right" echoed Lincoln's Second Inaugural Address. Truman's famous words, "the buck stops here", underscored the awesome, final responsibility of the President.

Mainly, however, Ford's words were aimed at conveying the difficulty of the decision – one that no one but he could make – and the reasons he made it. He advanced two arguments. The first was by far the harder sell – that Nixon "and his loyal wife and family" had suffered enough and that, given the current climate in the country, the former President would be unable to find the justice available to any other citizen. It was a measure of Ford's sincerity that he did not try to downplay his own long friendship with, or his sympathy for, Nixon.

Ford's repeated sympathetic references – as unwilling as the audience may have been to share them – served to emphasize his own personal qualities of candor and decency and, perhaps, actually increased the overall effectiveness of the speech.

Ford's second argument was that the nation needed to "shut and seal" the book on Watergate and Nixon, and that spending years on the process of putting him in prison would prevent that. "America needed recovery, not revenge," he later wrote in his autobiography. "The hate had to be drained and the healing begun."

As important as the speech was the speaker. Despite the shock and outrage that greeted the pardon, Ford managed to persuade the public that, even though they might disagree with his decision, he had made it honestly and according to his own convictions. It goes without saying that Spiro Agnew, or any other highly partisan politician of the time, could not have pardoned Nixon and gotten away with it.

Nevertheless, Ford was finished politically. In the weeks that followed, his approval rating dropped from 66.25 percent to 49.93 percent. He was called before the Congress to deny rumors that he had made a deal prior to Nixon's resignation to pardon him in return for the Presidency. He flatly denied it, and was believed. There was even a half-hearted call for his impeachment.

Ford lost the 1976 election to Jimmy Carter, and later attributed his loss to the pardon. Others were of the opinion that the country's economic troubles and Ford's own deficiencies as a candidate played significant roles. Ford never held public office again.

The mark of a successful speech is whether it accomplishes its objective. By that measure was the pardon speech a success? Despite its negative impact on the speaker himself, the conclusion must be that it was. The nation did get on with healing and the obsession with Nixon waned, though some of his subordinates did go to jail. Nixon's reputation eventually was rehabilitated, to some extent. He wrote books and made television appearances, an outcome that could not have occurred had he been prosecuted or further hounded.

History also seems to have validated Ford's action. In 2001, he received the John F. Kennedy Profile in Courage Award, given annually to acknowledge a courageous, selfless political act. In presenting the award, Senator Edward Kennedy admitted that he had spoken out against the pardon, but that " … time has a way of clarifying past events, and now we see that President Ford was right."

Gerald Ford defends his pardon of Richard Nixon at a press conference on September 20, 1974.

August 27, 1910	Born Agnes Gonxha Bojaxhiu in Skopje, in what is now Macedonia (formerly Yugoslavia), to Nikolai and Dranafile Bojaxhiu.
1928	Becomes a Roman Catholic Loretto nun and begins noviate training in Loretto Abbey, Dublin, Ireland.
1929	Arrives in Calcutta, India, and becomes a teacher at St. Mary's High School.
1937	Takes final vows as a nun and the name Sister Teresa.
September 1946	Receives a calling to serve among the poor and leaves the Convent to work in the slums of Calcutta.
1948	Sister Teresa is permitted to leave her order and moves to the slums where she starts a school. She also transfers her citizenship from Yugoslavia to India and travels to Paris where she receives medical training.
1950	Founds the Missionaries of Charity.
1952	Opens Nirmal Hriday ("Pure Heart"), a home for the dying.
1953	Opens an orphanage.
1957	Begins her work with lepers for which her order becomes well known around the world.
1958	The order's first facility outside of Calcutta opens in Drachi, India.
1971	Receives the Pope John XXIII Peace Prize and uses the $25,000 to build a leper colony.
1979	Awarded the Nobel Peace Prize for her work with the destitute and dying.
1982	Persuades the Israelis and Palestinians to cease fire long enough to enable the rescue of 37 mentally challenged children from Beirut.
1983	Suffers a heart attack while visiting Pope John Paul II.
1985	Awarded Presidential Medal of Freedom by President Reagan at a White House ceremony.
1989	Suffers a second heart attack and is subsequently fitted with a pacemaker.
1990	Mother Teresa is re-elected Superior General of her order of the Missionaries for Charity, despite her wish to step down.
1993	Falls and breaks three ribs in May, and is hospitalized with malaria in August. Mother Teresa later undergoes surgery for a blocked blood vessel in September.
March 13, 1997	Steps down as the head of her order and is succeeded by Sister Nirnalaof Charity.
September 5, 1997	Mother Teresa dies of a heart attack at age 87.
October 19, 2003	Beatified by the Roman Catholic Church and given the title "Blessed" after a miracle is attributed to her intercession.

Mother Teresa

"Love begins at home."

THE YEAR 1979 WAS NOT a promising one in which to find a recipient for the Nobel Peace Prize. The Nobel Prize Committee chairman summed up the situation succinctly in his announcement address:

"The year 1979 has not been a year of peace: disputes and conflicts between nations, peoples, and ideologies have been conducted with all the accompanying extremes of inhumanity and cruelty. We have witnessed wars, the unrestrained use of violence, we have witnessed fanaticism hand in hand with cynicism, we have witnessed contempt for human life and dignity.

"We are faced with new and overwhelming floods of refugees. Not without reason the word 'genocide' has been on many lips. In many countries completely innocent people have been the victims of acts of terror. In this year, moreover, we recall the way in which an entire ethnic group was virtually exterminated in Europe only a generation ago. The Holocaust film series has shaken us, not only as an evil memory from our own not-too-distant past and, as we consider the world of 1979, not one of us can be certain that the like may not recur in the future."

In short, it seemed to the Nobel Committee a perfect year to award the prize to a person who had devoted her life to charitable works and to nurturing "human life and dignity" among the poorest and most deprived peoples of the Earth.

Mother Teresa, the Albanian-born Roman Catholic nun who spent more than 45 years comforting the hungry, sick, and dying of Calcutta (now Kolkata) in India, was a safe choice in such a divisive, unpromising year. She was by this time an icon of international humanitarian activity and compassion, working and living in some of the worst slums in the world. She was also the founder of the Missionaries of Charity in India, which, by her death in 1997, had expanded to comprise more than 600 facilities in 123 countries.

NOBEL PEACE PRIZE ACCEPTANCE SPEECH

DECEMBER 11, 1979
OSLO, NORWAY

As we have gathered here together to thank God for the Nobel Peace Prize I think it will be beautiful that we pray the prayer of St. Francis of Assisi which always surprises me very much – we pray this prayer every day after Holy Communion,

Mother Teresa receives the Nobel Peace Prize in Oslo, December 11, 1979.

Mother Teresa addresses the crowd at the Catholic Convention in Berlin, West Germany, in 1950 – the year in which she received Vatican permission to start the diocesan congregation that would become the Missionaries of Charity.

that, where there are shadows, I may bring light;

that, where there is sadness, I may bring joy.

Lord, grant that I may seek rather to comfort than to be comforted,

to understand than to be understood;

to love than to be loved;

for it is by forgetting self that one finds;

it is forgiving that one is forgiven;

it is by dying that one awakens to eternal life.

Let us thank God for the opportunity that we all have together today, for this gift of peace that reminds us that we have been created to live that peace, and Jesus became man to bring that good news to the poor. He being God became man in all things like us except sin, and he proclaimed very clearly that he had come to give the good news. The news was peace to all of good will and this is something that we all want – the peace of heart – and God loved the world so much that he gave his son – it was a giving – it is as much as if to say it hurt God to give, because he loved the world so much that he gave his son, and he gave him to Virgin Mary, and what did she do with him?

As soon as he came in her life – immediately she went in haste to give that good news, and as she came into the house of her cousin, the child – the unborn child – the child in the womb of Elizabeth, leapt with joy. He was that little unborn child, was the first messenger of peace. He recognised the Prince of Peace, he recognised that Christ has come to bring the good news for you and for me. And as if that was not enough – it was not enough to become a man – he died on the cross to show that greater love, and he died for you and for me and for that leper and for that man dying of hunger and that naked person lying in the street not only of Calcutta, but of Africa, and New York, and London, and Oslo – and insisted that we love one another as he loves each one of us. And we read that in the Gospel very clearly – love as I have loved you – as I love you – as the Father has loved me, I love you – and the harder the Father loved him, he gave him to us, and how much we love one another, we, too, must give each other until it hurts. It is not enough for us to say: I love God, but I do not love my neighbour. St. John says you are a liar if you say you love God and you don't love your neighbour. How can you love God whom you do not see, if you do not love your neighbour whom you see, whom you touch, with whom you live. And so this is very important for us to realise that love, to be true, has to hurt. It hurt Jesus to love us, it hurt him. And to make sure we remember his great love he made himself the bread of life to satisfy our hunger for his love. Our hunger for God, because we have been created for that love. We have been created in his image. We have been created

because it is very fitting for each one of us, and I always wonder that 4-500 years ago as St. Francis of Assisi composed this prayer that they had the same difficulties that we have today, as we compose this prayer that fits very nicely for us also. I think some of you already have got it – so we will pray together.

Lord, make [me] a channel of Thy peace

that, where there is hatred, I may bring love;

that where there is wrong, I may bring the spirit of forgiveness;

that, where there is discord, I may bring harmony;

that, where there is error, I may bring truth;

that, where there is doubt, I may bring faith;

that, where there is despair, I may bring hope;

Mother Teresa greets children at the opening of two new missions in Anacostia.

to love and be loved, and then he has become man to make it possible for us to love as he loved us. He makes himself the hungry one – the naked one – the homeless one – the sick one – the one in prison – the lonely one – the unwanted one – and he says: You did it to me. Hungry for our love, and this is the hunger of our poor people. This is the hunger that you and I must find, it may be in our own home.

I never forget an opportunity I had in visiting a home where they had all these old parents of sons and daughters who had just put them in an institution and forgotten maybe. And I went there, and I saw in that home they had everything, beautiful things, but everybody was looking towards the door. And I did not see a single one with their smile on their face. And I turned to the Sister and I asked: How is that? How is it that the people they have everything here, why are they all looking towards the door, why are they not smiling? I am so used to see the smile on our people, even the dying one smile. And she said: This is nearly every day, they are expecting, they are hoping that a son

or daughter will come to visit them. They are hurt because they are forgotten," and see – this is where love comes. That poverty comes right there in our own home, even neglect to love. Maybe in our own family we have somebody who is feeling lonely, who is feeling sick, who is feeling worried, and these are difficult days for everybody. Are we there, are we there to receive them, is the mother there to receive the child?

I was surprised in the West to see so many young boys and girls given into drugs, and I tried to find out why – why is it like that, and the answer was: Because there is no one in the family to receive them. Father and mother are so busy they have no time. Young parents are in some institution and the child takes back to the street and gets involved in something. We are talking of peace. These are things that break peace, but I feel the greatest destroyer of peace today is abortion, because it is a direct war, a direct killing – direct murder by the mother herself. And we read in the Scripture, for God says very clearly: Even if a mother could forget her child – I will not forget you – I have carved

Pope John Paul II greets Mother Teresa. Following her death in 1997, she was beatified and given the title Blessed Teresa of Calcutta.

you in the palm of my hand. We are carved in the palm of His hand, so close to Him that unborn child has been carved in the hand of God. And that is what strikes me most, the beginning of that sentence, that even if a mother could forget something impossible – but even if she could forget – I will not forget you. And today the greatest means – the greatest destroyer of peace is abortion. And we who are standing here – our parents wanted us. We would not be here if our parents would do that to us. Our children, we want them, we love them, but what of

the millions. Many people are very, very concerned with the children in India, with the children in Africa where quite a number die, maybe of malnutrition, of hunger and so on, but millions are dying deliberately by the will of the mother. And this is what is the greatest destroyer of peace today. Because if a mother can kill her own child – what is left for me to kill you and you kill me – there is nothing between. And this I appeal in India, I appeal everywhere: Let us bring the child back, and this year being the child's year: What have we done for the child? At the beginning of the year I told, I spoke everywhere and I said: Let us make this year that we make every single child born, and unborn, wanted. And today is the end of the year, have we really made the children wanted? I will give you something terrifying. We are fighting abortion by adoption, we have saved thousands of lives, we have sent words to all the clinics, to the hospitals, police stations – please don't destroy the child, we will take the child. So every hour of the day and night it is always somebody, we have quite a number of unwedded mothers – tell them come, we will take care of you, we will take the child from you, and we will get a home for the child. And we have a tremendous demand from families who have no children, that is the blessing of God for us. And also, we are doing another thing which is very beautiful – we are teaching our beggars, our leprosy patients, our slum dwellers, our people of the street, natural family planning.

And in Calcutta alone in six years – it is all in Calcutta – we have had 61,273 babies less from the families who would have had, but because they practise this natural way of abstaining, of self-control, out of love for each other. We teach them the temperature meter which is very beautiful, very simple, and our poor people understand. And you know what they have told me? Our family is healthy, our family is united, and we can have a baby whenever we want. So clear – those people in the street, those beggars – and I think that if our people can do like that how much more you and all the others who can know the ways and means without destroying the life that God has created in us.

The poor people are very great people. They can teach us so many beautiful things. The other day one of them came to thank and said: "You people who have vowed chastity you are the best people to teach us family planning. Because it is nothing more than self-control out of love for each other." And I think they said a beautiful sentence. And these are people who maybe have nothing to eat, maybe they have not a home where to live, but they are great people. The poor are very wonderful people. One evening we went out and we picked up four people from the street. And one of them was in a most terrible condition – and I told the Sisters: You take care of the other three, I take of this one that looked worse. So I did for her all that my love can do. I put her in bed, and there was such a beautiful smile on her face. She took hold of my hand, as she said one word only: Thankyou – and she died.

I could not help but examine my conscience before her, and I asked what would I say if I was in her place. And my answer was very simple. I would have tried to draw a little attention to myself, I would have said I am hungry, that I am dying, I am cold, I am in pain, or something, but she gave me much more – she gave me her grateful love. And she died with a smile on her face. As that man whom we picked up from the drain, half eaten with worms, and we brought him to the home. I have lived like an animal in the street, but I am going to die like an angel, loved and cared for. And it was so wonderful to see the greatness of that man who could speak like that, who could die like that without blaming anybody, without cursing anybody, without comparing anything. Like

an angel – this is the greatness of our people. And that is why we believe what Jesus had said: I was hungry – I was naked – I was homeless – I was unwanted, unloved, uncared for – and you did it to me.

I believe that we are not real social workers. We may be doing social work in the eyes of the people, but we are really contemplatives in the heart of the world. For we are touching the Body of Christ 24 hours. We have 24 hours in this presence, and so you and I. You too try to bring that presence of God in your family, for the family that prays together stays together. And I think that we in our family don't need bombs and guns, to destroy to bring peace – just get together, love one another, bring that peace, that joy, that strength of presence of each other in the home. And we will be able to overcome all the evil that is in the world.

There is so much suffering, so much hatred, so much misery, and we with our prayer, with our sacrifice are beginning at home. Love begins at home, and it is not how much we do, but how much love we put in the action that we do. It is to God Almighty – how much we do it does not matter, because He is infinite, but how much love we put in that action. How much we do to Him in the person that we are serving.

Some time ago in Calcutta we had great difficulty in getting sugar, and I don't know how the word got around to the children, and a little boy of four years old, Hindu boy, went home and told his parents: I will not eat sugar for three days, I will give my sugar to Mother Teresa for her children. After three days his father and mother brought him to our home. I had never met them before, and this little one could scarcely pronounce my name, but he knew exactly what he had come to do. He knew that he wanted to share his love.

And this is why I have received such a lot of love from you all. From the time that I have come here I have simply been surrounded with love, and with real, real understanding love. It could feel as if everyone in India, everyone in Africa is somebody very special to you. And I felt quite at home I was telling Sister today. I feel in the Convent with the Sisters as if I am in Calcutta with my own Sisters. So completely at home here, right here.

And so here I am talking with you – I want you to find the poor here, right in your own home first. And begin love there. Be that good news to your own people. And find out about your next-door neighbour – do you know who they are? I had the most extraordinary experience with a Hindu family who had eight children. A gentleman came to our house and said: Mother Teresa, there is a family with eight children, they had not eaten for so long – do something. So I took some rice and I went there immediately. And I saw the children – their eyes shinning with hunger – I don't know if you have ever seen hunger. But I have seen it very often. And she took the rice, she divided the rice, and she went out. When she came back I asked her – where did you go, what did you do? And she gave me a very simple answer: They are hungry also. What struck me most was that she

knew – and who are they, a Muslim family – and she
knew. I didn't bring more rice that evening because
I wanted them to enjoy the joy of sharing. But there
were those children, radiating joy, sharing the joy with
their mother because she had the love to give. And you
see this is where love begins – at home. And I want
you – and I am very grateful for what I have received.
It has been a tremendous experience and I go back to
India – I will be back by next week, the 15th I hope –
and I will be able to bring your love.

And I know well that you have not given from your
abundance, but you have given until it has hurt you.
Today the little children they have – I was so surprised
– there is so much joy for the children that are hungry.
That the children like themselves will need love and care
and tenderness, like they get so much from their parents.
So let us thank God that we have had this opportunity
to come to know each other, and this knowledge of each
other has brought us very close. And we will be able to
help not only the children of India and Africa, but will be
able to help the children of the whole world, because as
you know our Sisters are all over the world. And with this
prize that I have received as a prize of peace, I am going
to try to make the home for many people that have no
home. Because I believe that love begins at home, and if
we can create a home for the poor – I think that more and
more love will spread. And we will be able through this
understanding love to bring peace, be the good news to
the poor. The poor in our own family first, in our country
and in the world.

To be able to do this, our Sisters, our lives have to be
woven with prayer. They have to be woven with Christ
to be able to understand, to be able to share. Because
today there is so much suffering – and I feel that the
passion of Christ is being relived all over again – are
we there to share that passion, to share that suffering
of people. Around the world, not only in the poor
countries, but I found the poverty of the West so much
more difficult to remove. When I pick up a person from
the street, hungry, I give him a plate of rice, a piece of
bread, I have satisfied. I have removed that hunger. But
a person that is shut out, that feels unwanted, unloved,
terrified, the person that has been thrown out from
society – that poverty is so hurtable and so much, and I
find that very difficult. Our Sisters are working amongst

Mourners watch as the casket of Mother Teresa
moves toward the Netaji Stadium in Calcutta.

A man places flowers on a statue of Mother Teresa in her native city of Skopje, Macedonia.

That we may remain faithful to the gift of God, to love Him and serve Him in the poor together with you. What we have done we should not have been able to do if you did not share with your prayers, with your gifts, this continual giving. But I don't want you to give me from your abundance, I want that you give me until it hurts.

The other day I received 15 dollars from a man who has been on his back for 20 years, and the only part that he can move is his right hand. And the only companion that he enjoys is smoking. And he said to me: I do not smoke for one week, and I send you this money. It must have been a terrible sacrifice for him, but see how beautiful, how he shared, and with that money I bought bread and I gave to those who are hungry with a joy on both sides, he was giving and the poor were receiving. This is something that you and I – it is a gift of God to us to be able to share our love with others. And let it be as it was for Jesus. Let us love one another as he loved us. Let us love Him with undivided love. And the joy of loving Him and each other – let us give now – that Christmas is coming so close. Let us keep that joy of loving Jesus in our hearts. And share that joy with all that we come in touch with. And that radiating joy is real, for we have no reason not to be happy because we have no Christ with us. Christ in our hearts, Christ in the poor that we meet, Christ in the smile that we give and the smile that we receive. Let us make that one point: That no child will be unwanted, and also that we meet each other always with a smile, especially when it is difficult to smile.

I never forget some time ago about 14 professors came from the United States from different universities. And they came to Calcutta to our house. Then we were talking about that they had been to the home for the dying. We have a home for the dying in Calcutta, where we have picked up more than 36,000 people only from the streets of Calcutta, and out of that big number more than 18,000 have died a beautiful death. They have just gone home to God; and they came to our house and we talked of love, of compassion, and then one of them asked me: Say, Mother, please tell us something that we will remember, and I said to them: Smile at each other, make time for each other in your family. Smile at each other. And then another one asked me: Are you married, and I said: Yes, and I find it sometimes very difficult to smile at Jesus because he can be very demanding sometimes. This is really something true, and there is where love comes – when it is demanding, and yet we can give it to Him with joy. Just as I have said today, I have said that if I don't go to Heaven for anything else I will be going to Heaven for all the publicity because it has purified me and sacrificed me and made me really ready to go to Heaven. I think that this is something, that we must live life beautifully, we have Jesus with us and He loves us. If we could only remember that God loves me, and I have an opportunity to love others as he loves me, not in big things, but in small things with great love, then Norway becomes a nest of love. And how beautiful it will be that from here a center for peace has been given. That from here the joy of life of the unborn child comes out. If you become a burning light in the world of peace, then really the Nobel Peace Prize is a gift of the Norwegian people. God bless you!

that kind of people in the West. So you must pray for us that we may be able to be that good news, but we cannot do that without you, you have to do that here in your country. You must come to know the poor, maybe our people here have material things, everything, but I think that if we all look into our own homes, how difficult we find it sometimes to smile at each other, and that the smile is the beginning of love.

And so let us always meet each other with a smile, for the smile is the beginning of love, and once we begin to love each other naturally we want to do something. So you pray for our Sisters and for me and for our Brothers, and for our Co-Workers that are around the world.

Analysis

As is noted elsewhere in this book, the Greek founders of rhetoric, notably Aristotle, divided the elements of a speech into three: *logos*, *ethos*, and *pathos*. *Logos* is the appeal to logic – the information contained in a speech. A lawyer's courtroom address would be a good example of a *logos*-heavy speech. *Ethos* is the character of the speaker him or herself – the personal credentials that makes the audience "buy" the rhetorical content the speaker is offering. *Pathos* is emotional appeal. Every speech is made up of a combination of these three, with the percentage varying according to the occasion.

In rigidly stratified societies such as Korea and Japan, much more than in the individualistic societies of the West, it matters much less what a speaker says than who the speaker is. That was precisely the case with Mother Teresa. If her Nobel acceptance speech was successful, it was entirely because of her *ethos* – because of who she was and the way she had lived her life: the *ethos* of a tiny, humble, old figure in the familiar habit bent over the lectern.

The speech contains some *pathos*, to be sure, as would be expected in any sermon – because that is essentially what the speech is – and it is deeply personal. Her words that day were as authentic and unpolished as the woman herself – delivered in her heavily accented English, rambling somewhat, and consisting of the recitation of the articles of her faith and belief in the redemptive powers of love and charity, as well as appeals to join her in the acceptance of that faith and those practices. Her words were limited by the fact that English was her language – she had learned it as a young nun in order to work effectively in India, which was still under British rule when she arrived there.

One might think that a speech by such a beloved figure would be non-controversial, but neither the speech, nor the speaker, was bland. Beloved and wholly dedicated to her admirable work she was. Meek and mild, she was not. The energy and drive that led her to create a worldwide organization are readily discernible in her words. One of her major themes was a strong anti-abortion message, a feature of virtually all of her public statements. That, and her vigorous proselytizing for her Catholic faith, were the source of much of the criticism leveled at her during her lifetime, and such criticism as was directed at the speech.

Mother Teresa and her work had been known to Roman Catholics for decades before she won the Nobel Prize, but her fame had gradually become more widely known, in part because of a documentary and book on her work that was published in 1971. By the end of that decade she was world famous. She became the face of human charity and goodness in the eyes of the world for the remaining 18 years of her life. Donations to her Missionaries of Charity multiplied, and she traveled the world almost constantly, opening up new facilities. In effect, she became the Chief Executive of a multi-national organization devoted to good works. In that role, she drew criticism both for the focus and quality of the care her organization delivered. Critics complained that

her clinics were more concerned that patients die good deaths than that they return to health. Questions were raised about where and how donations were spent. Such criticisms were, perhaps, to be expected, and they did little damage to her reputation. After her death, she was beatified by Pope John Paul II, and given the title Blessed Teresa of Calcutta. Beatification is an intermediate step toward canonization. Whether she proceeds to sainthood no longer depends on her life's achievements, but on whether miracles can be attributed to prayers to her.

Her personal achievements speak for themselves. However, the international renown her good works realized was largely due to the public recognition she received, and the Nobel Peace Prize was the single greatest of her many honors. It elevated her stature enormously. Her acceptance speech did nothing to detract from that stature. Her words were exactly what the Nobel Committee, and the rest of the world, expected, and were entirely consistent with her admirable work and life.

A Christian devotee touches a portrait of Mother Teresa on the anniversary of her death.

President Ronald Reagan

"The crew of the space shuttle *Challenger* honored us by the manner in which they lived their lives."

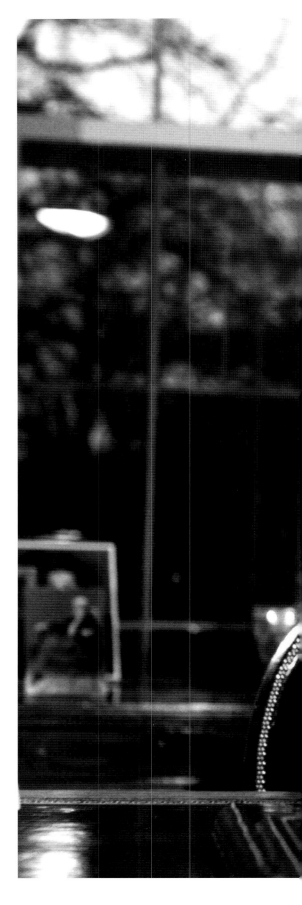

THE SPACE SHUTTLE *CHALLENGER* BROKE apart and plunged into the ocean live on national television at 11:39 a.m., Eastern Standard Time, January 28, 1986. Not many people watched the broadcast live, since space shuttle flights had become relatively routine and it was carried only on CNN and not on the networks. However, many schoolchildren were watching in their classrooms on special NASA hookups, because of the presence on the flight of Christa McAuliffe, winner of a national contest to become the first schoolteacher in space. However, word spread quickly and it is estimated that 85 percent of the American people saw footage within an hour of the catastrophe. It was characterized as an explosion, but later investigations showed that neither the shuttle nor its booster rockets exploded – the shuttle and rocket broke up due to the failure of some connecting "O-rings" and the plumes emanating from the craft and rocket were from the liquid hydrogen and oxygen propellants coming into contact with the atmosphere. The shuttle plunged into the ocean and that, in all probability, is what killed the crew.

In more than 25 years of launching manned flights, the U.S. space program had never known such a public tragedy. Three astronauts had perished in a launch pad fire in 1967, but there was little television footage. Astronauts had been killed in training accidents, again out of public view. However, this accident was horrifically visible and was made even worse by the publicity given to McAuliffe's participation in what she called "the ultimate field trip" in the months leading up to the event.

President Reagan had been scheduled to deliver his State of the Union Address that night, but postponed that by a week and instead went on national television live from the Oval Office at 5 p.m. to console the American people and lead the mourning for the seven dead astronauts.

FOR RONALD REAGAN TIMELINE, PLEASE SEE PAGE 102

Ronald Reagan addresses the nation from the White House on January 28, 1986, following the explosion of the space shuttle *Challenger*.

JANUARY 28, 1986

WHITE HOUSE, WASHINGTON, D.C.

Ladies and gentlemen, I'd planned to speak to you tonight to report on the state of the Union, but the events of earlier today have led me to change those plans. Today is a day for mourning and remembering. Nancy and I are pained to the core by the tragedy of the shuttle *Challenger*. We know we share this pain with all of the people of our country. This is truly a national loss.

Nineteen years ago, almost to the day, we lost three astronauts in a terrible accident on the ground. But we've never lost an astronaut in flight; we've never had a tragedy like this. And perhaps we've forgotten the courage it took for the crew of the shuttle. But they, the *Challenger* Seven, were aware of the dangers, but overcame them and did their jobs brilliantly. We mourn seven heroes: Michael Smith, Dick Scobee, Judith Resnik, Ronald McNair, Ellison Onizuka, Gregory Jarvis, and Christa McAuliffe. We mourn their loss as a nation together.

For the families of the seven, we cannot bear, as you do, the full impact of this tragedy. But we feel the loss, and we're thinking about you so very much. Your loved ones were daring and brave, and they had that special grace, that special spirit that says, "Give me a challenge, and I'll meet it with joy." They had a hunger to explore the universe and discover its truths. They wished to serve, and they did. They served all of us. We've grown used to wonders in this century. It's hard to dazzle us. But for 25 years the United States space program has been doing just that. We've grown used to the idea of space, and perhaps we forget that we've only just begun. We're still pioneers. They, the members of the *Challenger* crew, were pioneers.

And I want to say something to the schoolchildren of America who were watching the live coverage of the shuttle's takeoff. I know it is hard to understand, but sometimes painful things like this happen. It's all part of the process of exploration and discovery. It's all part of taking a chance and expanding man's horizons. The future doesn't belong to the fainthearted; it belongs to the brave. The *Challenger* crew was pulling us into the future, and we'll continue to follow them.

I've always had great faith in and respect for our space program, and what happened today does nothing to diminish it. We don't hide our space program. We don't keep secrets and cover things up. We do it all up front and in public. That's the way freedom is, and we wouldn't change it for a minute. We'll continue our quest in space. There will be more shuttle flights and more shuttle crews and, yes, more volunteers, more civilians, more teachers in space. Nothing ends here; our hopes and our journeys continue. I want to add that I wish I could talk to every man and woman who works for NASA or who worked on this mission and tell them: "Your dedication and professionalism have moved and impressed us for decades. And we know of your anguish. We share it."

There's a coincidence today. On this day 390 years ago, the great explorer Sir Francis Drake died aboard ship off the coast of Panama. In his lifetime the great frontiers were the oceans, and an historian later said, "He lived by the sea, died on it, and was buried in it." Well, today we can say of the *Challenger* crew: Their dedication was, like Drake's, complete.

The crew of the space shuttle *Challenger* honored us by the manner in which they lived their lives. We will never forget them, nor the last time we saw them, this morning, as they prepared for their journey and waved goodbye and "slipped the surly bonds of earth" to "touch the face of God."

Analysis

This short address to the American people perfectly captured the speaking style of Ronald Reagan – deceptively simple and homely, yet delivered with perfect emotional pitch. Reagan rarely spoke as the "imperial" President, but rather as a friend and neighbor. He signalled this low-key approach in this instance, as in so many others, by invoking his wife's name as the joint deliverer of the message. "Nancy and I are pained to the core …." He also, commendably, took care to address personal words to the schoolchildren who had witnessed the disaster in their classrooms in terms they could understand.

Simple sentences, words of one syllable, sincerely delivered; that was the Reagan style and it rarely worked better than in this instance. The simple words were enhanced by Reagan's peerless delivery. Critics carped that of course his delivery was great; he had been a professional actor. That was said as if his former profession somehow devalued his oratorical achievements. In fact, movie critics have noted that Reagan was not much of an actor – he essentially played a version of himself in nearly every screen role. His personal qualities of likeability and sincerity came across on the screen, as they did in his political career. As a public speaker, he only did what every speaker should – value the oratorical process and pay attention to the words as he was speaking them. In fact, he was a masterful speaker, and his addresses consistently did what he wanted them to do, which is the point of public speaking in the first place.

Reagan did not draft his own speeches, as is well known – though all his speechwriters say that he helped shape them and laid out the ideas on which they were based. The *Challenger* speech was written by the now-famous Peggy Noonan who, as in so many other instances, admirably captured Reagan's voice. The tone was solemn, but the words hopeful – nowhere does it say that America will quit space. Reagan made an instant commitment to keep the shuttle program going, which only a President, and not a speechwriter, can do.

Interestingly, at the beginning Reagan made the same argument that President Kennedy had made years earlier, saying "We don't hide our

Challenger takes off from the Kennedy Space Center, Florida, on January 28, 1986.

space program. We don't keep secrets and cover things up. We do it all up front and in public." That statement was as clearly aimed at the Soviet Union as was Kennedy's, and is indicative that in Reagan's mind space remained political, as it had in Kennedy's.

The closing reference to Sir Francis Drake was a little clunky at the start, but Reagan/Noonan closed the loop effectively with the analogy between the challenges of the sea centuries ago and space now.

Reagan's final words were the final lines of the poem "High Flight" by John Gillespie Magee, Jr., an Anglo-American pilot in the Royal Canadian Air Force who was killed at age 19 early in World War II, shortly after writing the poem. The *Challenger* astronauts, Reagan said in conclusion, had "slipped the surly bonds of earth" to "touch the face of God." The words themselves are poetic and poignant, but the reference itself was illustrative of how completely Reagan, and Noonan, were culturally attuned to the American people. "High Flight" became widely known in many parts of the U.S. in the 1950s,

when local television stations across the country were still signing off the air overnight. For many Americans – including children and adolescents enjoying the secret thrill of staying up until the TV went off – the inspiring film of "High Flight" was the last thing shown before the snow appeared on the old black and white set. Therefore, many Americans, hearing Reagan's final words, were doubly consoled – by the words themselves and, subliminally, by a cherished old memory from decades past.

Reagan's address provided the necessary comfort to get people past this horrendous day and the graphically distressing images of certain death they had witnessed. Afterwards came the work of finding the causes of the disaster and addressing the culture of complacency at NASA that had led it to ignore the potential dangers of the flight. It took three years, but the shuttles flew again. After Reagan's performance on that day there was little doubt in the minds of the American people that they would.

President Ronald Reagan

"Mr. Gorbachev, tear down this wall."

W HEN PRESIDENT KENNEDY VISITED BERLIN in 1963, Cold War tensions were high. Berliners lived in constant fear that their enclave of democracy, located well within East Germany, would be invaded and subsumed into the Communist state. The Berlin Wall, surrounding West Berlin, had loomed over them since 1961, and the situation was precarious. However, Kennedy's strong support caused the Soviets and their East German vassals to back off.

By 1971, the era of détente was beginning and East-West tensions over Berlin had eased. The four wartime powers that had divided Berlin and Germany at the end of World War II (the United States, the United Kingdom, France, and the Soviet Union) signed a new agreement on the status of Berlin. It was not a formal treaty, and was purposely vague. Berlin was not even mentioned by name. However, the effect was to re-establish ties between the two parts of Berlin and improve travel and communications. The agreement also recognized the existence of the two German states and established diplomatic ties. Tacitly, West Berlin was recognized as part of West Germany. With uncertainties about its status resolved, West Berlin prospered along with the rest of West Germany. Nevertheless, despite the thaw in relations, the Berlin Wall still stood.

Presidents Richard Nixon and Jimmy Carter rather routinely visited West Berlin during the era of détente. The Reagan Presidency, however, brought about heightened tensions, as Reagan initiated a record peacetime defense build-up, including the "Star Wars" space defense program and the stationing of short-range missiles in Europe. The U.S.S.R. bristled at the escalation. However, also during this time, Mikhail Gorbachev came to power in the Soviet Union and began a series of economic and social reforms known as *perestroika*. Reagan saw some hope for increased freedoms within the Soviet bloc, including Berlin, and decided to visit West Berlin after an economic summit meeting in Italy. He set his speech at the historic Brandenburg Gate, which had been kept closed since the city was divided.

FOR RONALD REAGAN TIMELINE, PLEASE SEE PAGE 102

Ronald Reagan addresses West Berliners on June 12, 1987, in front of the Brandenburg Gate, West Berlin.

SPEECH AT THE BRANDENBURG GATE

JUNE 12, 1987

BRANDENBURG GATE, WEST BERLIN

Thank you very much. Chancellor Kohl, Governing Mayor Diepgen, ladies and gentlemen: Twenty four years ago, President John F. Kennedy visited Berlin, speaking to the people of this city and the world at the City Hall. Well, since then two other presidents have come, each in his turn, to Berlin. And today I, myself, make my second visit to your city.

We come to Berlin, we American Presidents, because it's our duty to speak, in this place, of freedom. But I must confess, we're drawn here by other things as well: by the feeling of history in this city, more than 500 years older than our own nation; by the beauty of the Grunewald and the Tiergarten; most of all, by your courage and determination. Perhaps the composer, Paul Lincke, understood something about American Presidents. You see, like so many Presidents before me, I come here today because wherever I go, whatever I do: "Ich hab noch einen Koffer in Berlin." [I still have a suitcase in Berlin.]

Our gathering today is being broadcast throughout Western Europe and North America. I understand that it is being seen and heard as well in the East. To those listening throughout Eastern Europe, I extend my warmest greetings and the good will of the American people. To those listening in East Berlin, a special word: Although I cannot be with you, I address my remarks to you just as surely as to those standing here before me. For I join you, as I join your fellow countrymen in the West, in this firm, this unalterable belief: Es gibt nur ein Berlin. [There is only one Berlin.]

Behind me stands a wall that encircles the free sectors of this city, part of a vast system of barriers that divides the entire continent of Europe. From the Baltic, south, those barriers cut across Germany in a gash of barbed wire, concrete, dog runs, and guard towers. Farther south, there may be no visible, no obvious wall. But there remain armed guards and checkpoints all the same – still a restriction on the right to travel, still an instrument to impose upon ordinary men and women the will of a totalitarian state. Yet it is here in Berlin where the wall emerges most clearly; here, cutting across your city, where the news photo and the television screen have imprinted this brutal division of a continent upon the mind of the world. Standing before the Brandenburg Gate, every man is a German, separated from his fellow men. Every man is a Berliner, forced to look upon a scar.

President von Weizsacker has said: "The German question is open as long as the Brandenburg Gate is closed." Today I say: As long as this gate is closed, as long as this scar of a wall is permitted to stand, it is not the German question alone that remains open, but the question of freedom for all mankind. Yet I do not come here to lament. For I find in Berlin a message of hope, even in the shadow of this wall, a message of triumph.

The Reagans join in celebrations for the city's 750th birthday.

President Reagan and West German Chancellor Helmut Kohl (left) view the Berlin Wall from the balcony of the Reichstag.

In this season of spring in 1945, the people of Berlin emerged from their air raid shelters to find devastation. Thousands of miles away, the people of the United States reached out to help. And in 1947 Secretary of State – as you've been told – George Marshall announced the creation of what would become known as the Marshall plan. Speaking precisely 40 years ago this month, he said: "Our policy is directed not against any country or doctrine, but against hunger, poverty, desperation, and chaos."

In the Reichstag a few moments ago, I saw a display commemorating this 40th anniversary of the Marshall plan. I was struck by the sign on a burnt-out, gutted structure that was being rebuilt. I understand that Berliners of my own generation can remember seeing signs like it dotted throughout the Western sectors of the city. The sign read simply: "The Marshall plan is helping here to strengthen the free world." A strong, free world in the West, that dream became real. Japan rose from ruin to become an economic giant. Italy, France, Belgium – virtually every nation in Western Europe saw political and economic rebirth; the European Community was founded.

In West Germany and here in Berlin, there took place an economic miracle, the Wirtschaftswunder. Adenauer, Erhard, Reuter, and other leaders understood the practical importance of liberty – that just as truth can flourish only when the journalist is given freedom of speech, so prosperity can come about only when the farmer and businessman enjoy economic freedom. The German leaders reduced tariffs, expanded free trade, lowered taxes. From 1950 to 1960 alone, the standard of living in West Germany and Berlin doubled.

Where four decades ago there was rubble, today in West Berlin there is the greatest industrial output of any city in Germany – busy office blocks, fine homes and apartments, proud avenues, and the spreading lawns of park land. Where a city's culture seemed to have been destroyed, today there are two great universities, orchestras and an opera, countless theaters, and museums. Where there was want, today there's abundance – food, clothing, automobiles – the wonderful goods of the Ku'damm. From devastation, from utter ruin, you Berliners have, in freedom, rebuilt a city that once again ranks as one of the greatest on Earth. The Soviets may have had other plans. But, my friends, there were a few things the Soviets didn't count on: Berliner Herz, Berliner Humor, ja, und Berliner Schnauze. [Berliner heart, Berliner Humor, yes, and a Berliner Schnauze.]

In the 1950s, Khrushchev predicted: "We will bury you." But in the West today, we see a free world that has achieved a level of prosperity and well-being unprecedented in all human history. In the Communist world, we see failure, technological backwardness, declining standards of health, even want of the most basic kind – too little food. Even today, the Soviet Union still cannot feed itself. After these four decades, then, there stands before the entire world one great and inescapable conclusion: Freedom leads to prosperity. Freedom replaces the ancient hatreds among the nations with comity and peace. Freedom is the victor.

And now the Soviets themselves may, in a limited way, be coming to understand the importance of freedom. We hear much from Moscow about a new policy of reform and openness. Some political prisoners have been released. Certain foreign news broadcasts are no longer being jammed. Some economic enterprises have been permitted to operate with greater freedom from state control. Are these the beginnings of profound changes in the Soviet state? Or are they token gestures, intended to raise false hopes in the West, or to strengthen the Soviet system without changing it? We welcome change and openness; for we believe that freedom and security go together, that the advance of human liberty can only strengthen the cause of world peace.

There is one sign the Soviets can make that would be unmistakable, that would advance dramatically the cause of freedom and peace. General Secretary Gorbachev, if you seek peace, if you seek prosperity for the Soviet Union and Eastern Europe, if you seek liberalization: Come here to this gate! Mr. Gorbachev, open this gate! Mr. Gorbachev, tear down this wall!

I understand the fear of war and the pain of division that afflict this continent – and I pledge to you my country's efforts to help overcome these burdens. To be sure, we in the West must resist Soviet expansion. So we must maintain defenses of unassailable strength. Yet we seek peace; so we must strive to reduce arms on both sides. Beginning 10 years ago, the Soviets challenged the Western alliance with a grave new threat, hundreds of new and more deadly SS-20 nuclear missiles, capable of striking every capital in Europe. The Western alliance responded by committing itself to a counter-deployment unless the Soviets agreed to negotiate a better solution; namely, the elimination of such weapons on both sides. For many months, the Soviets refused to bargain in earnestness. As the alliance, in turn, prepared to go forward with its counter-deployment, there were difficult days – days of protests

like those during my 1982 visit to this city – and the Soviets later walked away from the table.

But through it all, the alliance held firm. And I invite those who protested then – I invite those who protest today – to mark this fact: Because we remained strong, the Soviets came back to the table. And because we remained strong, today we have within reach the possibility, not merely of limiting the growth of arms, but of eliminating, for the first time, an entire class of nuclear weapons from the face of the Earth. As I speak, NATO ministers are meeting in Iceland to review the progress of our proposals for eliminating these weapons. At the talks in Geneva, we have also proposed deep cuts in strategic offensive weapons. And the Western allies have likewise made far-reaching proposals to reduce the danger of conventional war and to place a total ban on chemical weapons.

While we pursue these arms reductions, I pledge to you that we will maintain the capacity to deter Soviet aggression at any level at which it might occur. And in cooperation with many of our allies, the United States is pursuing the Strategic Defense Initiative – research to base deterrence not on the threat of offensive retaliation, but on defenses that truly defend; on systems, in short, that will not target populations, but shield them. By these means we seek to increase the safety of Europe and all the world. But we must remember a crucial fact: East and West do not mistrust each other because we are armed; we are armed because we mistrust each other. And our differences are not about weapons but about liberty. When President Kennedy spoke

Ronald Reagan displays some souvenirs of his trip to Berlin.

at the City Hall those 24 years ago, freedom was encircled, Berlin was under siege. And today, despite all the pressures upon this city, Berlin stands secure in its liberty. And freedom itself is transforming the globe.

In the Philippines, in South and Central America, democracy has been given a rebirth. Throughout the Pacific, free markets are working miracle after miracle of economic growth. In the industrialized nations, a technological revolution is taking place – a revolution marked by rapid, dramatic advances in computers and telecommunications.

In Europe, only one nation and those it controls refuse to join the community of freedom. Yet in this age of redoubled economic growth, of information and innovation, the Soviet Union faces a choice: It must make fundamental changes, or it will become obsolete. Today thus represents a moment of hope. We in the West stand ready to cooperate with the East to promote true openness, to break down barriers that separate people, to create a safer, freer world.

And surely there is no better place than Berlin, the meeting place of East and West, to make a start. Free people of Berlin: Today, as in the past, the United States stands for the strict observance and full implementation of all parts of the Four Power Agreement of 1971. Let us use this occasion, the 750th anniversary of this city, to usher in a new era, to seek a still fuller, richer life for the Berlin of the future. Together, let us maintain and develop the ties between the Federal Republic and the Western sectors of Berlin, which is permitted by the 1971 agreement.

And I invite Mr. Gorbachev: Let us work to bring the Eastern and Western parts of the city closer together, so that all the inhabitants of all Berlin can enjoy the benefits that come with life in one of the great cities of the world. To open Berlin still further to all Europe, East and West, let us expand the vital air access to this city, finding ways of making commercial air service to Berlin more convenient, more comfortable, and more economical. We look to the day when West Berlin can become one of the chief aviation hubs in all central Europe.

With our French and British partners, the United States is prepared to help bring international meetings to Berlin. It would be only fitting for Berlin to serve as the site of United Nations meetings, or world conferences on human rights and arms control or other issues that call for international cooperation. There is no better way to establish hope for the future than to enlighten young minds, and we would be honored to sponsor summer youth exchanges, cultural events, and other programs for young Berliners from the East. Our French and British friends, I'm certain, will do the same. And it's my hope that an authority can be found in East Berlin to sponsor visits from young people of the Western sectors.

One final proposal, one close to my heart: Sport represents a source of enjoyment and ennoblement, and you many have noted that the Republic of Korea – South Korea – has offered to permit certain events

of the 1988 Olympics to take place in the North. International sports competitions of all kinds could take place in both parts of this city. And what better way to demonstrate to the world the openness of this city than to offer in some future year to hold the Olympic games here in Berlin, East and West?

In these four decades, as I have said, you Berliners have built a great city. You've done so in spite of threats – the Soviet attempts to impose the East-mark, the blockade. Today the city thrives in spite of the challenges implicit in the very presence of this wall. What keeps you here? Certainly there's a great deal to be said for your fortitude, for your defiant courage. But I believe there's something deeper, something that involves Berlin's whole look and feel and way of life – not mere sentiment. No one could live long in Berlin without being completely disabused of illusions. Something instead, that has seen the difficulties of life in Berlin but chose to accept them, that continues to build this good and proud city in contrast to a surrounding totalitarian presence that refuses to release human energies or aspirations. Something that speaks with a powerful voice of affirmation, that says yes to this city, yes to the future, yes to freedom. In a word, I would submit that what keeps you in Berlin is love – love both profound and abiding.

Perhaps this gets to the root of the matter, to the most fundamental distinction of all between East and West. The totalitarian world produces backwardness because it does such violence to the spirit, thwarting the human impulse to create, to enjoy, to worship. The totalitarian world finds even symbols of love and of worship an affront. Years ago, before the East Germans began rebuilding their churches, they erected a secular structure: the television tower at Alexander Platz. Virtually ever since, the authorities have been working to correct what they view as the tower's one major flaw, treating the glass sphere at the top with paints and chemicals of every kind. Yet even today when the Sun strikes that sphere – that sphere that towers over all Berlin – the light makes the sign of the cross. There in Berlin, like the city itself, symbols of love, symbols of worship, cannot be suppressed.

As I looked out a moment ago from the Reichstag, that embodiment of German unity, I noticed words crudely spray-painted upon the wall, perhaps by a young Berliner, "This wall will fall. Beliefs become reality." Yes, across Europe, this wall will fall. For it cannot withstand faith; it cannot withstand truth. The wall cannot withstand freedom.

And I would like, before I close, to say one word. I have read, and I have been questioned since I've been here about certain demonstrations against my coming. And I would like to say just one thing, and to those who demonstrate so. I wonder if they have ever asked themselves that if they should have the kind of government they apparently seek, no one would ever be able to do what they're doing again.

Thank you and God bless you all.

West Berliners watch as East German border guards demolish a section of the Berlin Wall on November 11, 1989. The previous day Gunter Schabowski, the East Berlin Communist Party leader, declared that starting from midnight, East Germans would be free to leave the country without permission, at any point along the border.

NOTE: The President spoke at 2:20 p.m. at the Brandenburg Gate. In his opening remarks, he referred to West German Chancellor Helmut Kohl. Prior to his remarks, President Reagan met with West German President Richard von Weizsacker and the Governing Mayor of West Berlin Eberhard Diepgen at Schloss Bellevue, President Weizsacker's official residence in West Berlin. Following the meeting, President Reagan went to the Reichstag, where he viewed the Berlin Wall from the East Balcony.

Analysis

Reagan's speech is famous for one quote: "Mr. Gorbachev, open this gate! Mr. Gorbachev, tear down this wall!" It was a great sound bite, one of Reagan's most famous, and has been shown countless times on television and in various documentaries. Logically, it should have been the conclusion of the speech, but it was not. The phrase occurred halfway through and was followed by about 10 minutes worth of anticlimactic detail. Ironically, the immortal words almost did not make it into the speech at all. Only Reagan's rhetorical instincts, and the arguments of his speechwriter, preserved them for history.

Reagan chose the Brandenburg Gate for his speech to highlight his belief that encouragement of democracy would eventually bring the wall down. He offered several initiatives in the speech to that end, and the "tear down this wall" line was to be the logical conclusion of the recitation of the initiatives. As in so many political instances, his senior staffers were timid, worrying that a strong call for such a move would heighten tensions, or would anger Gorbachev at a critical time. They recommended that the line be eliminated, and the overall tone softened. Reagan overruled them, but the speech as a whole suffered from too many fingerprints and the great line wound up buried in the middle.

Early in the speech Reagan followed the tradition inaugurated by Kennedy by making not one but three forays into German. In the first, he invoked the name of Paul Lincke, known as the "Father of German Musical Comedy", and the composer of "Berlin Luft" (the Berlin Air), which is otherwise known as the hymn of Berlin. Lincke is best known to Americans as the composer of "Glow, Little Glowworm", a 1930s hit, but was well known to Reagan's Berlin audience, and the "Ich hab noch einen Koffer in Berlin," the title of a tune by Lincke, was a good local touch and doubtless well received.

The second and third German phrases were somewhat gratuitous, with the second, the basic "There is only one Berlin," not adding much to the speech. The third is a laugh-line reference to "Berliner Schnauze", the Berlin dialect, which would be the equivalent of Cockney Rhyming Slang in Britain or Brooklynese in America. It seems as if either Reagan or his speechwriter was showing off. One German phrase would have been enough.

Reagan preceded the "tear down this wall" phrase by complimenting the Soviets in a backhanded way on their efforts toward reform and openness, but then went on to delineate his policy of resistance to Soviet expansionism and peace through strength, citing the Strategic Defense Initiative (Star Wars) and other defence programs. Reagan also made an extended reference to the Soviet SS-20 nuclear weapons program, the initial failure then resumption of talks, and the possibility "not merely of limiting the growth of arms, but of eliminating, for the first time, an entire class of nuclear weapons from the face of the Earth."

He ended the speech with another allusion to the Berlin Wall, quoting from graffiti on the wall itself, "This wall will fall. Beliefs become reality," and ending with "For it cannot withstand faith; it cannot withstand truth. The wall cannot withstand freedom." A nice ending, but nowhere as powerful as "tear down this wall."

The speech received little Western media coverage at the time, and Soviet news agencies dismissed it as warmongering and "provocative," despite the intermittently conciliatory tone. It was only two years later, when the Berlin Wall actually fell, that it came into prominence, with former West German Chancellor Helmut Kohl, among others, pointing to it as a seminal moment.

In the final analysis, the speech as a whole is a rather ordinary recitation of many things Reagan said before or after, and as an oratorical exercise is a classic example of the fate of so many Presidential speeches – the victim of a mixture of overzealous editing and overcautious policymaking by a staff anxious to prove its value. However, its weaknesses aside, it will live on because it contains what are arguably the most famous six words of the Reagan Presidency, "Mr. Gorbachev, tear down this wall!"

Ronald Reagan greets Mikhail Gorbachev upon his arrival in the U.S., during Gorbachev's first visit to America after he stepped down as President of the former Soviet Union.

March 18, 1936	Born Frederik Willem (F.W.) de Klerk in Johannesburg, South Africa, into a prominent political family long identified with apartheid.
1958	Graduates from Potchefstroom University with a law degree and begins practicing law in Vereeniging.
1959	Marries Marike Willemse.
1969	De Klerk is elected to the whites-only House of Assembly as the member for Vereeniging.
1978	Appointed to the first of a series of Cabinet posts in the National Party government.
1985	Becomes Chairman of the Minister's Council in the House of Assembly.
1986	Becomes Leader of the House of Assembly.
February 2, 1989	Elected leader of the National Party. Calls for reform and a non-racist South Africa in his first speech.
August 15, 1989	Becomes Acting State President.
September 20, 1989	After the General Election, de Klerk is inaugurated as State President.
1989–1994	As State President de Klerk initiates and presides over inclusive negotiations that lead to the dismantling of apartheid and the adoption of South Africa's first fully democratic constitution in December 1993.
December 10, 1993	Shares the Nobel Peace Prize and Philadelphia Peace Prize with Nelson Mandela.
1994	Nelson Mandela is elected State President.
1994–1996	De Klerk serves as one of two Deputy Presidents under Mandela.
June 1996–1998	De Klerk becomes Leader of the Opposition until his retirement from active party politics.
1998	Divorces his wife after an extramarital scandal and remarries, effectively ending his political career.
2004	De Klerk brings together a number of respected former national leaders to join him as founding members of the Global Leadership Foundation, a non-profit organization that aims to play a constructive role in the promotion of peace, democracy, and development in countries across the world.
Present	De Klerk lives in retirement in Cape Town.

President F. W. (Frederik Willem) de Klerk

"The time for negotiation has arrived."

F W. DE KLERK CAME FROM a family of politicians who had helped to shape, and staunchly supported, the apartheid policies that made South Africa an international pariah for decades, yet he was the last white President of South Africa by his own choice and through his own actions.

During his career, de Clerk rose through the ranks of the ruling National Party and eventually became Minister of Education after South Africa changed its form of government in the 1980s from a parliamentary system headed by a Prime Minister to one with a stronger executive branch. As in the parliamentary system, the leader of the majority party became the state president. The new system was a way for Prime Minister P.W. Botha, a fierce advocate of apartheid, to further consolidate his power and he subsequently continued the harsh repression of political dissent imposed by his predecessors. Opposition parties such as Nelson Mandela's African National Congress remained outlawed and many of their leaders, including Mandela, were jailed without charges or trial on national security grounds. Some were tortured or killed. Many nations, including the U.S. and Great Britain, began economic and diplomatic sanctions on the country. By the late 1980s, South Africa's economy was feeling the impact of international disinvestment and its people the impact of worldwide disapproval.

After Botha suffered a stroke, de Klerk was unexpectedly named to head the National Party and thus become State President. When Botha tried to reassume his office, de Klerk fought him off and then called (whites only) elections in which the National Party retained power and he retained the Presidency.

De Klerk had campaigned during the elections as a reformist, but his actions surpassed all expectations. He legalized opposition parties, freed Nelson Mandela

F .W. de Klerk speaks at the final National Party rally before the 1989 South African election.

as well as hundreds of other prominent dissidents, and started South Africa down the path to power sharing with the black majority, finally giving the nation respectability in the eyes of the world. In his initial speech to the South African Parliament, he laid out his policies and spelled out his intentions.

OPENING OF THE SECOND SESSION OF THE NINTH PARLIAMENT

FEBRUARY 2, 1990

HOUSES OF PARLIAMENT, CAPE TOWN

Mr Speaker, Members of Parliament.

The general election on September the 6th, 1989, placed our country irrevocably on the road of drastic change. Underlying this is the growing realisation by an increasing number of South Africans that only a negotiated understanding among the representative leaders of the entire population is able to ensure lasting peace.

The alternative is growing violence, tension and conflict. That is unacceptable and in nobody's interest. The well-being of all in this country is linked inextricably to the ability of the leaders to come to terms with one another on a new dispensation. No-one can escape this simple truth.

On its part, the Government will accord the process of negotiation the highest priority. The aim is a totally new and just constitutional dispensation in which every inhabitant will enjoy equal rights, treatment and opportunity in every sphere of endeavour – constitutional, social and economic.

I hope that this new Parliament will play a constructive part in both the prelude to negotiations and the negotiating process itself. I wish to ask all of you who identify yourselves with the broad aim of a new South Africa, and that is the overwhelming majority:

- Let us put petty politics aside when we discuss the future during this Session.

- Help us build a broad consensus about the fundamentals of a new, realistic and democratic dispensation.

- Let us work together on a plan that will rid our country of suspicion and steer it away from domination and radicalism of any kind.

During the term of this new Parliament, we shall have to deal, complimentary to one another, with the normal processes of legislation and day-to-day government, as well as with the process of negotiation and renewal.

Within this framework I wish to deal first with several matters more closely concerned with the normal process of government before I turn specifically to negotiation and related issues.

1. FOREIGN RELATIONS

The Government is aware of the important part the world at large has to play in the realisation of our country's national interests.

Without contact and co-operation with the rest of the world we cannot promote the well-being and security of our citizens. The dynamic developments in international politics have created new opportunities for South Africa as well. Important advances have been made, among other things, in our contacts abroad, especially where these were precluded previously by ideological considerations.

I hope this trend will be encouraged by the important change of climate that is taking place in South Africa.

For South Africa, indeed for the whole world, the past year has been one of change and major upheaval. In Eastern Europe and even the Soviet Union itself, political and economic upheaval surge forward in an unstoppable tide. At the same time, Beijing temporarily smothered with brutal violence the yearning of the people of the Chinese mainland for greater freedom.

The year of 1989 will go down in history as the year in which Stalinist Communism expired.

These developments will entail unpredictable consequences for Europe, but they will also be of decisive importance to Africa. Those who seek to force this failure of a system on South Africa, should engage in a total revision of their point of view. It should be clear to all that it is not the answer here either. The new situation in Eastern Europe also shows that foreign intervention is no recipe for domestic change. It never succeeds, regardless of its ideological motivation. The upheaval in Eastern Europe took place without the involvement of the Big Powers or of the United Nations.

The countries of Southern Africa are faced with a particular challenge; Southern Africa now has an historical opportunity to set aside its conflicts and ideological differences and draw up a joint programme of reconstruction. It should be sufficiently attractive to ensure that the Southern African region obtains adequate investment and loan capital from the industrial countries of the world. Unless the countries of Southern Africa achieve stability and a common approach to economic development rapidly, they will be faced by further decline and ruin.

The Government is prepared to enter into discussions with other Southern African countries with the aim of formulating a realistic development plan. The Government believes that the obstacles in the way of a conference of Southern African states have now been removed sufficiently.

Hostile postures have to be replaced by co-operative ones; confrontation by contact; disengagement by engagement; slogans by deliberate debate.

The season of violence is over. The time for reconstruction and reconciliation has arrived.

Recently there have, indeed, been unusually positive results in South Africa's contacts and relations with other African states. During my visits to their countries I was received cordially, both in private and in public, by Presidents Mobutu, Chissano, Houphouet-Boigny and Kaunda. These leaders expressed their sincere concern about the serious economic problems in our part of the world. They agreed that South Africa could and should play a positive part in regional co-operation and development.

Our positive contribution to the independence process in South West Africa has been recognised internationally. South Africa's good faith and reliability as a negotiator made a significant contribution to the success of the events. This, too, was not unnoticed. Similarly, our efforts to help bring an end to the domestic conflict situations in Mozambique and Angola have received positive acknowledgement.

At present the Government is involved in negotiations concerning our future relations with an independent Namibia and there are no reasons why good relations should not exist between the two

An anti-apartheid rally at Johannesburg's Wits medical school before the 1989 South African elections.

countries. Namibia needs South Africa and we are prepared to play a constructive part.

Nearer home I paid fruitful visits to Venda, Transkei and Ciskei and intend visiting Bophuthatswana soon. In recent times there has been an interesting debate about the future relationship of the TBVC countries with South Africa and specifically about whether they should be re-incorporated into our country.

Without rejecting this idea out of hand, it should be borne in mind that it is but one of many possibilities. These countries are constitutionally independent. Any return to South Africa will have to be dealt with, not only by means of legislation in their parliaments, but also through legislation in this Parliament. Naturally this will have to be preceded by talks and agreements.

2. HUMAN RIGHTS

Some time ago the Government referred the question of the protection of fundamental human rights to the South African Law Commission. This resulted in the Law Commission's interim working document on individual and minority rights. It elicited substantial public interest.

I am satisfied that every individual and organisation in the country has had ample opportunity to make representations to the Law Commission, express criticism freely and make suggestions. At present, the Law Commission is considering the representations received. A final report is expected in the course of this year.

In view of the exceptional importance of the subject of human rights to our country and all its people, I wish to ask the Law Commission to accord this task high priority.

The whole question of protecting individual and minority rights, which includes collective rights and the rights of national groups, is still under consideration by the Law Commission. Therefore, it would be inappropriate of the Government to express a view on the details now. However, certain matters of principle have emerged fairly clearly and I wish to devote some remarks to them.

The Government accepts the principle of the recognition and protection of the fundamental individual rights which form the constitutional basis of most Western democracies. We acknowledge, too, that the most practical way of protecting those rights is vested in a declaration of rights justiciable by an independent judiciary. However, it is clear that a system for the protection of the rights of individuals, minorities and national entities has to form a well-rounded and balanced whole. South Africa has its own national composition and our constitutional dispensation has to take this into account. The formal recognition of individual rights does not mean that the problem of a heterogeneous population will simply disappear. Any new constitution which disregards this reality will be inappropriate and even harmful.

Naturally, the protection of collective, minority and national rights may not bring about an imbalance in respect of individual rights. It is neither the Government's policy nor its intention that any group – in whichever way it may be defined – shall be favoured above or in relation to any of the others.

The Government is requesting the Law Commission to undertake a further task and report on it. This task is directed at the balanced protection in a future constitution of the human rights of all our citizens, as well as of collective units, associations, minorities and nations. This investigation will also serve the purpose of supporting negotiations towards a new constitution.

The terms of reference also include:

- the identification of the main types and models of democratic constitutions which deserve consideration in the aforementioned context;

- an analysis of the ways in which the relevant rights are protected in every model; and

- possible methods by means of which such constitutions may be made to succeed and be safeguarded in a legitimate manner.

3. THE DEATH PENALTY

The death penalty has been the subject of intensive discussion in recent months. However, the Government has been giving its attention to this extremely sensitive issue for some time. On April the 27th, 1989, the honourable Minister of Justice indicated that there was merit in suggestions for reform in this area. Since 1988 in fact, my predecessor and I have been taking decisions on reprieves which have led, in proportion, to a drastic decline in executions.

We have now reached the position in which we are able to make concrete proposals for reform. After the Chief Justice was consulted, and he in turn had consulted the Bench, and after the Government had noted the opinions of academics and other interested parties, the Government decided on the following broad principles from a variety of available options:

- that reform in this area is indicated;

- that the death penalty should be limited as an option of sentence to extreme cases, and specifically through broadening judicial discretion in the imposition of sentence; and

- that an automatic right of appeal be granted to those under sentence of death.

Should these proposals be adopted, they should have a significant influence on the imposition of death sentences on the one hand, and on the other, should ensure that every case in which a person has been sentenced to death, will come to the attention of the Appellate Division.

These proposals require that everybody currently awaiting execution, be accorded the benefit of the proposed new approach. Therefore, all executions have been suspended and no executions will take place until Parliament has taken a final decision on the new proposals. In the event of the proposals being adopted, the case of every person involved will be dealt with in accordance with the new guidelines. In the mean time, no executions have taken place since November the 14th, 1989.

New and uncompleted cases will still be adjudicated in terms of the existing law. Only when the death sentence is imposed, will the new proposals be applied, as in the case of those currently awaiting execution.

The legislation concerned also entails other related principles which will be announced and elucidated in due course by the Minister of Justice. It will now be formulated in consultation with experts and be submitted to Parliament as soon as possible.

I wish to urge everybody to join us in dealing with this highly sensitive issue in a responsible manner.

4. SOCIO-ECONOMIC ASPECTS

A changed dispensation implies far more than political and constitutional issues. It cannot be pursued successfully in isolation from problems in other spheres of life which demand practical solutions. Poverty, unemployment, housing shortages, inadequate education and training, illiteracy, health needs and numerous other problems still stand in the way of progress and prosperity and an improved quality of life.

Nelson Mandela and his then-wife Winnie raise their fists to salute the cheering crowd upon Mandela's release from prison on February 11, 1990.

The conservation of the physical and human environment is of cardinal importance to the quality of our existence. For this the Government is developing a strategy with the aid of an investigation by the President's Council.

All of these challenges are being dealt with urgently and comprehensively. The capability for this has to be created in an economically accountable manner. Consequently, existing strategies and aims are undergoing a comprehensive revision.

From this will emanate important policy announcements in the socio-economic sphere by the responsible Ministers during the course of the session. One matter about which it is possible to make a concrete announcement, is the Separate Amenities Act, 1953. Pursuant to my speech before the President's Council late last year, I announce that this Act will be repealed during this Session of Parliament.

The State cannot possibly deal alone with all of the social advancement our circumstances demand. The community at large, and especially the private sector, also have a major responsibility towards the welfare of our country and its people.

5. THE ECONOMY

A new South Africa is possible only if it is bolstered by a sound and growing economy, with particular emphasis on the creation of employment. With a view to this, the Government has taken thorough cognisance of the advice contained in numerous reports by a variety of advisory bodies. The central message is that South Africa, too, will have to make certain structural changes to its economy, just as its major trading partners had to do a decade or so ago.

The period of exceptionally high economic growth experienced by the Western world in the sixties, was brought to an end by the oil crisis in 1973. Drastic structural adaptations became inevitable for these countries, especially after the second oil crisis in 1979, when serious

Newly-elected South African President F. W. de Klerk shakes hands with African National Congress (ANC) President Nelson Mandela at a 1990 press conference after historic "talks about talks" between the South African government and the ANC in Cape Town.

imbalances occurred in their economies. After considerable sacrifices, those countries which persevered with their structural adjustment programmes, recovered economically so that lengthy periods of high economic growth and low inflation were possible.

During that particular period, South Africa was protected temporarily by the rising gold price from the necessity of making similar adjustments immediately. In fact, the high gold price even brought prosperity with it for a while. The recovery of the world economy and the decline in the price of gold and other primary products, brought with them unhealthy trends. These included high inflation, a serious weakening in the productivity of capital, stagnation in the economy's ability to generate income and employment opportunities. All of this made a drastic structural adjustment of our economy inevitable.

The Government's basic point of departure is to reduce the role of the public sector in the economy and to give the private sector maximum opportunity for optimal performance. In this process, preference has to be given to allowing the market forces and a sound competitive structure to bring about the necessary adjustments.

Naturally, those who make and implement economic policy have a major responsibility at the same time to promote an environment optimally conducive to investment, job creation and economic growth

by means of appropriate and properly co-ordinated fiscal and monetary policy. The Government remains committed to this balanced and practical approach.

By means of restricting capital expenditure in parastatal institutions, privatisation, deregulation and curtailing government expenditure, substantial progress has been made already towards reducing the role of the authorities in the economy. We shall persist with this in a well-considered way.

This does not mean that the State will forsake its indispensable development role, especially in our particular circumstances. On the contrary, it is the precise intention of the Government to concentrate an equitable portion of its capacity on these aims by means of the meticulous determination of priorities.

Following the progress that has been made in other areas of the economy in recent years, it is now opportune to give particular attention to the supply side of the economy.

Fundamental factors which will contribute to the success of this restructuring are:

- the gradual reduction of inflation to levels comparable to those of our principal trading partners;

- the encouragement of personal initiative and savings;

- the subjection of all economic decisions by the authorities to stringent financial measures and discipline;

- rapid progress with the reform of our system of taxation; and

- the encouragement of exports as the impetus for industrialisation and earning foreign exchange.

These and other adjustments, which will require sacrifices, have to be seen as prerequisites for a new period of sustained growth in productive employment in the nineties.

The Government is very much aware of the necessity of proper co-ordination and consistent implementation of its economic policy. For this reason, the establishment of the necessary structures and expertise to ensure this co-ordination is being given preference. This applies both to the various functions within the Government and to the interaction between the authorities and the private sector.

This is obviously not the occasion for me to deal in greater detail with our total economic strategy or with the recent course of the economy.

I shall confine myself to a few specific remarks on one aspect of fiscal policy that has been a source of criticism of the Government for some time, namely State expenditure.

The Government's financial year ends only in two month's time and several other important economic indicators for the 1989 calendar year are still subject to refinements at this stage. Nonetheless, several important trends are becoming increasingly clear. I am grateful to be able to say that we have apparently succeeded to a substantial degree in achieving most of our economic aims in the past year.

In respect of Government expenditure, the budget for the current financial year will be the most accurate in many years. The financial figures will show:

- that Government expenditure is thoroughly under control;

- that our normal financing programme has not exerted any significant upward pressure on rates of interest; and

- that we will close the year with a surplus, even without taking the income from the privatisation of Iscor into account.

- Without pre-empting this year's main budget, I wish to emphasise that it is also our intention to co-ordinate fiscal and monetary policy in the coming financial year in a way that will enable us to achieve the ensuing goals – namely:

- that the present downturn will take the form of a soft landing which will help to make adjustments as easy as possible;

- that our economy will consolidate before the next upward phase so that we will be able to grow from a sound base; and

- that we shall persist with the implementation of the required structural adaptations in respect, among other things, of the following: easing the tax burden, especially on individuals; sustained and adequate generation of surpluses on the current account of the balance of payments; and the reconstruction of our gold and foreign exchange reserves.

It is a matter of considerable seriousness to the Government, especially in this particular period of our history, to promote a dynamic economy which will make it possible for increasing numbers of people to be employed and share in rising standards of living.

6. NEGOTIATION

In conclusion, I wish to focus the spotlight on the process of negotiation and related issues. At this stage I am refraining deliberately from discussing the merits of numerous political questions which undoubtedly will be debated during the next few weeks. The focus, now, has to fall on negotiation.

Practically every leader agrees that negotiation is the key to reconciliation, peace and a new and just dispensation. However, numerous excuses for refusing to take part are advanced. Some of the reasons being advanced are valid. Others are merely part of a political chess game. And while the game of chess proceeds, valuable time is being lost.

Against this background I committed the Government during my inauguration to giving active attention to the most important obstacles in the way of negotiation. Today I am able to announce far-reaching decisions in this connection.

I believe that these decisions will shape a new phase in which there will be a movement away from measures which have been seized upon as a justification for confrontation and violence. The emphasis has to move, and will more now, to a debate and discussion of political and economic points of view as part of the process of negotiation.

I wish to urge every political and community leader, in and outside Parliament, to approach the new opportunities which are being created, constructively. There is no time left for advancing all manner of new conditions that will delay the negotiating process.

The steps that have been decided, are the following:

- The prohibition of the African National Congress, the Pan Africanist Congress, the South African Communist Party and a number of subsidiary organisations is being rescinded.

- People serving prison sentences merely because they were members of one of these organisations or because they committed another offence which was merely an offence because a prohibition on one of the organisations was in force, will be identified and released. Prisoners who have been sentenced for other offences such as murder, terrorism or arson are not affected by this.

- The media emergency regulations as well as the education emergency regulations are being abolished in their entirety.

- The security emergency regulations will be amended to still make provision for effective control over visual material pertaining to scenes of unrest.

- The restrictions in terms of the emergency regulations on 33 organisations are being rescinded. The organisations include the following:

  National Education Crisis Committee

  South African National Students Congress

  United Democratic Front

  Cosatu

  Die Blanke Bevrydingsbeweging van Suid-Afrika.

- The conditions imposed in terms of the security emergency regulations on 374 people on their release, are being rescinded and the regulations which provide for such conditions are being abolished.

- The period of detention in terms of the security emergency regulations will be limited henceforth to six months. Detainees also acquire the right to legal representation and a medical practitioner of their own choosing.

These decisions by the Cabinet are in accordance with the Government's declared intention to normalise the political process in South Africa without jeopardising the maintenance of the good order. They were preceded by thorough and anonymous advice by a group of officials which included members of the security community.

Implementation will be immediate and, where necessary, notices will appear in the Government Gazette from tomorrow.

The most important facets of the advice the Government received in this connection; are the following:

- The events in the Soviet Union and Eastern Europe, to which I have referred already, weaken the capability of organisations which were previously supported strongly from those quarters.

- The activities of the organisations from which the prohibitions are now being lifted, no longer entail the same degree of threat to internal security which initially necessitated the imposition of the prohibition.

- There have been important shifts of emphasis in the statements and points of view of the most important of the organisations concerned, which indicate a new approach and a preference for peaceful solutions.

- The South African Police is convinced that it is able, in the present circumstances, to combat violence and other crimes perpetrated also by members of these organisations and to bring offenders to justice without the aid of prohibitions on organisations.

About one matter there should be not doubt. The lifting of the prohibition on the said organisations does not signify in the least the approval or condonation of terrorism or crimes of violence committed under their banner or which may be perpetrated in the future. Equally, it should not be interpreted as a deviation from the Government's principles, among other things, against their economic policy and aspects of their constitutional policy. This will be dealt with in debate and negotiation.

At the same time I wish to emphasise that the maintenance of law and order are not to be jeopardised. The Government will not forsake its duty in this connection. Violence from whichever source, will be fought with all available might. Peaceful protest may not become the springboard for lawlessness, violence and intimidation. No democratic country can tolerate that.

Strong emphasis will be placed as well on even more effective law enforcement. Proper provision of manpower and means for the police, and all who are involved with the enforcement of the law, will be ensured. In fact, the budget for the coming financial year will already begin to give effect to this.

I wish to thank the members of our security forces and related services for the dedicated service they have rendered the Republic of South Africa. Their dedication makes reform in a stable climate possible.

On the state of emergency I have been advised that an emergency situation, which justifies these special measures which have been retained, still exists. There is still conflict which is manifesting itself mainly in Natal, but as a consequence of the country-wide political power struggle. In addition, there are indications that radicals are still trying to disrupt the possibilities of negotiations by means of mass violence.

It is my intention to terminate the state of emergency completely as soon as circumstances justify it and I request the co-operation of everybody towards this end. Those responsible for unrest and conflict have to bear the blame for the continuing state of emergency. In the mean time, the state of emergency is inhibiting only those who use chaos and disorder as political instruments. Otherwise the rules of the game under the state of emergency are the same for everybody.

Against this background the Government is convinced that the decisions I have announced are justified from the security point of view. However, these decisions are justified from a political point of view as well.

Our country and all its people have been embroiled in conflict, tension and violent struggle for decades. It is time for us to break out of the cycle of violence and break through the peace and reconciliation. The silent majority is yearning for this. The youth deserve it.

With the steps the Government has taken it has proven its good faith and the table is laid for sensible leaders to begin talking about a new dispensation, to reach an understanding by way of dialogue and discussion.

The agenda is open and the overall aims to which we are aspiring should be acceptable to all reasonable South Africans.

Among other things, those aims include a new, democratic constitution; universal franchise; no domination; equality before an independent judiciary; the protection of minorities as well as of individual rights; freedom of religion; a sound economy based on proven economic principles and private enterprise; dynamic programmes directed at better education, health services, housing and social conditions for all.

In this connection Mr Nelson Mandela could play an important part. The Government has noted that he has declared himself to be willing to make a constructive contribution to the peaceful political process in South Africa.

I wish to put it plainly that the Government has taken a firm decision to release Mr Mandela unconditionally. I am serious about bringing this matter to finality without delay. The Government will take a decision soon on the date of his release. Unfortunately, a further short passage of time is unavoidable.

Normally there is a certain passage of time between the decision to release and the actual release because of logistical and administrative requirements. In the case of Mr Mandela there are

Nelson Mandela and F. W. de Klerk receive the Nobel Peace Prize together at City Hall in Oslo, Norway, on December 10, 1993.

factors in the way of his immediate release, of which his personal circumstances and safety are not the least. He has not been an ordinary prisoner for quite some time. Because of that, his case requires particular circumspection.

Today's announcements, in particular, go to the heart of what Black leaders – also Mr Mandela – have been advancing over the years as their reason for having resorted to violence. The allegation has been that the Government did not wish to talk to them and that they were deprived of their right to normal political activity by the prohibition of their organisations.

Without conceding that violence has ever been justified, I wish to say today to those who argued in this manner:

- The Government wishes to talk to all leaders who seek peace.

Well-heeled white people join with squatters to vote on April 28, 1994, in South Africa's first multi-racial elections.

· The unconditional lifting of the prohibition on the said organisations places everybody in a position to pursue politics freely.

· The justification for violence which was always advanced, no longer exists.

These facts place everybody in South Africa before a *fait accompli*. On the basis of numerous previous statements there is no longer any reasonable excuse for the continuation of violence. The time for talking has arrived and whoever still makes excuses does not really wish to talk.

Therefore, I repeat my invitation with greater conviction than ever:

Walk through the open door, take your place at the negotiating table together with the Government and other leaders who have important power bases inside and outside of Parliament.

Henceforth, everybody's political points of view will be tested against their realism, their workability and their fairness. The time for negotiation has arrived.

To those political leaders who have always resisted violence I say thank you for your principled stands. This includes all the leaders of parliamentary parties, leaders of important organisations and movements, such as Chief Minister Buthelezi, all of the other Chief Ministers and urban community leaders.

Through their participation and discussion they have made an important contribution to this moment in which the process of free political participation is able to be restored. Their places in the negotiating process are assured.

CONCLUSION

In my inaugural address I said the following:

· "All reasonable people in this country – by far the majority – anxiously await a message of hope. It is our responsibility as leaders in all spheres to provide that message realistically, with courage and conviction. If we fail in that, the ensuing chaos, the demise of stability and progress, will for ever be held against us.

· "History has thrust upon the leadership of this country the tremendous responsibility to turn our country away from its present direction of conflict and confrontation. Only we, the leaders of our peoples, can do it.

· "The eyes of responsible governments across the world are focused on us. The hopes of millions of South Africans are centred around us. The future of Southern Africa depends on us. We dare not falter or fail."

This is where we stand:

· Deeply under the impression of our responsibility.

· Humble in the face of the tremendous challenges ahead.

· Determined to move forward in faith and with conviction.

I ask of Parliament to assist me on the road ahead. There is much to be done.

I call on the international community to re-evaluate its position and to adopt a positive attitude towards the dynamic evolution which is taking place in South Africa.

I pray that the Almighty Lord will guide and sustain us on our course through uncharted waters and will bless your labours and deliberations.

Mr Speaker, Members of Parliament. I now declare this Second Session of the Ninth Parliament of the Republic of South Africa to be duly opened.

Analysis

DeKlerk's hour-long maiden speech to the South African Parliament was, on the surface, a run-of-the-mill recitation of the aims of a new Administration. For most of its length, in tone and rhetorical technique, it was virtually indistinguishable from dozens of its type delivered by presidents and prime ministers all over the world.

The words in the early sections were bureaucratically careful, full of circumlocutions. The use of the weaker passive voice was pervasive. To anyone unfamiliar with the situation in South Africa, it would have seemed dull. However, the truly revolutionary nature of the policies de Klerk was announcing must have kept his audience, and the rest of the country, riveted.

The speech is divided into six sections, covering the major topics he wished to address. In the first, "Foreign Relations", de Klerk had two major points. He alluded briefly and without elaboration to the "ideological considerations" that had limited "our contacts abroad," and to the opportunity to improve the situation. He then moved on to international developments, specifically the collapse of the Soviet Union and, with it, the implosion of international Communism. Dissidents in South Africa had been strongly supported by the Soviets, both financially and organizationally and, with the presumed end of that support, they should engage in "a total revision of their points of view." It provided an opportunity, he said, for the government of South Africa to replace repression with constructive engagement and debate.

The next section includes a strong statement of support for human rights, requesting the expansion and acceleration of the efforts of the Law Commission, a group convened by his predecessor in response to international pressure. De Klerk followed with a call for reforms in the death penalty and an announcement that all executions would be suspended until reforms had been considered.

His next section – again couched in the same bland language – contained another bombshell. Under the heading "Socio-Economic Aspects," he announced that the Parliament would, during the coming

session, repeal the Separate Amenities Act of 1953, a cornerstone of apartheid. That act legalized the racial segregation of public amenities and facilities, and had been used to exclude non-whites entirely from some areas of the country. As leader of the majority party, de Klerk could order a Parliamentary repeal. In fact, the act was repealed during that session.

After a lengthy section devoted to economic privatization, de Klerk came to the final, powerful sections of the speech. The section is headed "Negotiation" and he, in rapid succession, announced the end to the prohibition of the African National Congress and related organizations, the release of political prisoners, the end to suppression of the media, and of other emergency regulations. This amounted to a statement that the police state had ended and the time of confrontation and segregation was to be replaced by negotiation and inclusion.

De Klerk took care to emphasize that the government would maintain public order during this transition and that those who had committed violent acts in the past would remain in jail and those who were violent in the future would be incarcerated.

At the end of the speech, he began to replace the flat, matter-of-fact tone of the speech with some rhetorical flourishes calculated to inspire. "Our country and all its people have been embroiled in conflict, tension and violent struggle for decades," he said. "It is time for us to break out of the cycle of violence and break through to peace and reconciliation. The silent majority is yearning for this. The youth deserve it."

In this final section, the speech moves toward simple, declarative sentences in the active voice – the basic constructions of any orator who wants to appear forceful. De Klerk, for the first time, mentioned Nelson Mandela by name, stating, "I wish to put it plainly that the Government has taken a firm decision to release Mr. Mandela unconditionally."

The section on "Negotiation" builds toward a powerful and moving conclusion, in which de Klerk quoted his own Inaugural Address and effectively used rhetorical devices such as the Rule of Three, saying: "This is where we stand: Deeply under the impression of our responsibility. Humble in the face of the tremendous challenges ahead. Determined to move forward in faith and with conviction."

De Klerk's words were followed by deeds that fundamentally changed South Africa. Nelson Mandela led his organizations to the negotiating table and, together with de Klerk's party, created a new government that included all races. In 1994, South Africa saw the first election in which blacks, mixed-race people, and the country's Indian minority could vote. Mandela was elected President of the National Unity government. De Klerk became one of his Deputy Presidents. He and Mandela shared the Nobel Peace Prize in 1993.

July 18, 1918	Rolihlahla Dalibhunga Mandela is born at Mvezo in the Transkei, South Africa. He is a member of the Madiba clan and the first member of his family to attend school (where a teacher gives him his English name, Nelson).
1927	Mandela's father dies and the chief of his clan becomes his guardian.
1939–1940	Mandela attends Fort Hare University, but is expelled for protesting against university policies.
1941–1942	Works as a clerk in a law firm and completes a B.A. degree through correspondence from the University of South Africa. Begins to study for a law degree.
1943	Joins the African National Congress (ANC).
1944	Marries his first wife, Evelyn Ntolo Mase. They divorce in 1957.
June 1952	Mandela is prominent in the ANC launch of the Defiance Campaign, which advocates non-violent mass resistance.
December 1952	With Oliver Tambo, Mandela opens the first black law firm in South Africa. They provide free or low-cost legal counsel to blacks.
December 5, 1956	Mandela is one of 155 blacks arrested and charged with high treason. By 1961 they are all acquitted.
June 1958	Marries his second wife, Nomzamo "Winnie" Madikizela. They separate in 1992 and divorce in March 1996.
1960	After the Sharpeville massacre, the ANC is banned and Mandela goes into hiding, forming a military group for armed resistance.
August 1962	Mandela is arrested and sentenced to five years in prison.
October 1962	Escapes from prison.
June 1964	Mandela is recaptured. At the Rivonia Trial he is convicted of treason and sentenced to life in prison.
February 1990	The ban on ANC is lifted and Mandela released from prison.
1991	Mandela is elected President of the ANC at the first national conference held in South Africa.
December 1993	Awarded the Nobel Peace Prize jointly with South African President F.W. de Klerk.
April 26–29, 1994	Wins the South African Presidential election, the first in which blacks are allowed to vote. He appoints de Klerk as Deputy President and forms a racially mixed government.
1998	Marries his third wife, Graça Machel.
June 14, 1999	Mandela's Presidential term ends. He is succeeded by Thabo Mbeki.
2004	Retires from public life.
November 2009	The United Nations General Assembly announces that his birthday, July 18, will be known as "Mandela Day".

President Nelson Rolihlahla Mandela

"Never, never and never again shall it be that this beautiful land will again experience the oppression of one by another."

NELSON MANDELA SPENT 27 YEARS in prison after his conviction for leading the armed wing of the African National Congress in its fight against apartheid. An adherent of Mahatma Gandhi's philosophy of non-violence, he had turned to sabotage only when he became convinced that it was the only way to get the attention of the white minority power structure.

He spent 18 of those years doing hard labor in a limestone quarry at the notorious Robben Island prison. The white South African government had hoped to silence him by limiting his visitors and letters to one each every six months, but they were disappointed in that aim. During his time in prison, Mandela became, *in absentia*, the single most prominent and respected black political leader in South Africa. Internationally, he became a symbol of the struggle against the repressive minority government that, over time, made South Africa a pariah in the international community. Many prominent world leaders vocally supported the movement to free him.

As Mandela became a focal point of international outrage over apartheid, the South African government began making overtures to him, transferring him from Robben Island and offering to free him if he would renounce armed struggle. Mandela rejected the offer. World political and economic pressure continued to build throughout the 1980s, with international trade sanctions severely damaging South Africa's economy. Finally, in the late 1980s, F.W. de Klerk took over the ruling National Party and became State President. De Klerk was determined to end South Africa's status as

Nelson Mandela takes the oath during his Inauguration at the Union Building in Pretoria, South Africa, on May 10, 1994.

an international outlaw. He ended the ban on the African National Congress and other opposition parties, released Mandela and hundreds of other dissidents from prison unconditionally in 1990, and, in 1994, engineered the first elections in which all races could freely participate.

The African National Congress won 62 percent of the vote and Mandela became State President. De Klerk was a Deputy President. The two had shared the Nobel Peace Prize the previous year.

Mandela took the podium for his inaugural address at a ceremony attended by many prominent world leaders.

INAUGURAL ADDRESS

MAY 10, 1994

UNION BUILDINGS, PRETORIA

Your Majesties, Your Highnesses, Distinguished Guests, Comrades and Friends.

Today, all of us do, by our presence here, and by our celebrations in other parts of our country and the world, confer glory and hope to newborn liberty.

Out of the experience of an extraordinary human disaster that lasted too long, must be born a society of which all humanity will be proud.

Our daily deeds as ordinary South Africans must produce an actual South African reality that will reinforce humanity's belief in justice, strengthen its confidence in the nobility of the human soul and sustain all our hopes for a glorious life for all.

All this we owe both to ourselves and to the peoples of the world who are so well represented here today.

To my compatriots, I have no hesitation in saying that each one of us is as intimately attached to the soil of this beautiful country as are

Nelson Mandela together with Archbishop Desmond Tutu (left), Mandela's then-wife Winnie (center), Walter Sisulu, ANC Secretary General and former Robben Island prison inmate (second right), and Sisulu's wife Albertina, in the garden of Tutu's residence in Cape Town, the day after Mandela's release from jail.

the famous jacaranda trees of Pretoria and the mimosa trees of the bushveld.

Each time one of us touches the soil of this land, we feel a sense of personal renewal. The national mood changes as the seasons change.

We are moved by a sense of joy and exhilaration when the grass turns green and the flowers bloom.

That spiritual and physical oneness we all share with this common homeland explains the depth of the pain we all carried in our hearts as we saw our country tear itself apart in a terrible conflict, and as we saw it spurned, outlawed and isolated by the peoples of the world, precisely because it has become the universal base of the pernicious ideology and practice of racism and racial oppression.

We, the people of South Africa, feel fulfilled that humanity has taken us back into its bosom, that we, who were outlaws not so long ago, have today been given the rare privilege to be host to the nations of the world on our own soil.

We thank all our distinguished international guests for having come

to take possession with the people of our country of what is, after all, a common victory for justice, for peace, for human dignity.

We trust that you will continue to stand by us as we tackle the challenges of building peace, prosperity, non-sexism, non-racialism and democracy.

We deeply appreciate the role that the masses of our people and their political mass democratic, religious, women, youth, business, traditional and other leaders have played to bring about this conclusion. Not least among them is my Second Deputy President, the Honourable F.W. de Klerk.

We would also like to pay tribute to our security forces, in all their ranks, for the distinguished role they have played in securing our first democratic elections and the transition to democracy, from blood-thirsty forces which still refuse to see the light.

The time for the healing of the wounds has come.

The moment to bridge the chasms that divide us has come.

The time to build is upon us.

We have, at last, achieved our political emancipation. We pledge ourselves to liberate all our people from the continuing bondage of poverty, deprivation, suffering, gender and other discrimination.

We succeeded to take our last steps to freedom in conditions of relative peace. We commit ourselves to the construction of a complete, just and lasting peace.

We have triumphed in the effort to implant hope in the breasts of the millions of our people. We enter into a covenant that we shall build the society in which all South Africans, both black and white, will be able to walk tall, without any fear in their hearts, assured of their inalienable right to human dignity – a rainbow nation at peace with itself and the world.

As a token of its commitment to the renewal of our country, the new Interim Government of National Unity will, as a matter of urgency, address the issue of amnesty for various categories of our people who are currently serving terms of imprisonment.

We dedicate this day to all the heroes and heroines in this country and the rest of the world who sacrificed in many ways and surrendered their lives so that we could be free.

Their dreams have become reality. Freedom is their reward.

We are both humbled and elevated by the honour and privilege that you, the people of South Africa, have bestowed on us, as the first President of a united, democratic, non-racial and non-sexist government.

We understand it still that there is no easy road to freedom

We know it well that none of us acting alone can achieve success.

Mandela sits next to an election campaign poster after addressing some 20,000 supporters at the Soweto stadium in South Africa.

175

We must therefore act together as a united people, for national reconciliation, for nation building, for the birth of a new world.

Let there be justice for all.

Let there be peace for all.

Let there be work, bread, water and salt for all.

Let each know that for each the body, the mind and the soul have been freed to fulfil themselves.

Never, never and never again shall it be that this beautiful land will again experience the oppression of one by another and suffer the indignity of being the skunk of the world.

Let freedom reign.

The sun shall never set on so glorious a human achievement!

God bless Africa!

Thank you.

President Nelson Mandela outlines his vision for the new South Africa as he opens the first session of the country's first all-race parliament.

Analysis

Nelson Mandela had, by the time of his inauguration, become an international icon of the struggle for racial equality. He had earned his stature – his *ethos*, in rhetorical terms – through the grace and magnanimity he showed during decades of maltreatment and imprisonment by the apartheid government of South Africa. When he took the podium for his inaugural speech, it mattered less what he said than that he was there.

However, over the years, Mandela had also earned a reputation as a graceful and articulate spokesmen for his people and his inaugural speech – while brief – fully displayed his oratorical talents. He struck three main themes in the speech: the love of all South Africans for their country, a tribute to those who played positive roles in the relatively peaceful transition, and a strong call for unity. He effectively used rhetorical techniques, notably repetition and the rule of three (linking three words or phrases for emphasis), as well as some very lyrical turns of phrase, such as his opening sentence in which he said the occasion conferred "glory and hope to newborn liberty."

The speech itself is a hopeful one, evoking both the beauty of South Africa and the profound attachment of all South Africans of all races, to the country. That very beauty, Mandela said, intensified the pain of the consequences of the conflict caused by racism and racial oppression. Mandela's characterization of the apartheid period was frank. He acknowledged that "we were outlaws" and at the end said his country

would never again "suffer the indignity of being the skunk of the world." He used the pronoun "we" instead of "they", in referring to South Africa's apartheid period, to indicate the spirit of reconciliation and inclusion he wanted to convey.

Mandela singled out F.W. de Klerk for special mention as one who played a role in the transition, and then, surprisingly, paid tribute to South African security forces, so hated and feared, for the "distinguished role" they played. He was thus signalling, as de Klerk did before him in his own inauguration speech, that he would maintain the rule of law and that the "blood-thirsty forces which still refuse to see the light" would be put down.

Also interesting is that Mandela repeatedly put sexism on a par with racism as a challenge to be overcome. South Africa had been, historically, a male-dominated as well as white-dominated society, as had most of the rest of Africa. Mandela clearly wanted that to change. "We pledge ourselves," he said, "to liberate all our people from the continuing bondage of poverty, deprivation, suffering, gender and other discrimination." Later, he proclaimed his pride in becoming "the first President of a united, democratic, non-racial and non-sexist government."

Mandela also, consciously or not, gave a nod to America in the reference to his people's "inalienable right to human dignity," which echoed the Declaration of Independence." He followed with his aspiration for South Africa to become "a rainbow nation at peace with itself and the world."

Mandela's close was a powerful call for justice, peace, and freedom, and an eloquent promise that "Never, never and never again shall it be that this beautiful land will again experience the oppression of one by another."

The inaugural speech was viewed, and cheered, by millions around the world. Nelson Mandela, during his five-year term as President, did his best to make good on his promises of an open society. His South Africa was welcomed back into the community of nations, with a consequent salutary effect on its economy and diplomatic ties. Mandela acted symbolically on many occasions to try to heal the divide between black and white – most notably by publicly urging blacks to support the Springboks, South Africa's national rugby team, which had been a symbol of apartheid in the past. The team won the 1995 World Rugby Cup, the first major international sporting competition held in South Africa in many years.

Citing his advanced age, Mandela retired as head of the ANC at the time of the 1999 elections, thus effectively declining to seek election for another term. His term as President is deemed successful on most counts, and he is considered to have remained true to his principles while in power. In retirement, he has continued to amass international honors and has also remained a symbol of equality and the potential for peaceful reconciliation.

In less than five years, Nelson Mandela went from political prisoner to a world leader with the ear of Pope John Paul II.

July 6, 1946	George Walker Bush is born in New Haven, Connecticut. He is the eldest son of George H.W. Bush, who later becomes U.S. President from 1989 to 1993, and Barbara Pierce Bush.
June 1948	The Bush family moves from Connecticut to Texas.
1964–1968	Bush attends Yale University, majoring in history.
May 1968	Commissioned into the Texas Air National Guard, Bush serves as a pilot there and in the Alabama National Guard until 1973.
1973–1975	Attends the Harvard Business School, earning an MBA.
1975–1994	Employed in either his father's or his own oil companies in Texas.
November 5, 1977	Marries Laura Welch in Midland, Texas.
1978	Campaigns, unsuccessfully, for the U.S. House of Representatives.
1987–1988	Works on his father's (successful) Presidential campaign.
April, 1989	Purchases a share of the Texas Rangers Baseball Team, and serves as Managing General Partner for five years.
November 8, 1994	Elected Governor of Texas.
November 3, 1998	Re-elected Governor of Texas.
December 13, 2000	Declared winner of the controversial November 7 election for President of the United States. Dick Cheney is elected Vice-President.
September 11, 2001	Bush addresses the nation after the terrorist attacks, and declares a global war on terrorism.
2001–2003	U.S. invades Afghanistan and Iraq as part of the War on Terror.
November 2004	Re-elected President.
January 20, 2009	Having served two terms as President, Bush retires to Texas.

President George W. Bush

"A great people has been moved to defend a great nation."

WHAT MORE NEED BE SAID about the events of September 11, 2001? The images of the twin towers of the World Trade Center collapsing are indelibly imprinted on the minds of all Americans, and people around the world. Less visually appalling, but equally disturbing, was the footage of the burning Pentagon; the center of American defense capabilities. The crash of yet another commercial plane commandeered by terrorists who were overpowered by passengers was yet another blow. Any one of these events would have been a terrible landmark. Taken together, they placed the date right up beside December 7, 1941, as one of the worst in U.S. history.

America lost something on that day – a sense of inviolability. The World Trade Center had been bombed by terrorists once before, in 1993, and six people had been killed. But the twin towers had withstood the assault, and stayed standing. Somehow, the country was proud of that. It had taken the worst that terrorists could offer, or so Americans thought. When that proved not to be the case the country was stunned, and changed. The tactics used by the terrorists were incredibly vicious, and the suffering both of those on the planes and in the struck buildings was mind-boggling. Some of the televised images, such as the plane slicing through one of the towers, were so disturbing that after having been seen early that day they have not been aired since.

The horrified nation looked, as it had so many times in the past, to its leader, the new President, George W. Bush. In office less than nine months, this was President Bush's first real test and it was a big one. He went on national television that evening.

TELEVISED ADDRESS
SEPTEMBER 11, 2001
WHITE HOUSE, WASHINGTON, D.C.

Good evening. Today, our fellow citizens, our way of life, our very freedom came under attack in a series of deliberate and deadly terrorist acts. The victims were in

Hijacked United Airlines Flight 175 from Boston crashes into the south tower of the World Trade Center at 9:03 am on September 11, 2001.

airplanes, or in their offices; secretaries, businessmen and women, military and federal workers; moms and dads, friends and neighbors. Thousands of lives were suddenly ended by evil, despicable acts of terror.

The pictures of airplanes flying into buildings, fires burning, huge structures collapsing, have filled us with disbelief, terrible sadness, and a quiet, unyielding anger. These acts of mass murder were intended

to frighten our nation into chaos and retreat. But they have failed; our country is strong.

A great people has been moved to defend a great nation. Terrorist attacks can shake the foundations of our biggest buildings, but they cannot touch the foundation of America. These acts shattered steel, but they cannot dent the steel of American resolve.

George Bush addresses the nation from the Oval Office of the White House on September 11, 2001.

America was targeted for attack because we're the brightest beacon for freedom and opportunity in the world. And no one will keep that light from shining.

Today, our nation saw evil, the very worst of human nature. And we responded with the best of America – with the daring of our rescue workers, with the caring for strangers and neighbors who came to give blood and help in any way they could.

Immediately following the first attack, I implemented our government's emergency response plans. Our military is powerful, and it's prepared. Our emergency teams are working in New York City and Washington, D.C. to help with local rescue efforts.

Our first priority is to get help to those who have been injured, and to take every precaution to protect our citizens at home and around the world from further attacks.

The functions of our government continue without interruption. Federal agencies in Washington which had to be evacuated today are reopening for essential personnel tonight, and will be open for business tomorrow. Our financial institutions remain strong, and the American economy will be open for business, as well.

The search is underway for those who are behind these evil acts. I've directed the full resources of our intelligence and law enforcement communities to find those responsible and to bring them to justice. We will make no distinction between the terrorists who committed these acts and those who harbor them.

I appreciate so very much the members of Congress who have joined me in strongly condemning these attacks. And on behalf of the American people, I thank the many world leaders who have called to offer their condolences and assistance.

America and our friends and allies join with all those who want peace and security in the world, and we stand together to win the war against terrorism. Tonight, I ask for your prayers for all those who grieve, for the children whose worlds have been shattered, for all whose sense of safety and security has been threatened. And I pray they will be comforted by a power greater than any of us, spoken through the ages in Psalm 23: "Even though I walk through the valley of the shadow of death, I fear no evil, for You are with me."

This is a day when all Americans from every walk of life unite in our resolve for justice and peace. America has stood down enemies before, and we will do so this time. None of us will ever forget this day. Yet, we go forward to defend freedom and all that is good and just in our world.

Analysis

The occasion of a great national tragedy in the United States requires a carefully calibrated response from the White House. Perhaps the two closest parallels to the September 11 attacks were Pearl Harbor and the *Challenger* disaster and, for each, the President was equal to the event.

Thousands of Americans were killed at Pearl Harbor, but it took place thousands of miles away and seemed remote. Moreover, the threat of war had hung over America for years, so there was a sense that the inevitable had at last happened. President Roosevelt reassured the country that America would rise in righteous wrath, and would prevail. In effect, he gave the country permission to get mad and stay that way until America had won.

The *Challenger* disaster presented a different test to President Reagan. Deaths were involved, but there was no national threat. The task was to comfort a nation that had witnessed a terrible event, if not live, then in contemporaneous news accounts.

Essentially, President Bush's communications task was a combination of the previous two. The cataclysmic events of September 11 came, literally, out of the blue, and America watched the World Trade Center towers collapse on live television. Few, if any, of the nation's television sets were not tuned to the news coverage of the events by the time the second tower collapsed. The pictures shown were horrendous – planes puncturing the glass and steel towers, bodies raining down, fire and chaos.

The American people needed consolation in their collective grief as well as reassurance that they, individually and collectively, were not in mortal danger. Only when that fear had been assuaged could anger take hold.

The language of the statement is relatively plain, perhaps because time constraints did not allow his speechwriters to indulge in flights of eloquence, perhaps because they felt the events spoke for themselves. The closest thing to a memorable line is "A great people has been moved to defend a great nation," which does not come up to Roosevelt's "day which will live in infamy."

Bush's delivery was curiously flat and low key, seemingly detached – possibly stunned. He failed to infuse even the strongest lines of the speech with anything like real conviction. It was evident to viewers that he was reading from a script and strictly adhering to it. When he spoke of "disbelief, terrible sadness, and a quiet, unyielding anger," the viewing audience saw none of those emotions on his face. Even his evocation of the 23rd Psalm was delivered in a sort of monotone.

Crowds outside the service held on September 14, 2001, at the Washington National Cathedral for those killed and injured during the terrorist attacks, hold a sign demonstrating support for President Bush in the aftermath of the attacks.

President Bush's short statement was intended to restore perspective after a day of chaos and uncertainty. His message was that the terrorists had failed to destabilize America, as they had hoped. The country remained strong and its defenses were working. Bush spoke of those behind the "evil acts" being brought to justice, in effect relegating them to the status of criminals. However, he then broadened the response into a "war on terrorism", according enemy combatant status to the perpetrators of the acts and warning countries that might be favorably disposed to them that "we will make no distinction between the terrorists who committed these acts and those who harbor them." The war on terrorism was a theme on which he would expand, ultimately into war in Iraq and Afghanistan. This statement was the opening salvo of that war.

Nevertheless, the reaction to the address, and to Bush's other public statements and actions following the attacks, was undeniably positive. He was much more effective in remarks through a bullhorn at the disaster site in Lower Manhattan. Shortly after 9/11, his approval rating rose from 51 percent to 90 percent, and stayed above 70 percent for more than a year thereafter. Evidence therefore suggests that his remarks effectively communicated the situation to his audience and met their needs both for information and emotional support.

As such, the address must be regarded as among the most successful of George W. Bush's Presidency. For the remainder of his two terms, he developed and sustained a reputation as one of the least accomplished public speakers to hold the office in the modern era.

August 4, 1961	Barack Hussein Obama, Jr. is born in Honolulu, Hawaii.
1963	Obama's parents separate, divorcing in 1964.
1967	Obama's mother marries Lolo Soetoro and the family move to Jakarta, Indonesia.
1971	Obama returns to Hawaii to live with his maternal grandparents. His mother moves back with his younger half-sister in 1972.
1979	Graduates from Punahou School, a private college preparatory school in Honolulu.
1979–1981	Attends Occidental College in Los Angeles.
1981–1983	Attends Columbia University in New York, majoring in political science with a specialization in international relations.
1985	Moves to Chicago to become a full-time community organizer.
1988	Travels to Europe and then to Kenya, his father's home country, where he meets many of his paternal relatives. Returns to Kenya in 2006.
1988–1991	Attends Harvard Law School and becomes the first black president of the Harvard Law Review. He graduates *magna cum laude*.
October 3, 1992	Marries Michelle Robinson in Chicago.
1992–2004	Teaches constitutional law at the University of Chicago Law School
1995	Publishes his first book, a memoir titled *Dreams From My Father*. His second book, *The Audacity of Hope*, is published in 2006.
November 5, 1996	Elected to the Illinois Senate. Re-elected in 1998 and 2002.
October 2, 2002	In a speech in Chicago, Obama declares his opposition to the war in Iraq, a "war based not on reason, but on politics."
July 27, 2004	Delivers the keynote address at the Democratic National Convention in Boston.
November 2, 2004	Elected to the U.S. Senate.
November 5, 2008	Defeats Republican John McCain in the Presidential election. Delaware Senator Joseph R. Biden Jr. is elected Vice-President.
January 20, 2009	Inaugurated as the 44th President of the United States.

President Barack Hussein Obama

"What is required of us now is a new era of responsibility – a recognition on the part of every American that we have duties to ourselves, our nation and the world."

N O ONE BUT BARACK OBAMA knows exactly when he first dreamed of becoming President of the United States. Possibly it was when his first book, *Dreams From My Father*, was published in 1995. The Presidency was certainly on his mind by the time he wrote his second book, *The Audacity of Hope*, which has been called his "thesis submission" for the Presidency. It was full of policy positions and suffused with, as the title suggests, hope.

However, while writing those words Obama could not have imagined the national and international circumstances on the day his dreams finally came true. His predecessor, George W. Bush, on his own Inauguration day in 2001, thought that he would preside over a continuation of the economic prosperity of the Clinton years. Less than nine months later, he was disabused of that notion. Instead, his terms in office were dominated by the global war on terrorism with American troops on the ground in Iraq and Afghanistan.

Terrorism was a continuing issue when Obama began his successful campaign for the Democratic nomination, but America was prosperous – jobs were plentiful and

President Barack Obama gives his Inaugural Address on the West Front of the Capitol.

WORDS THAT CHANGED THE WORLD

the stock market soaring. By the time of the November election, the bottom had dropped out. The stock market had lost more than half its value – trillions of dollars in the net worth of both the mighty and the humble. The banking system was in shambles, huge corporations were failing, and the Bush Administration was scrambling in its waning days to hold the economic slide merely to severe recession. The financial crisis was acknowledged to be the most severe since the Great Depression of the 1930s.

The young President faced a record crowd from the steps of the U.S. Capitol as he stepped up to give his Inaugural Address, many of them African-Americans cheering the first of their race ever elected to the office. The much larger television and radio audience was not cheering, however. They were looking for assurance that the country was not crumbling into ruin before their eyes, and that their new President could, and would, reverse the calamity.

INAUGURAL ADDRESS

JANUARY 20, 2009

UNITED STATES CAPITOL, WASHINGTON, D.C.

My fellow citizens: I stand here today humbled by the task before us, grateful for the trust you've bestowed, mindful of the sacrifices borne by our ancestors.

I thank President Bush for his service to our nation – (applause) – as well as the generosity and cooperation he has shown throughout this transition.

Forty-four Americans have now taken the presidential oath. The words have been spoken during rising tides of prosperity and the still waters of peace. Yet, every so often, the oath is taken amidst gathering clouds and raging storms. At these moments, America has carried on

Barack Hussein Obama is sworn into office as his wife, Michelle, looks on.

not simply because of the skill or vision of those in high office, but because we, the people, have remained faithful to the ideals of our forebears and true to our founding documents.

So it has been; so it must be with this generation of Americans.

That we are in the midst of crisis is now well understood. Our nation is at war against a far-reaching network of violence and hatred. Our economy is badly weakened, a consequence of greed and irresponsibility on the part of some, but also our collective failure to make hard choices and prepare the nation for a new age. Homes have been lost, jobs shed, businesses shuttered. Our health care is too costly, our schools fail too many – and each day brings further evidence that the ways we use energy strengthen our adversaries and threaten our planet.

These are the indicators of crisis, subject to data and statistics. Less measurable, but no less profound, is a sapping of confidence across our land; a nagging fear that America's decline is inevitable, that the next generation must lower its sights.

Today I say to you that the challenges we face are real. They are serious and they are many. They will not be met easily or in a short span of time. But know this America: They will be met. (Applause.)

On this day, we gather because we have chosen hope over fear, unity of purpose over conflict and discord. On this day, we come to proclaim an end to the petty grievances and false promises, the recriminations and worn-out dogmas that for far too long have strangled our politics. We remain a young nation. But in the words of Scripture, the time has come to set aside childish things. The time has come to reaffirm our enduring spirit; to choose our better history; to carry forward that precious gift, that noble idea passed on from generation to generation: the God-given promise that all are equal, all are free, and all deserve a chance to pursue their full measure of happiness. (Applause.)

In reaffirming the greatness of our nation we understand that greatness is never a given. It must be earned. Our journey has never been one of short-cuts or settling for less. It has not been the path for the faint-hearted, for those that prefer leisure over work, or seek only the pleasures of riches and fame. Rather, it has been the risk-takers, the doers, the makers of things – some celebrated, but more often men and women obscure in their labor – who have carried us up the long rugged path towards prosperity and freedom.

For us, they packed up their few worldly possessions and traveled across oceans in search of a new life. For us, they toiled in sweatshops, and settled the West, endured the lash of the whip, and plowed the hard earth. For us, they fought and died in places like Concord and Gettysburg, Normandy and Khe Sahn.

Time and again these men and women struggled and sacrificed and worked till their hands were raw so that we might live a better life. They saw America as bigger than the sum of our individual ambitions, greater than all the differences of birth or wealth or faction.

This is the journey we continue today. We remain the most prosperous, powerful nation on Earth. Our workers are no less productive than when this crisis began. Our minds are no less inventive, our goods and services no less needed than they were last week, or last month, or last year. Our capacity remains undiminished. But our time of standing pat, of protecting narrow interests and putting off unpleasant decisions – that time has surely passed. Starting today, we must pick ourselves up, dust ourselves off, and begin again the work of remaking America. (Applause.)

For everywhere we look, there is work to be done. The state of our economy calls for action, bold and swift. And we will act, not only to create new jobs, but to lay a new foundation for growth. We will build the roads and bridges, the electric grids and digital lines that feed our commerce and bind us together. We'll restore science to its rightful place, and wield technology's wonders to raise health care's quality and lower its cost. We will harness the sun and the winds and the soil to fuel our cars and run our factories. And we will transform our schools and colleges and universities to meet the demands of a new age. All this we can do. All this we will do.

Now, there are some who question the scale of our ambitions, who suggest that our system cannot tolerate too many big plans. Their memories are short, for they have forgotten what this country has already done, what free men and women can achieve when imagination is joined to common purpose, and necessity to courage. What the cynics fail to understand is that the ground has shifted beneath them, that the stale political arguments that have consumed us for so long no longer apply.

The question we ask today is not whether our government is too big or too small, but whether it works – whether it helps families find jobs at a decent wage, care they can afford, a retirement that is dignified. Where the answer is yes, we intend to move forward. Where the answer is no, programs will end. And those of us who manage the public's dollars will be held to account, to spend wisely, reform bad habits, and do our business in the light of day, because only then can we restore the vital trust between a people and their government.

Nor is the question before us whether the market is a force for good or ill. Its power to generate wealth and expand freedom is unmatched. But this crisis has reminded us that without a watchful eye, the market can spin out of control. The nation cannot prosper long when it favors only the prosperous. The success of our economy has always depended not just on the size of our gross domestic product, but on the reach of our prosperity, on the ability to extend opportunity to every willing heart – not out of charity, but because it is the surest route to our common good. (Applause.)

As for our common defense, we reject as false the choice between our safety and our ideals. Our Founding Fathers – (applause) – our Founding Fathers, faced with perils that we can scarcely imagine, drafted a charter to assure the rule of law and the rights of man – a charter expanded by the blood of generations. Those ideals still light the world, and we will not give them up for expedience sake. (Applause.)

And so, to all the other peoples and governments who are watching today, from the grandest capitals to the small village where my father was born, know that America is a friend of each nation, and every man, woman and child who seeks a future of peace and dignity. And we are ready to lead once more. (Applause.)

Recall that earlier generations faced down fascism and communism not just with missiles and tanks, but with the sturdy alliances and enduring convictions. They understood that our power alone cannot protect us, nor does it entitle us to do as we please. Instead they knew that our power grows through its prudent use; our security emanates from the justness of our cause, the force of our example, the tempering qualities of humility and restraint.

We are the keepers of this legacy. Guided by these principles once more we can meet those new threats that demand even greater effort, even greater cooperation and understanding between nations. We will begin to responsibly leave Iraq to its people and forge a hard-earned peace in Afghanistan. With old friends and former foes, we'll work tirelessly to lessen the nuclear threat, and roll back the specter of a warming planet.

We will not apologize for our way of life, nor will we waver in its defense. And for those who seek to advance their aims by inducing terror and slaughtering innocents, we say to you now that our spirit is stronger and cannot be broken – you cannot outlast us, and we will defeat you. (Applause.)

For we know that our patchwork heritage is a strength, not a weakness. We are a nation of Christians and Muslims, Jews and Hindus, and non-believers. We are shaped by every language and culture, drawn from every end of this Earth; and because we have tasted the bitter swill of civil war and segregation, and emerged from that dark chapter stronger and more united, we cannot help but believe that the old hatreds shall someday pass; that the lines of tribe shall soon dissolve; that as the world grows smaller, our common humanity shall reveal itself; and that America must play its role in ushering in a new era of peace.

To the Muslim world, we seek a new way forward, based on mutual interest and mutual respect. To those leaders around the globe who seek to sow conflict, or blame their society's ills on the West, know

that your people will judge you on what you can build, not what you destroy. (Applause.)

To those who cling to power through corruption and deceit and the silencing of dissent, know that you are on the wrong side of history, but that we will extend a hand if you are willing to unclench your fist. (Applause.)

To the people of poor nations, we pledge to work alongside you to make your farms flourish and let clean waters flow; to nourish starved bodies and feed hungry minds. And to those nations like ours that enjoy relative plenty, we say we can no longer afford indifference to the suffering outside our borders, nor can we consume the world's resources without regard to effect. For the world has changed, and we must change with it.

As we consider the role that unfolds before us, we remember with humble gratitude those brave Americans who at this very hour patrol far-off deserts and distant mountains. They have something to tell us, just as the fallen heroes who lie in Arlington whisper through the ages.

We honor them not only because they are the guardians of our liberty, but because they embody the spirit of service – a willingness to find meaning in something greater than themselves.

And yet at this moment, a moment that will define a generation, it is precisely this spirit that must inhabit us all. For as much as government can do, and must do, it is ultimately the faith and determination of the American people upon which this nation relies. It is the kindness to take in a stranger when the levees break, the selflessness of workers who would rather cut their hours than see a friend lose their job which sees us through our darkest hours. It is the firefighter's courage to storm a stairway filled with smoke, but also a parent's willingness to nurture a child that finally decides our fate.

Our challenges may be new. The instruments with which we meet them may be new. But those values upon which our success depends – honesty and hard work, courage and fair play, tolerance and curiosity, loyalty and patriotism – these things are old. These things are true. They have been the quiet force of progress throughout our history.

What is demanded, then, is a return to these truths. What is required of us now is a new era of responsibility – a recognition on the part of every American that we have duties to ourselves, our nation and the world; duties that we do not grudgingly accept, but rather seize gladly, firm in the knowledge that there is nothing so satisfying to the spirit, so defining of our character than giving our all to a difficult task.

This is the price and the promise of citizenship. This is the source of our confidence – the knowledge that God calls on us to shape an uncertain destiny. This is the meaning of our liberty and our creed, why

President Obama dances with First Lady Michelle Obama at the Commander-In-Chief's Inaugural Ball.

men and women and children of every race and every faith can join in celebration across this magnificent mall; and why a man whose father less than 60 years ago might not have been served in a local restaurant can now stand before you to take a most sacred oath. (Applause.)

So let us mark this day with remembrance of who we are and how far we have traveled. In the year of America's birth, in the coldest of months, a small band of patriots huddled by dying campfires on the shores of an icy river. The capital was abandoned. The enemy was advancing. The snow was stained with blood. At the moment when the outcome of our revolution was most in doubt, the father of our nation ordered these words to be read to the people:

"Let it be told to the future world... that in the depth of winter, when nothing but hope and virtue could survive... that the city and the country, alarmed at one common danger, came forth to meet [it]."

Vice-President Joe Biden (left) and White House Clerk Lisa Brown (right) welcome the latest incumbent to the Oval Office.

America: In the face of our common dangers, in this winter of our hardship, let us remember these timeless words. With hope and virtue, let us brave once more the icy currents, and endure what storms may come. Let it be said by our children's children that when we were tested we refused to let this journey end, that we did not turn back nor did we falter; and with eyes fixed on the horizon and God's grace upon us, we carried forth that great gift of freedom and delivered it safely to future generations.

Thank you. God bless you. And God bless the United States of America. (Applause.)

Analysis

Barack Obama is a masterful speaker whose oratorical prowess played a major role in his meteoric rise. His speech before the Democratic Convention in 2004 electrified both the party and the television audience and took him from candidate for the U.S. Senate from Illinois at that convention to the Oval Office a little over four years later.

While Obama's lean and dignified presence, deep voice, and clipped cadences add up to a superb delivery, he also is a fine writer. Much has been made about the fact that 27-year-old rising star Jon Favreau, and several other writers, worked on the Inaugural speech, but Obama's input cannot be discounted. An accomplished writer knows a good line

some Presidents have, but as others have, "amidst gathering clouds and raging storms." This was followed by a concise summation of a situation of which his audience was only too aware.

Obama did not shy away from controversy. Despite his conciliatory words to President Bush at the outset of the speech, he went on to verbally savage the opposition for their role in the economic meltdown. His rhetorical tactics included setting up a series of "straw men" to be knocked down. In the straw man technique, the speaker states, or misstates, the opponent's position, then refutes it. For instance, he said, "There are some who question the scale of our ambition," adding that the "stale political arguments no longer apply." Later uses included the rejection of supposed Republican beliefs in his statements that, "The nation cannot prosper long when it favors only the prosperous," and, "We reject as false the choice between our safety and our ideals."

In fact, the speech is full of not-so-subtle digs at the previous Administration and the financial establishment for leading America into harm's way, starting with " … we gather because we have chosen hope over fear, unity of purpose over conflict and discord," with the clear implication that the outgoing Administration represents the fear, conflict, and discord. One of Obama's major concerns was a desire to rebuild alliances with other countries, rich and poor, around the world. In making this point, he drew another contrast between his intentions and the previous Administration, to which he attributed the attitude that America's power "entitle[s] us to do as we please."

Almost throughout, the speech lacks a unifying theme, but toward the end one emerges: Americans are too self-indulgent and "childish" and must grow up and face a bad situation. Obama placed some blame on Wall Street, but essentially said there is enough blame to go around: "Our economy is badly weakened, a consequence of greed and irresponsibility on the part of some, but also our collective failure to make hard choices and prepare the nation for a new age." America needs "a new era of responsibility" if the country is to discharge its duties to the nation and the world.

There is very little self-congratulation in the speech – only one reference to his history-making election, and himself as "a man whose father less than 60 years ago might not have been served in a local restaurant" taking the oath of office. Other than that, Obama stuck to business.

The speech has drawn criticism that it is more workmanlike than eloquent, with no really memorable lines of the calibre of Roosevelt's "rendezvous with destiny" or Kennedy's "Ask not …" That may be true – it certainly has come to be a widely accepted judgment in the time since the speech was delivered – but it is probable that the tone and content of the speech was a matter of conscious strategy rather than oratorical deficiency. Apparently, Barack Obama decided that America needed a wakeup call more than a bugle call, and that is exactly what he delivered.

from a bad one. And even more important, an orator of Obama's stature can contribute something more than rhetorical flourishes – he (or she) will know what kind of speech to deliver. The context – the issues of importance to the audience, the circumstances at the time of delivery – is of primary importance. Given the state of the country, a fluffy, conceptual speech full of high-sounding ambiguities would have dropped like a rock. Obama knew that. The times demanded substance and Obama's Inauguration Address was a hard-hitting, muscular, plain-language speech that turned on the simple declaration that though the challenges are many and serious, " … know this America. They will be met."

The new President began by establishing the context for the speech. He was taking the oath not during a period of peace and prosperity, as

Index

Index

Picture Credits